TISS-NET

National Entrance Test

Latest Edition
Practice Kit

20 Tests
08 Mock Test
03 Previous Year Paper
09 Sectional Test

Based On Real Exam Pattern

✓ Thoroughly Revised and Updated

✓ Sample Papers with Answer Keys

Title	: TISS-NET National Entrance Test
Author Name	: Mr. Rohit Manglik
Published By	: EduGorilla Community Pvt. Ltd.
Publishers Address	: 12/651, First Floor Opp. Arvindo Park, Near Jama Masjid, Indira Nagar, Lucknow, Uttar Pradesh-226016, India

Copyright EduGorilla

Disclaimer EduGorilla

Compiled and created by EduGorilla Community Pvt. Ltd

Printed By EduGorilla Community Pvt. Ltd.

ROHIT MANGLIK
CEO, EduGorilla

Dear Applicants,

People say *"Success comes to those who work hard."* But I've seen people working hard for their exams day in and day out for marginal success. While others succeed in their examinations by putting in just half the work. So are they God Gifted? No! I believe that it's because they work *smart* and not just *hard*. Similarly, for your exams, you should strategize your preparation so as to increase the likelihood of success. Well with EduGorilla get ready to increase your *chances of selection* in your exam by *16x*.

EduGorilla helps you in not only working *hard* but also working in a *smart and strategic* manner. With EduGorilla's preparation package, you get a chance to make your exam preparation easy, and a fun learning path towards selection. Finding the right path to your preparations can be difficult if you don't know in which direction to head. Don't worry, we have you covered! EduGorilla will be your guide to success in your journey. With our Preparation Package, you can prepare strategically and beat the exam in just one attempt.

EduGorilla's Preparation Package includes-

• **Test Series**   • **Books**

Our preparation package is handcrafted as per the latest changes, expert opinions, and students' discretion. Thus, enabling you to get through each stage of the selection process for your exam.

Our Books are designed by the teachers and experts of the respective exam with a combined 150+ years of experience; to provide you with easy, efficient, and effective learning. Our books are smart, in the sense that not only do they give you the answers to the questions but also provide similar questions for practice.

EduGorilla's competent Test Series gives you real-time experience and confidence through which you can clear your offline or online exam in just one attempt. We currently host 83,000+ mock tests for 1,440+ competitive and academic exams.

Thus, EduGorilla misses no chance to assist you in your preparation and covers all stages of the exam, so that you don't have to look anywhere else.

We provide complete preparation packages for defense, banking, teaching, and other National & State-Level exams. Hence, it doesn't matter which exam you aspire to because you will reach your success.

ALL THE BEST !
Let EduGorilla be your Guide to Success.

Rohit Manglik,
Founder and CEO, EduGorilla

INTRODUCTION

EduGorilla focuses on guiding students to succeed in their examinations. With that in mind, our book, titled "TISS-NET : National Entrance Test", has been drafted through the collective efforts of our distinguished experts with 150+ years of combined experience. This book consists of questions that are created following the latest changes in the syllabus and exam pattern. We compiled the book on the basis of questions that are most likely to appear in the TISS-NET Exam. Through EduGorilla's "TISS-NET : National Entrance Test" your chances of success will increase 16x.

EduGorilla does this through our Complete Preparation Package. This package consists of well-conceptualized and structured content in the form of questions that are tailor-made according to your needs and will help you practice for exams in a smart way by pinpointing all the necessary information. It also provides smart answer sheet for your self-evaluation. You can assess your shortcomings and work accordingly on areas that may require more of your attention.

EduGorilla promises to help you succeed in your examination and accomplish your dream goals. We believe in our aspirants and see them at the top of the merit list. And the first step towards the top is to start preparing with us. EduGorilla's "TISS-NET : National Entrance Test" includes the following attributes.

➤ Well-Researched Content

➤ Top-Notch Quality

➤ Smart Answer Sheet

➤ Exam Relevant Questions

Therefore, EduGorilla fortifies your preparation and makes it durable enough to help you stand tall and beat the examination.

TISS-NET Exam

Scan QR code for Eligibility, Exam Pattern, Syllabus and more.

Book ID: 0807

TABLE OF CONTENTS

General Awareness

Q.1 The second edition of the "DUSTLIK II" joint military exercise has been organized in which place in India?
A. Nainital
B. Ranikhet
C. Dehradun
D. Haldwani

Q.2 What was the theme of International Girls in ICT Day 2022 which is observed annually on the fourth Thursday in April?
A. Access and safety
B. Inspiring the Next Generation
C. Case For Change, Connected Women, IoT and Tech4Girls
D. Powering Change: Women in Innovation and Creativity

Q.3 Which Country was ranked as 1st in Global peace Index 2019?

[Territorial Army Officer, 2019]

A. Norway
B. Iceland
C. Nepal
D. Australia

Q.4 What is the unit for measuring the amplitude of a sound?
A. Decibel
B. Coulomb
C. Hum
D. Cycles

Q.5 What is Ekaboron that was an element predicted by Mendeleev and he leaved a space for it in his periodic table, identified with?
A. Germanium
B. Technitium
C. Scandium
D. Gallium

Q.6 The instrument used for measuring electric current is?
A. Electrometer
B. Dynamometer
C. Ammeter
D. Gravimeter

Q.7 Wellington Trophy is related to which of the following games?
A. Cricket
B. Football
C. Hockey
D. Rowing

Q.8 Which among the following statements involves the principle of capillary action?
A. It is enhanced in trees by branching, evaporation at the leaves creating depressurization
B. Oil raise up the wick in a lamp
C. Both A and B
D. Oil remains in the stable condition

Q.9 The leader who established the Tattvabodhini Sabha in 1839 at Calcutta was_______.
A. Sivanatha Sasri
B. Raja Rammohan Roy
C. Debendranath Tagore
D. Keshab Chandra Sen

Q.10 Which of the following is an air-borne disease?
A. Typhoid
B. Cholera
C. Measles
D. None of these

Q.11 Brihadeshwara Temple which is dedicated to shiva was built by __________.
A. Chandra Gupta
B. Raja Chola III
C. Raja Chola I
D. None of these

Q.12 Which health insurance re-branded itself as Care Health Insurance?
A. Birla
B. Bajaj
C. Reliance
D. Religare

Q.13 Consider the statements about the Harappan people which is incorrect-
A. They placed their gods in temples.
B. They looked upon the earth as a fertility goddess.
C. They worshipped gods in the form of human beings.
D. The Harappans were phallus worshippers.

Q.14 The neighboring country which sources its entire requirement of petrol, diesel and jet fuel from India is___________.
A. Mauritius
B. Maldives
C. Nepal
D. Bangladesh

Q.15 The special provisions have been made for National SCs/STs, OBCs and Anglo Indians in _______.
A. Part XIII of the Indian constitution
B. Part XI of the Indian constitution
C. Part XVI of the Indian constitution
D. Part XXI of the Indian constitution

Q.16 With which sports "Formula-1" is associated?
A. Motor racing
B. Cricket
C. Ice Hockey
D. Polo

Q.17 The Supreme Court decisions which stated that the Directive Principles of State policy cannot override fundamental rights is ______.
A. In Minerva Mills vs. UOI
B. In Unna Krishnan vs. State of Andhra Pradesh
C. In Keshavananda Bharti vs. UOI
D. In state of Madras vs. Champakam Dorairajan

Q.18 Which of the following feature is NOT associated with Nagara School of art ?
A. High Plinth
B. Mandapam
C. Gopuram
D. Shikhara

Q.19 The Gender Inequality Index (GII) was introduced in _______.
A. 1998
B. 2005
C. 2010
D. 2011

Q.20 Who propounded the group displacement law?
A. Rutherford and Soddy
B. Rutherford and Madam Curie
C. Soddy and Fajans
D. Rutherford and Fajans

Q.21 Who among the following was conferred "Global Goalkeeper" award?
A. Donald Trump
B. Emmanuel Macron
C. Angela Merkel
D. Narendra Modi

Q.22 Where does the Sabarmati river originate in?
A. The Western Ghats
B. The Vindhyas
C. The Aravallis
D. The Satpuras

Q.23 What is the National Sports of Nepal?
A. Volleyball
B. Cricket
C. Trekking
D. Baseball

Q.24 The frequency of alternating current produced in India is __________.
A. 65 Hz
B. 60 Hz
C. 50 Hz
D. 40 Hz

Q.25 Which of the following statements regarding the Speaker is NOT correct?
A. Speaker can be removed by Lok Sabha only
B. Speaker doesn't vote in the first instance
C. Speaker tenders resignation to the President
D. Speaker guards the rights and privileges of members of Lok Sabha

Q.26 What is the average salinity of the water present in the oceans?
A. 65 per thousand
B. 35 per thousand
C. 10 per thousand
D. 80 per thousand

Q.27 The Gandhara Art was mainly patronized by:
A. Satvahanas
B. Guptas
C. Mauryas
D. Sakas and Kushans

Q.28 What was the name of the person who first discovered the ruins of 'Mohenjo-daro'?
A. R. D. Banerji
B. Daya ram Sahni
C. Marshall
D. John Clay

Q.29 Which of the following city have the remains of the Vijayanagara dynasty?
A. Hampi
B. Baroda
C. Golconda
D. Bijapur

Q.30 Which of the following is not a significant event of Indian National Movement in 1919?
A. Montagu - Chelmsford Reforms
B. Rowlatt Act
C. Jallianwala Bagh Massacre
D. Khilafat Movement

Q.31 The 36th Raising Day of the National Security Guard (NSG) was observed on which date?
A. 14 October
B. 17 October
C. 16 October
D. 15 October

Q.32 'Chukker' is a sports term is related to:
A. Cricket
B. Polo
C. Football
D. Basketball

Q.33 'Good Governance Day' is celebrated on the 25th of December every year in India to mark the birth anniversary of:
A. Atal Bihari Vajpayee
B. Anna Hazare
C. Rajiv Gandhi
D. Pratibha Patil

Q.34 Which of the following statements about the Preamble is NOT correct?
A. The Preamble to the Indian Constitution is based on the 'Objectives Resolution' drafted by BR Ambedkar
B. It has been amended only once
C. The Preamble states that the Constitution derives its authority from the people of India
D. It stipulates November 26, 1949 as the date of adoption of the Constitution

Q.35 The technique of foreshortening in Indian Painting was introduced by
A. Turks
B. Afghans
C. Greeks
D. Mughals

Q.36 Fundamental Rights are enshrined in the Constitution of India in _______.
A. Part I
B. Part III
C. Part IV
D. Part V

Q.37 "Durand Line" is a boundary which lies between:
A. India and Bangladesh
B. India and Pakistan
C. Pakistan and Afghanistan
D. China and Mongolia

Q.38 Which is the largest bank in the world by assets?
A. Bank of America
B. Industrial & Commercial Bank of China
C. Royal Bank of Scotland Group
D. Citigroup Inc

Q.39 What was the most unique feature found in paintings of Jahangir's era?
A. 3-D figures
B. Calligraphy
C. Foreshortening
D. Decorated margins

Q.40 Which of the following was used as a medium in mural paintings of India?
A. Vegetable dye
B. Milk
C. Oil
D. Brick

English Proficiency

Ques (41-42):Direction: In the following question, some of the sentences have errors and some have none. Find out which part of the sentence has an error. The number of that part is your answer. If there is no error, the answer would be (D).

Q.41 The Bhagavad Gita is more than a religious or philosophical text (A)/ its 700 plus verses offer insight into (B)/ every aspect of life and are universal relevant. (C)/ No Error (D)
A. A
B. B
C. C
D. D

Q.42 Perfection is attained when our real self completely eliminates (A)/ our worldly egoistic covering, becomes aware of (B)/ an existence of Supreme Power. (C)/ No Error (D)

A. A   **B.** B   **C.** C   **D.** D

Q.43 Direction: Sentences are given with blanks to be filled in with an appropriate Preposition. Some alternatives are suggested for each question. Choose the correct alternative out of the given alternatives.

He has to be motivated to exercise restraint, change lifestyle and comply________ medical advice.

A. to   **B.** with   **C.** for   **D.** from

Q.44 Direction: In the following question, a sentence is given with a blank to be filled in with appropriate word(s). Some alternatives are suggested for each question. Choose the correct alternative from the given alternatives.

We learn two things from the __________ of Buddha, the first is how to handle suffering and the second is how to create happiness.

A. teaching   **B.** teachings
C. lives   **D.** entire life

Ques (45-48):Direction: In the following question, out of the four alternatives, choose the one which gives the opposite meaning of the given word.

Q.45 Flinch
A. Forge   **B.** Plunder   **C.** Slovenly   **D.** Grin

Q.46 Deplored
A. Endorse   **B.** Execrate   **C.** Costraint   **D.** Relish

Q.47 Charlatan
A. Swindler   **B.** Hoaxer
C. Exponent   **D.** Cajole

Q.48 Forbid
A. Permit   **B.** Deprive
C. Prohibit   **D.** Expropriate

Ques (49-50):Direction: In the following question a part of the sentence is bold. Below are given alternatives to the part of the sentence given in bold, which may improve the sentence. Choose the alternative which makes the sentence grammatically and contextually correct. In case the sentence is correct as it is, chooses 'No Improvement' as your option.

Q.49 Unfortunately, many amongst us may find it difficult to follow values such as honesty, forgiveness in our lives because we have not perceived the subtle gains **which** come to us by following these values.

A. That   **B.** When
C. Which will   **D.** No improvement

Q.50 I think every one of us **know** that we have to handle one's suffering first and we have to make the choice right away to pick what is in front of us first.

A. Knew   **B.** Knowing
C. Knows   **D.** No improvement

Ques (51-55):Direction: Read the given passage carefully and select the best answer to each question out of the five given alternatives.

The Chinese economy is seeing the first signs of trouble after long years of sustained growth that rode on cheap labor and high volumes of exports. Data released by the National Bureau of Statistics on Monday revealed that the economy grew by 6.2% in the second quarter, its slowest pace in 27 years. This is in contrast to the growth rates of 6.4% and 6.6% reported for the first quarter and the full year of 2018, respectively. The faltering growth rate was due to a slump in exports in June amidst China's ongoing trade war with the United States and the downturn witnessed by sectors such as housing construction, where investor sentiments play a major role.

Many economists believe that the worst may not yet be over for China and that economic growth could further worsen in the coming quarters. But just as growth seems to be faltering, the latest growth figures also showed that the retail sales and industrial output components of the growth numbers witnessed steady growth, suggesting that domestic demand may be compensating for the dropping appetite for Chinese exports weighed down by high tariffs. But with China still heavily reliant on exports and its trade war with the U.S. showing no signs of coming to an end, the pressure on growth is likely to remain for some more time. So the Chinese government, which has tried to boost the economy through measures such as tax cuts, increased public spending, and relaxation in bank reserve requirements to encourage banks to increase lending, will hope that domestic demand for its goods will hold up the economy.

China's quarterly GDP numbers, while useful in many ways, don't reveal very much about the underlying challenges facing the country. One is the need to improve the credibility of data released by the Chinese government. An even larger challenge is the urgent need to restructure the Chinese economy from one that is driven heavily by state-led investment and exports to one that is driven primarily by market forces. The high-growth years of the Chinese economy were made possible by the huge amount of liquidity provided by the Chinese state and the large and affordable workforce that helped build China into an export powerhouse. But now, with China's tried and tested growth model facing the threat of getting derailed as the export and investment boom comes to an end, the Chinese will have to build a more sustainable model or forfeit hopes of double-digit economic growth in the future. As of now, there are no signs to suggest that the Chinese authorities are looking at implementing deep-seated structural reforms reminiscent of its early decades of liberalization that can help fundamentally restructure the economy.

Q.51 Which of the following can be correctly inferred from the above passage?

A. There might not be a need for radical macroeconomic changes in China

B. China and the United States have been engaged in a trade war through increasing tariffs and other measures since 2018

C. Reducing the reliance on exports can end China's economic troubles

D. China has planned to lift restrictions on foreign investment in the automotive industry in 2022

Q.52 Which of the following is a synonym of "Faltering"?

A. Construing

B. Assimilating

C. Wavering

D. Procuring

Q.53 Which of the following can be correctly inferred from the 2nd paragraph?

A. The faltering Chinese economic growth rate was due to a slump in exports in June.

B. If the Chinese banks can be encouraged to increase lending, the domestic demand for the goods might be able to hold up the economy

C. China is currently not in an ongoing trade war with the United States

D. Data for June showed money supply and credit expanding at a record low pace for a fourth consecutive month

Q.54 According to the above passage, what measures has the Chinese government adopted to boost the economy?

A. The PBoC has cut the required reserve ratio (RRR) for some banks three times this year in a bid to boost the money supply

B. The State Council has pledged to ensure "appropriate" credit growth

C. Local governments are urged to speed up disbursal of unused fiscal revenue and called on financial institutions to ensure adequate lending to local governments' off-budget financing vehicles so that projects are not delayed

D. The government has introduced tax cuts, increased public spending and a relaxation in bank reserve requirements

Q.55 According to the above passage, what are the two main challenges China is facing?

A. U.S. officials, businesspeople, and organizations have accused China of stealing American intellectual property and military technology

B. Improving the credibility of data released by the government and converting the Chinese economy into one that is primarily driven by market forces

C. China is being accused of adopting and enforcing policies which put U.S. patent holders at a disadvantage in Chinese markets

D. China faces the twin challenges of a global financial crisis and worldwide recession

Q.56 Direction: Pick out the appropriate words from the options given below the sentence to complete it meaningfully.

I was late _____ the cab was not on time.

A. because

B. though

C. if

D. in order to

Q.57 In the following question, a sentence has been given in Active Voice/ Passive Voice. Out of the four alternatives suggested, select the one which best expresses the same sentence in Passive/Active Voice.

Satish chose Praveen's job with intelligence.

A. Praveen's job is chosen with intelligence by Satish

B. Praveen's job was chosen by Satish intelligence

C. Praveen's job was chosen with intelligence

D. Praveen's job was chosen with intelligence by Satish

Q.58 Direction: In the following question , a sentence has been given in Direct/Indirect . Out of the four alternatives suggested, select the one which best expresses the same sentence in Indirect/ Direct .

Rahul said, "my parents are arriving tomorrow".

A. Rahul said that his parents were arriving the next day

B. Rahul said that his parents will arrive the next day

C. Rahul said that his parents were arriving tomorrow

D. Rahul said that my parents will arrive tomorrow

Q.59 Direction: Select the most appropriate word to fill in the blank.

The volcanic eruption _____ destroyed the whole village.

A. near

B. nearest

C. nearly

D. nearer

Q.60 Direction: In the following question, the given sentence has four parts marked as A, B, C and D. Choose the part of the sentence with the error and mark it as your answer. If there is no error, mark 'D' as your answer.

Neha in addition to her friends(A)/ were accused of not telling(B)/ the truth in the court of law. (C)/No error.

A. (D)

B. (B)

C. (C)

D. (A)

Ques (61-65):Direction: Read the following passage carefully and answer the question given below it.

How many really suffer as a result of labor market problems? This is one of the most critical yet contentious social policy questions. In many ways, our social statistics exaggerate the degree of hardship. Unemployment does not have the same dire consequences today as it did in the 1930's when most of the unemployed were primary breadwinners, when income and earnings were usually much closer to the margin of subsistence, and when there were no countervailing social programs for those failing in the labor market. Increasing affluence, the rise of families with more than one wage earner, the growing predominance of secondary earners among the unemployed, and improved social welfare protection have unquestionably mitigate the consequences of joblessness. Earnings and income data also overstate the dimensions of hardship. Among the millions with hourly earnings at or below the minimum wage level, the overwhelming majority are from multiple-earner, relatively affluent families. Most of those counted by the poverty statistics are elderly or handicapped or have family responsibilities which keep them out of the labor force, so the poverty statistics are by no means an accurate indicator of labor market pathologies.

Yet there are also many ways our social statistics underestimate the degree of labor-market-related hardship. The unemployment counts exclude the millions of fully employed workers whose wages are so low that their families remain in poverty. Low wages and repeated or prolonged unemployment frequently interact to undermine the capacity for self-support. Since the number experiencing joblessness at some time during the year is several times the number unemployed in any month, those who suffer as a result of forced idleness can equal or exceed average annual unemployment, even though only a minority of the jobless in any month really suffers. For every person counted in the monthly unemployment tallies, there is another working part-time because of the inability to find full-time work, or else outside the labor force but wanting a job. Finally, income transfers in our country have always focused on the elderly, disabled, and dependent, neglecting the needs of the working poor, so that the dramatic expansion of cash and in-kind transfers does not necessarily mean that those failing in the labor market are adequately protected.

As a result of such contradictory evidence, it is uncertain whether those suffering seriously as a result of labor market problems number in the hundreds of thousands or the tens of millions, and, hence, whether high levels of joblessness can be tolerated or must be countered by job creation and economic stimulus. There is only one area of agreement in this debate—that the existing poverty, employment, and earnings statistics are inadequate for one their primary applications, measuring the consequences of labor market problems.

Q.61 What is the main theme of the passage?

A. The causes of labor market pathologies which lead to suffering

B. The reason for the imprecise income measures in determining rate of poverty

C. The way by which social figures provide a vague picture of the extent of hardship due to low wages and inadequate job opportunities

D. The areas of agreement among employment, income figures and poverty

Q.62 The words "labor market problems" used by the author in the passage refer to:

A. All the factors responsible for poverty
B. Inefficiency in the training of the work force
C. Trade links between producers of goods and commodities
D. Scarcity of jobs that provide sufficient income

Q.63 The author of the passage compares the 1930s with the modern-day to prove that

A. There was more redundancy in the 1930's
B. Redundancy now has less rigorous effects
C. More social and employment programs are required to be implemented
D. Poverty has decreased since the 1930s

Q.64 The author mentions that the justifying effect of social programs concerning transfers of income on the level of income of low-income people is usually not realized by:

A. Retired people
B. Full time workers who turn jobless
C. Reliant children in single-earner families
D. The employed poor

Q.65 A factor that leads to unemployment and earnings figures to over expect the extent of economic hardship is the:

A. Dominance, among low-income earners and the jobless, of members of families in which are working

B. Repetition of periods of redundancy for a group of low-income earners

C. Probability that income might be received from more than one job per worker

D. Setting up of a system of record-keeping which makes it feasible to pile up poverty statistics

Q.66 Direction: Select the most appropriate synonym of the given word.

DESPISE

A. Adore   B. Admire   C. Abhor   D. Approve

Q.67 Direction: Select the most appropriate synonym of the given word.

SUMPTUOUS

A. Bereft   B. Meager   C. Stingy   D. Opulent

Q.68 Direction: Select the most appropriate word to fill in the blank.

The watchdogs _________ asleep when the bulls ran riot.

A. were   B. was   C. is   D. are

Q.69 Direction: Select the most appropriate word to fill in the blank.

The thorns on a rose plant are for protection ____predators.

A. by   B. through   C. between   D. against

Q.70 Direction: Fill in the blanks with the most appropriate word from the options given below:

I used to _____ on the right.

A. driving   B. drive   C. driven   D. drove

Maths and Logical Reasoning

Q.71 A student can reach the exam center from his house in 10 hours. If he reduces his speed by $\left(\frac{1}{20}\right)^{th}$, he will cover 10 km less in that time. Find the distance of the exam center from his house.

A. 1000   B. 250 km   C. 200 km1500   D. 150 km2000

Q.72 If A, B, C are the angle of a triangle, then $cotAcotB + cotBcotC + cotCcotA$ will be equal to:

A. $\tan0°$ B. $\tan45°$ C. $\tan30°$ D. $\tan60°$

Q.73 The present age of Kavya is 35% of the sum of ages of Geet and Tanu. Tanu's age is 3 times more than the age of Geet. Find the ratio of ages of Tanu and Kavya.

A. $16:5$ B. $14:9$ C. $16:7$ D. $14:5$

Q.74 The ratio of the three sides of a triangle is 3 : 4 : 5 and the perimeter of the triangle is 180 m, then find the area of the triangle.

A. 1080 m²   B. 1550 m²   C. 1200 m²   D. 1350 m²

Q.75 The simplified value of $\left(1 - \frac{2xy}{x^2+y^2}\right) \div \left(\frac{x^3-y^3}{x-y} - 3xy\right)$ is

A. $\frac{1}{x^2-y^2}$ B. $\frac{1}{x^2+y^2}$ C. $\frac{1}{x-y}$ D. $\frac{1}{x+y}$

Q.76 One of the diagonals of a rhombus is 18 cm and the area of the rhombus is 216 cm². Find the length of the side of the rhombus.

A. 16 cm   B. 15 cm   C. 12 cm   D. 14 cm

Q.77 The length, breadth and height of a room are 21 metres, 12 metres and 16 metres. What will be the length of the largest rod that can be placed in that room?

A. 32 meters   B. 25 meters
C. 31 meters   D. 29 meters

Q.78 The breadth of a rectangular hall is $\frac{4}{5}$ of its length. If the area of the floor is 500 m², then what is the difference (in meters) between the length and breadth of the hall?

A. 5   B. 10   C. 20   D. 15

Q.79 If $A = \tan 11^o \tan 29^o, B = 2\cot 61^o \cot 79^o$ then

A. $A = 2B$ B. $A = -2B$
C. $2A = B$ D. $2A = -B$

Q.80 One of the angles of a parallelogram is $65°$. The remaining angles are respectively?

A. 105°, 125°, 55°   B. 115°, 65°, 135°
C. 115°, 115°, 65°   D. 25°, 135°, 135°

Q.81 The pairs of equations $9x + 3y + 12 = 0$ and $18x + 6y + 26 = 0$ have

A. Unique solution
B. Exactly two solutions
C. Infinitely many solutions
D. No solution

Q.82 If $a = 2 + \sqrt{3}$, then find the value of $a - \frac{1}{a}$

A. $1\sqrt{2}$ B. $2\sqrt{1}$ C. $2\sqrt{3}$ D. $3\sqrt{2}$

Ques (83-85): The bar graph given below shows the foreign exchange reserves of a country (in million US $) from $1991 - 1992$ to $1998 - 1999$.

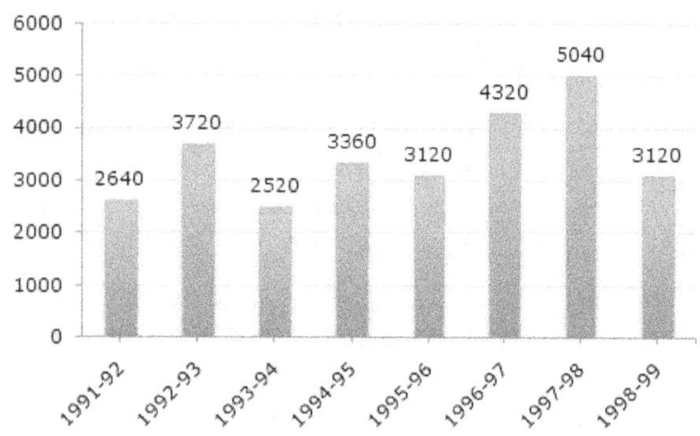

Q.83 The ratio of the number of years, in which the foreign exchange reserves are above the average reserves, to those in which the reserves are below the average reserves is?

[NCHM JEE (Hotel Mgmt & Catering), 2016]

A. 2 : 6   B. 6 : 2   C. 5 : 3   D. 3 : 5

Q.84 The foreign exchange reserves $1996 - 97$ were approximately what percent of the average foreign exchange reserves over the period under review?

A. 125%   B. 115%   C. 105%   D. 119%

Q.85 What was the percentage increase in the foreign exchange reserves in $1997 - 98$ over $1993 - 94$?

A. 95%   B. 90%   C. 110%   D. 100%

Q.86 If $2x + 3y : 3x + 5y = 18 : 29$ then $\frac{x}{y}$ is equal to

A. $\frac{3}{4}$ B. $\frac{4}{3}$ C. $\frac{2}{3}$ D. $\frac{5}{6}$

Q.87 Select the related words from the given alternatives.

Pullover : Wool : : Wall : ?

A. Color   B. Brick   C. Metal   D. Gold

Q.88 Find the odd one out from the given responses?

A. 48 – 54   B. 38 – 44   C. 34 – 40   D. 32 − 39

Q.89 Find the odd one from the given responses?

$13, 17, 23, 63, 71$

A. 63   B. 17   C. 23   D. 71

Q.90 If mode of the following data is 6, then the value of k in the 3, 8, 6, 7, 1, 6, 10, 6, 7, 2k + 4, 9, 7, and 13 is:

A. 0   B. 7   C. 1   D. 6

Q.91 What is tan 15° equal to?

A. $2 - \sqrt{3}$ B. $2 + \sqrt{3}$ C. $1 - \sqrt{3}$ D. $1 + \sqrt{3}$

Q.92 In the following question, select the missing number from the options given below?

$$\begin{matrix} 12 & 15 & 13 \\ 3 & 4 & 8 \\ 5 & 6 & 7 \\ 68 & 210 & ? \end{matrix}$$

A. 156   B. 255   C. 140   D. 152

Q.93 In a row of people facing north, Rakesh is 15th from the left end and Arun is 19th from the right end they interchange their positions and Bunny who sits 24th from the left end sits at the 5th place to the left of new position of Rakesh. Find the total number of people in the row?

A. 46   B. 47   C. 36   D. 37

Q.94 Rita and Sita are sisters. Prem is Sita's father. Prem has no siblings other than Reena who is the sister of Prem. Renu is Prem's niece. Rohan is Reena's grandson. How is Prem related to Rohan?

A. Maternal grandfather
B. Aunt
C. Grandson
D. Son

Q.95 What is sin² 20° + sin² 70° equal to?

A. 1   B. 0   C. -1   D. $\frac{1}{2}$

Q.96 Direction: In this series, you will be looking at a letter pattern. Fill the blank in the middle of the series or end of the series.

SCD, TEF, UGH, ___, WKL

A. VIJ   **B.** CMN   **C.** UJI   **D.** IJT

Q.97 Direction: In the following question, a series is given with one term missing. Choose the correct alternatives from the given ones that will complete the series.

DMOX, FKQV, HIST,?

A. JGVR   **B.** JGVS   **C.** JGUR   **D.** JKUR

Ques (98-99):Direction: What will come in place of the question mark (?) in the following number series?

Q.98 11, 27, 59, 123, ?

A. 351   **B.** 400   **C.** 251   **D.** 525

Q.99 10, 17, 48, 165, 688, 3475, ?

A. 27584   **B.** 25670   **C.** 21369   **D.** 20892

Q.100 The mean of the five observations $x, (x + 2), (x + 4), (x + 6), (x + 8)$ is 11. Then the mean of the first three observations is:

A. 20   **B.** 9   **C.** 12   **D.** 2

// Smart Answer Sheet //

Correct   Indicates percentage of students who answered questions correctly.

Skipped   Indicates percentage of students who skipped questions.

Q.	Ans.	Correct / Skipped	Q.	Ans.	Correct / Skipped	Q.	Ans.	Correct / Skipped	Q.	Ans.	Correct / Skipped	Q.	Ans.	Correct / Skipped
1	B	25.0 % / 20.0 %	17	D	26.67 % / 13.33 %	33	A	63.33 % / 16.67 %	49	A	20.0 % / 28.33 %	65	A	28.33 % / 28.34 %
2	A	13.33 % / 18.34 %	18	C	20.0 % / 6.67 %	34	A	21.67 % / 13.33 %	50	C	45.0 % / 28.33 %	66	C	36.67 % / 23.33 %
3	B	21.67 % / 16.66 %	19	C	28.33 % / 20.0 %	35	D	46.67 % / 20.0 %	51	C	21.67 % / 23.33 %	67	D	23.33 % / 30.0 %
4	A	63.33 % / 21.67 %	20	C	33.33 % / 13.34 %	36	B	53.33 % / 10.0 %	52	C	36.67 % / 23.33 %	68	A	58.33 % / 28.34 %
5	C	30.0 % / 21.67 %	21	D	43.33 % / 13.34 %	37	C	41.67 % / 16.66 %	53	B	25.0 % / 23.33 %	69	D	60.0 % / 23.33 %
6	C	45.0 % / 21.67 %	22	C	25.0 % / 23.33 %	38	B	40.0 % / 10.0 %	54	D	45.0 % / 21.67 %	70	B	51.67 % / 28.33 %
7	D	36.67 % / 16.66 %	23	A	51.67 % / 20.0 %	39	D	30.0 % / 20.0 %	55	B	28.33 % / 23.34 %	71	C	16.67 % / 25.0 %
8	C	56.67 % / 18.33 %	24	C	26.67 % / 15.0 %	40	A	46.67 % / 15.0 %	56	A	66.67 % / 28.33 %	72	B	20.0 % / 25.0 %
9	C	43.33 % / 11.67 %	25	C	16.67 % / 21.66 %	41	C	35.0 % / 26.67 %	57	D	45.0 % / 21.67 %	73	C	26.67 % / 25.0 %
10	C	31.67 % / 13.33 %	26	B	20.0 % / 23.33 %	42	C	23.33 % / 18.34 %	58	A	33.33 % / 20.0 %	74	D	20.0 % / 25.0 %
11	C	45.0 % / 18.33 %	27	D	26.67 % / 20.0 %	43	B	31.67 % / 30.0 %	59	C	63.33 % / 23.34 %	75	B	21.67 % / 25.0 %
12	D	31.67 % / 13.33 %	28	A	45.0 % / 10.0 %	44	B	41.67 % / 28.33 %	60	B	31.67 % / 16.66 %	76	B	13.33 % / 18.34 %
13	A	23.33 % / 15.0 %	29	A	61.67 % / 11.66 %	45	D	30.0 % / 21.67 %	61	C	23.33 % / 28.34 %	77	D	13.33 % / 25.0 %
14	A	15.0 % / 13.33 %	30	D	21.67 % / 20.0 %	46	D	18.33 % / 21.67 %	62	D	25.0 % / 26.67 %	78	A	20.0 % / 25.0 %
15	C	33.33 % / 18.34 %	31	C	36.67 % / 20.0 %	47	C	21.67 % / 21.66 %	63	B	8.33 % / 28.34 %	79	C	23.33 % / 25.0 %
16	A	65.0 % / 13.33 %	32	B	73.33 % / 11.67 %	48	A	53.33 % / 21.67 %	64	D	11.67 % / 23.33 %	80	C	40.0 % / 23.33 %

Q.	Ans.	Correct	
		Skipped	
81	D	15.0 %	
		25.0 %	
82	C	33.33 %	
		21.67 %	
83	D	26.67 %	
		23.33 %	
84	A	20.0 %	
		23.33 %	

Q.	Ans.	Correct	
		Skipped	
85	D	31.67 %	
		23.33 %	
86	A	41.67 %	
		18.33 %	
87	B	60.0 %	
		25.0 %	
88	D	68.33 %	
		16.67 %	

Q.	Ans.	Correct	
		Skipped	
89	A	50.0 %	
		25.0 %	
90	C	35.0 %	
		18.33 %	
91	A	10.0 %	
		25.0 %	
92	B	13.33 %	
		25.0 %	

Q.	Ans.	Correct	
		Skipped	
93	B	16.67 %	
		25.0 %	
94	A	48.33 %	
		25.0 %	
95	A	13.33 %	
		25.0 %	
96	A	61.67 %	
		21.66 %	

Q.	Ans.	Correct	
		Skipped	
97	C	45.0 %	
		23.33 %	
98	C	56.67 %	
		21.66 %	
99	D	11.67 %	
		21.66 %	
100	B	43.33 %	
		25.0 %	

Performance Analysis

Avg. Score (%)	38.0%
Toppers Score (%)	68.0%
Your Score	

General Awareness

Q.1 Under which mission did INS Gharial arrived at Colombo to deliver critical lifesaving medicines on 29 April 2022?

A. MAITRI-22
B. DOSTI-IV
C. MISSION DOSTI
D. SAGAR IX

Q.2 The Mahanadi Coalfields Limited (MCL) has crossed how many million tonnes (MT) in coal production in the financial year of 2021-22?

A. 142
B. 157
C. 169
D. 175

Q.3 How many marks has India got in Human Development Index - 2016?

[UPPSC Staff Nurse, 2017], [UPSSSC Rajasva Lekhpal, 2015]

A. 0.623
B. 0.624
C. 0.625
D. 0.626

Q.4 The Sati Pratha was declared illegal during The Governor Generalship of:

A. Dalhousie
B. Canning
C. William Bentinck
D. Cornwallis

Q.5 Potassium Permanganate is used for purifying drinking water, because

A. It is a sterilizing agent
B. It dissolves the impurities of water
C. It is a reducing agent
D. It is an oxidizing agent

Q.6 Which among the following is a well-known classical dance of Kerala?

A. Kuchipudi
B. Mohiniyattam
C. Garba
D. Bharatanatyam

Q.7 Which state observes 'Sangai Festival' every year?

A. Nagaland
B. Arunachal Pradesh
C. Manipur
D. Assam

Q.8 The Industrial Revolution began in:

A. Britain
B. Germany
C. France
D. None of these

Q.9 Which metal pollutes the air of a big city?

A. Copper
B. Chromium
C. Lead
D. Cadmium

Q.10 Which Indian player has become the first Indian athlete to qualify for Tokyo Olympics 2020 in individual competition?

A. KT Irfan
B. Mridul Pandey
C. Kapil Patra
D. Yogesh Awasthi

Q.11 The blue colour of the clear sky is due to

A. Diffraction of light
B. Dispersion of light
C. Reflection of light
D. Refraction of light

Q.12 Which of the following temporarily shifted the capital of Magadh to Vaishali?

A. Udayin
B. Shishunaga
C. Kalasoka
D. Mahapadma Nanda

Q.13 Which of the following caves consists of the rock sculpture of the front part of an elephant?

A. Lomasha Risi cave
B. Dhauli caves
C. Ajanta caves
D. Elephanta Caves

Q.14 The weight of an object will be minimum when it is placed at?

A. The North Pole
B. The South Pole
C. The Equator
D. The center of the Earth

Q.15 Which unit of a computer is the Arithmetic Logic Unit a part of?

A. Input Unit
B. Output Unit
C. Central Processing Unit
D. Memory Unit

Q.16 Which state has established India's first Centre for Animal Law?

A. Telangana
B. Maharashtra
C. Uttar Pradesh
D. Madhya Pradesh

Q.17 In which state is the agricultural festival Nuakhai mainly observed?

A. Assam
B. Odisha
C. Tamil Nadu
D. Haryana

Q.18 Global Atmosphere Watch is a global atmosphere monitoring system established by:

A. United Nations Environment Programme
B. World Meteorological Organization
C. United Nations Framework Convention on Climate Change
D. All of the above

Q.19 Who among the following called the Revolt of 1857 as a feudal Revolt?

A. Jawahar Lal Nehru
B. Subhash Chandra Bose
C. Mahatma Gandhi
D. Lala Lajpat Rai

Q.20 Which among the following is not an example of a storage device?

A. Hard disk drive
B. Pen drive
C. Mouse
D. CD drive

Q.21 Who is known as the Frontier Gandhi?

A. Abdul Ghaffar Khan

B. Syed Ahmed Khan

C. Maulana Abul Azad

D. None of these

Q.22 'Natya Shastra', the main source of India's classical dances, was written by:

A. Narad Muni

B. Bharat Muni

C. Abhinavagupta

D. Tandu Muni

Q.23 Cattle, sheep and termites are responsible for the release of which of the following greenhouse gases?

A. Methane

B. Carbon dioxide

C. Nitrous oxide

D. All of the above

Q.24 The first Indian to claim the World Amateur Billiards title was:

A. Geet Sethi

B. Wilson Jones

C. Michael Ferreira

D. Pankaj Advani

Q.25 Which dress was the sign of purity, simplicity and poverty for Mahatma Gandhi?

A. Western Clothes

B. Indian dhoti and kurta

C. Khadi

D. Three piece suits

Q.26 Which of the following is awarded to institutions having record merit and integrity in developing the Olympic Movement?

A. Olympic Cup

B. Olympic Town

C. Olympic Order

D. Olympic Laurel

Q.27 Who was the winner in Javelin Throw in the 2018 Diamond League event for men?

A. Andreas Hofmann

B. Jakub Vadlejch

C. Tomas Walsh

D. Darrell Hill

Q.28 What is the full form of LSI used in computer technology?

A. Large Scale Integration

B. Leveled Scale Implementation

C. Large Spot Integration

D. Light Spot Integration

Q.29 The main aim of Integrated Rural Development Programme is

A. To provide education to all rural poor

B. To increase the income generation capacity of rural poor

C. To provide subsidized food grains to rural poor

D. All of the above

Q.30 Which continent has sent the maximum number of teams to the Uber Cup?

A. Europe

B. Asia

C. Africa

D. North America

Q.31 Acid rain is caused by:

A. Carbon monoxide

B. Sulphur dioxide

C. Oxygen

D. All of the above

Q.32 Ozone holes exist over:-

1. Antarctica

2. Arctic

3. Tibet

Which of the above points is/are correct?

A. Only 1

B. 2 and 3

C. 1 and 2

D. 1, 2 and 3

Q.33 Which of these is the biggest cause of pollution of surface and groundwater in India?

A. Untreated sewage

B. Dumping partially cremated bodies

C. Open defecation

D. Communal violence related to distribution of water

Q.34 Which is the national sport of Bangladesh?

A. Hockey **B.** Football **C.** Kabaddi **D.** Cricket

Q.35 Who is called the 'Father of Indian Cinema'?

A. Raj Kapoor

B. Ashok Kumar

C. Prithviraj Kapoor

D. Dadasaheb Phalke

Q.36 Who was the first Chief election commissioner of India?

A. KVK Sundaram

B. SP Sen Verma

C. Sukumar Sen

D. Rajmannar

Q.37 Which of the following chemicals is/are linked with the depletion of ozone in the atmosphere?

A. Chlorofluorocarbons

B. Hydrogen peroxide

C. Carbon dioxide

D. Sulphur dioxide

Q.38 Who roped in as a brand ambassador of Vega?

A. Virat Kohli

B. Rohit Sharma

C. Jasprit Bumrah

D. Brett lee

Q.39 Which among the following articles of the Constitution of India abolishes the untouchablity?

A. Article 15

B. Article 16

C. Article 17

D. Article 18

Q.40 Which act provided for the right to vote to women?

A. Indian Councils Act, 1909

B. Government of India Act, 1919

C. Government of India Act, 1935

D. Indian Independence Act, 1947

English Proficiency

Q.41 Direction: The sentence is divided into four parts. Find out which part has an error and mark it as your answer. If there is no error, mark 'No error' as your answer.

I need (A) / the kind of person which (B) / will understand me. (C) / No error (D)

A. (A) **B.** (B) **C.** (C) **D.** (D)

Q.42 Direction: The sentence is divided into four parts. Find out which part has an error and mark it as your answer. If there is no error, mark 'No error' as your answer.

The members of family(A) / who live next to our home (B) / is adorable. (C) / No error (D)

A. (A) **B.** (B) **C.** (C) **D.** (D)

Q.43 Direction: Which of the option (A), (B), and (C) given below, should replace the phrase printed in bold in the sentence to make it grammatically correct? If the sentence is correct as it is given and no correction is required, mark (D) as the answer.

The prospects for Britain's orderly withdrawal from the European Union on March 29 **have receded further**, even as MPs rallied to stop a no-deal scenario.

A. had recede further
B. did receded further
C. has receded further
D. No correction required

Q.44 Direction: The sentence has four phrases, marked as (1), (2), (3), and (4). Identify the one phrase that must be changed in order for the sentence to be correct.

Each (1) of the department heads (2) are going to (3) be present at the (4) graduation ceremony.

A. (1) **B.** (2) **C.** (3) **D.** (4)

Q.45 Direction: A sentence/a part of the sentence is underlined. Four alternatives are given to the underlined part which will improve the sentence. Choose the correct alternative and click the button corresponding to it. In case no improvement is needed, click the button corresponding to "No improvement".

His wife is <u>as tall if not</u>, taller than him.

A. As tall as, if not
B. As taller if not
C. Not as tall but as
D. No improvement

Q.46 Direction: Select the word that is antonymous to the word given in bold letters.
NARCISSISM

A. Nihilism
B. Altruism
C. Insolence
D. Virtuous

Q.47 Fill in the blank with an appropriate word.
Fate smiles _________ those who untiringly grapple with stark realities of life.

A. Over **B.** On **C.** With **D.** Round

Q.48 Select the most appropriate synonym of the given word.
REMORSE

A. Affection
B. Indiffierence
C. Regret
D. Reproach

Q.49 Select the most appropriate ANTONYM of the given word.
CONSPICUOUS

A. Distinct
B. Obscure
C. Noticeable
D. Apparent

Q.50 Select the appropriate synonym of the given word.
TIMID

A. Willful **B.** Shy **C.** Kind **D.** Strong

Q.51 Select the most appropriate ANTONYM of the given word.
BENEVOLENT

A. Generous
B. Friendly
C. Stingy
D. Liberal

Q.52 Direction: The given sentence has four phrases, which are marked as (1), (2), (3) and (4). Identify the one phrase that must be changed in order for the sentence to be correct.

The (1) emergence of the railroad (2) during the 1900s (3) does much (4) to accelerate the settlement of the mid-western United States.

A. (1) **B.** (2) **C.** (3) **D.** (4)

Q.53 Direction: Choose the appropriate word to complete the given sentence.

He was brought up to be ________ and never to get into debt.

A. Immoderate
B. Thrifty
C. Extravagant
D. Compassionate

Q.54 Direction: Choose the appropriate word to complete the given sentence.

The U.S. ________ the most intensely disputed presidential election in our history.

A. Confronted
B. Appeased
C. Softened
D. Penalized

Ques (55-59):Direction: In the following passage, some words have been left out. Read the passage carefully and select the correct answer for the given blank out of the four alternatives.

Sharks are some ____ (A)____ the most regal and amazing creatures in the sea, though sometimes referred to as 'beasts' or 'killing machines' they are way more docile than human kind is____(B)____ to believe. Sharks are more____(C)____ than the common Great White shark that is so often portrayed in the movies. Sharks have some of the strongest olfactory senses in the marine world _____(D)____ This is why there is a common belief that a shark can sense 1 drop of blood mixed in a hundred drops of water. ____(E)____ the violent enactment of this amazing creature of the seas they are surprisingly calm until they are poked and prodded.

Q.55 Which of the following fits in the blank labelled (A)?
A. Off **B.** Of **C.** As **D.** To

Q.56 Which of the following fits in the blank labelled (B)?
A. Lead **B.** Leading **C.** Led **D.** Leaden

Q.57 Which of the following fits in the blank labelled (C)?
A. Variant
B. Immutable
C. Invariable
D. Variable

Q.58 Which of the following fits in the blank labelled (D)?
A. What **B.** Which **C.** Why **D.** How

Q.59 Which of the following fits in the blank labelled (E)?
A. Despite
B. Despite of
C. In spite
D. Irrelevant

Ques (60-61):Direction: Read the sentence to find out whether there is any grammatical or idiomatic error in it. The error, if any, will be in one part of the sentence. The number of that part is the answer. If there is no error, the answer is (d).

Q.60 Enjoy your own (a) living without comparing it (b) with that of another (c) No error (d).

A. (a)   **B.** (b)   **C.** (c)   **D.** (d)

Q.61 (a) Don't take yourself (b) so seriously (c) no one else does (d) No error.

A. (a)   **B.** (b)   **C.** (c)   **D.** (d)

Q.62 Direction: Choose the best option to fill in the blanks.
When there is complete _______ of division between the observer and the observed, then 'what is' is no longer _______.

A. Truce, existential
B. Impasse, paramount
C. Assent, of importance
D. Cessation, is what is

Q.63 Direction: From the given alternatives, choose the correct antonym for the given word:
IGNORE

A. Redress   **B.** Avoid   **C.** Accept   **D.** Favour

Q.64 Direction: Select the best option to fill in the blank.
Ballpoint pens require ___ as compared to fountain pens.

A. The thicker ink   **B.** An thicker ink
C. A thicker ink   **D.** Very thicker ink

Q.65 Direction: Read the sentence to find out whether there is any grammatical or idiomatic error in it. The error, if any, will be in one part of the sentence. The number of that part is the answer. If there is no error, the answer is (d).
We have hundred (a) of pages (b) of reading to do (c) No error (d).

A. (a)   **B.** (b)   **C.** (c)   **D.** (d)

Ques (66-70):Direction: Read the following passage and answer the given question.

This rule of always trying to do things as well as one can do them has an important bearing upon the problem of ambition. No man or woman should be without ambition, which is the inspiration of activity. But if one allows ambition to drive one to attempt things which are beyond one's own personal capacity, then unhappiness will result. If one imagines that one can do everything better than other people, then envy and jealousy, those twin monsters, will come to sadden one's days. But if one concentrates one's attention upon developing one's own special capacities, the things one is best at, then one does not worry overmuch if other people are more successful.

Q.66 The meaning of 'to have a bearing upon' is to:

A. Have an effect on
B. Carry the weight on oneself
C. Put up with
D. Decrease friction

Q.67 Which of the following statements is correct?

A. There is a close relationship between ambition and activity
B. Ambition and activity belong to two different areas
C. Ambition is useless
D. Activity is responsible for ambition

Q.68 The statement "if one allows ambition to drive one to attempt things which are beyond one's own personal capacity, then unhappiness will result" means that :-

A. One must always try to do less than one's capacity
B. One must always try to do more than one's capacity
C. Ambition must be consistent with one's capacity
D. There should be no ambition at all

Q.69 Which one of the following statements best reflects the underlying tone of the passage?

A. One ought to focus on what one considers oneself good at
B. One must try to be better than others
C. One must continuously worry about others
D. One must try beyond one's capacity to get results

Q.70 Which of the following statements can be assumed to be true?

A. It is good to imagine oneself better than others
B. One should not imagine oneself to be always better than others
C. All persons have equal capacity
D. One should have more ambitions than others

Maths and Logical Reasoning

Q.71 When an integer n is divided by 5, the remainder is 3. What is the remainder if 8n is divided by 5?

A. 1   **B.** 2   **C.** 3   **D.** 4

Q.72 If $r\sin\theta = 1, r\cos\theta = \sqrt{3}$, then the value of $\left(\sqrt{3}\tan\theta + 1\right) = ?$

A. $\sqrt{3}$ **B.** $\frac{1}{\sqrt{3}}$ **C.** 1   **D.** 2

Q.73 If a person walks at 14 km/hr instead of 10 km/hr, he would have walked 20 km more. The actual distance travelled by him is:

A. 89 km   **B.** 93 km   **C.** 56 km   **D.** 50 km

Q.74 A cord AB is such that AB is equal to the radius of circle and any point P is taken on the major arc of the AB. What will be the measure of angle ∠APB? Where AP≠BP.

A. 30°   **B.** 60°   **C.** 15°   **D.** 45°

Q.75 If a(a + 3) = 4, find the value of the expression $\frac{\left(a^6 + 63a^3 - 60\right)}{4}$?

A. 1   **B.** 0   **C.** 4   **D.** 2

Q.76 If a - b = 6 and ab = 15, then the value of $a^3 - b^3$ is:

A. 54   **B.** 270   **C.** 486   **D.** 216

Q.77 The minimum value of $2\sin^2\theta + 3\cos^2\theta$ is:

A. 1   **B.** 3   **C.** 2   **D.** 4

Q.78 A parallelogram ABCD has sides AB = 20 cm and AD = 24 cm. The distance between the sides AB and DC is 12 cm. Find the distance between the sides AD and BC.

A. 16 cm   **B.** 18 cm   **C.** 10 cm   **D.** 26 cm

Q.79 The diameter of a circle is 24 cm and the length of a chord is $12\sqrt{2}$ cm. Then find the length of the minor arc corresponding to the chord.

A. 12π cm   **B.** 4π cm   **C.** 8π cm   **D.** 6π cm

Q.80 The value of $\left[15 + (5 \times 4)\right] \div (5 + 2) + \left[20 - \left(\frac{3}{5} \text{ of } 15\right)\right]$ is:

A. 12   **B.** 16   **C.** 4   **D.** 18

Q.81 Direction: Select the option that is related to the third term in the same way as the second term is related to the first term.

JMP : HON :: ADG : ?

A. JKM   **B.** ZGF   **C.** YFE   **D.** CBI

Q.82 Choose the odd one out from the given alternatives.

A. 459   **B.** 306   **C.** 470   **D.** 153

Q.83 Find the wrong term in the following series.

EM, GO, IQ, KT, MU

A. KT   **B.** EM   **C.** GO   **D.** MU

Q.84 In a row of boys, A is thirteenth from the left and D is seventeenth from the right. If in this row, A is eleventh from the right, then what is the position of D from the left?

A. Sixth   **B.** Seventh   **C.** Tenth   **D.** Twelfth

Q.85 Direction: Find the number that will replace the question mark (?) in the following problem.

215	22	293
421	?	137

A. 20   **B.** 18   **C.** 19   **D.** 22

Ques (86-87):Direction: Study the following information carefully and answer the question beside:

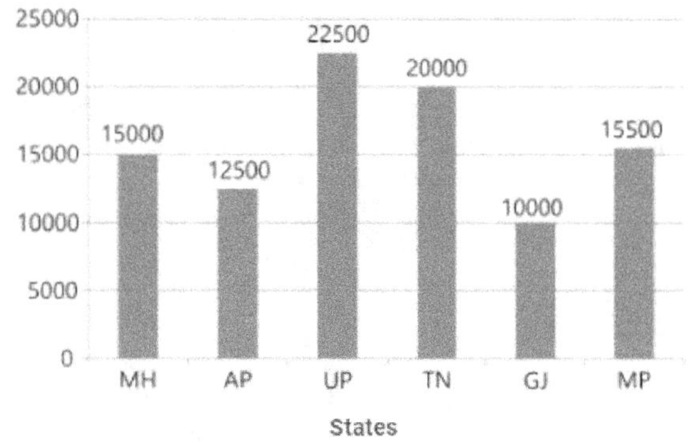

Q.86 By what per cent is the Sugarcane production of MH and GJ together more than that of AP?

A. 50%   **B.** 40%   **C.** 100%   **D.** 25%

Q.87 Which of the following states contributes less than 20 percent in the total Sugarcane production?

A. Only GJ   **B.** GJ, AP

C. GJ, AP, TN   **D.** GJ, MH, AP, MP

Q.88 Direction: Study the following information carefully and answer the question beside:

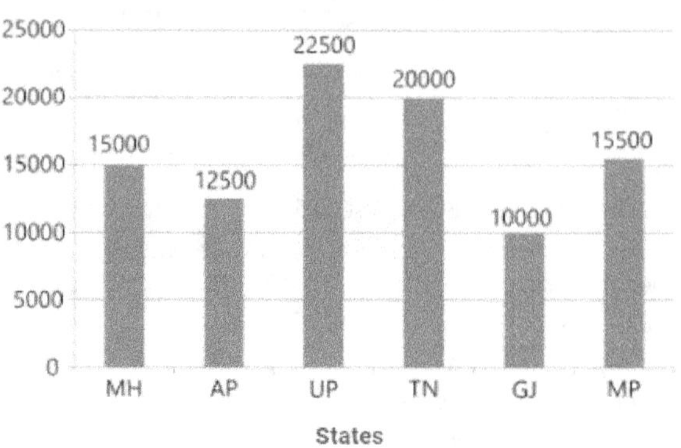

Approximately what percent of the total Sugarcane production is shared by UP and TN?

A. 40%   **B.** 44.5%   **C.** 25%   **D.** 48%

Q.89 Direction: Study the following information carefully and answer the question beside:

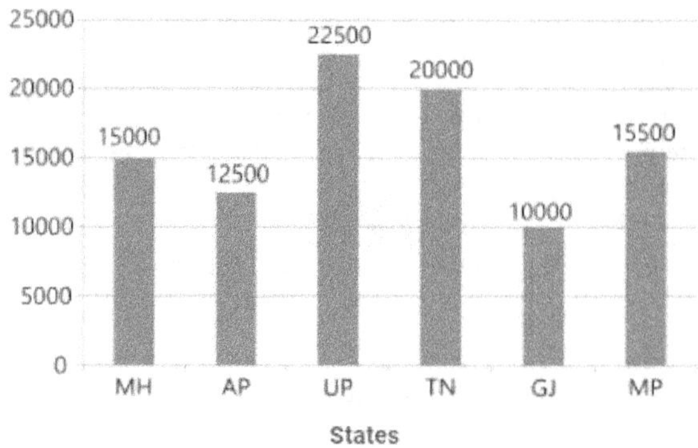

Due to the welfare scheme launched by the UP government, the production of sugarcane in UP in the year 2017 is increased by 2.4 times the average production of sugarcane taken all states together. Then by how much percentage more the production of sugarcane in the year 2017 than that of 2016 in UP?

A. 70%   **B.** 65%   **C.** 60%   **D.** 75%

Q.90 If angles P, Q, R and S of a quadrilateral PQRS are in the ratio of $3 : 7 : 6 : 4$, then PQRS is a

A. Rhombus   **B.** Parallelogram
C. Trapezium   **D.** Kite

Q.91 Christina is standing to the west of Broad and to the southwest of Andrew. Daniel is standing to the northwest of Andrew and to the north of Christina. What is the position of Broad with respect to Andrew, if Daniel, Andrew and Broad are standing in a straight line?

A. Southeast   **B.** Southwest
C. Northeast   **D.** Northwest

Q.92 A, B and C start running around a circular field having circumference 144 meters at the same time from the same point. Speeds of A, B and C are $6\ m/minute, 8\ m/minute$, and $12\ m/minute$. Find after how much time, they will meet again at the same point for the first time.

A. 72 minute **B.** 36 minute
C. 144 minute **D.** None of these

Q.93 A is two years older than B who is twice as old as C. If the total of the ages of A, B and C be 27, then how old is B?

A. 7 years **B.** 10 years **C.** 9 years **D.** 8 years

Q.94 Find the value of
$\frac{4}{3}\tan^2 30° + \sin^2 60° - 3\cos^2 60° + \frac{3}{4}\tan^2 60° - 2\tan^2 45°.$

A. $\frac{35}{36}$ **B.** $\frac{20}{36}$ **C.** $\frac{25}{36}$ **D.** $\frac{25}{40}$

Q.95 Find the value of $4(\sin^4 30° + \cos^4 60°) - 3(\cos^2 45° + \sin^2 90°).$

A. -1 **B.** -2 **C.** -3 **D.** -4

Q.96 Find the value of $\dfrac{\cot^2 A(\sec A - 1)}{(1 + \sin A)} + \dfrac{\sec^2 A(\sin A - 1)}{(1 + \sec A)}$

A. 0 **B.** 1 **C.** 2 **D.** 3

Ques (97-100):Direction: In this type of question, usually four groups of words are given. Three of them are similar to each other in some manner while one is different and this is to be chosen by the candidate as the answer.

Q.97 Arrange these letters of each group to make a meaningful word and then find the odd one out.

A. ORFU **B.** VIDEID **C.** GHIET **D.** VEENS

Q.98 Identify which one of the given alternatives will be another member of the group of that class.

Lucknow, Patna, Bhopal, Jaipur?

A. Pune **B.** Indore **C.** Shimla **D.** Mysore

Q.99 Four of the following five are alike in a certain way and so form a group. Which is the one that does not belong to that group?

A. Water **B.** Juice **C.** Petrol **D.** Sugar

Q.100 Select the one which is different from the other three responses.

A. Mayor **B.** Lawyer
C. Governor **D.** Legislator

// Smart Answer Sheet //

Correct   Indicates percentage of students who answered questions correctly.

Skipped   Indicates percentage of students who skipped questions.

Q.	Ans.	Correct / Skipped	Q.	Ans.	Correct / Skipped	Q.	Ans.	Correct / Skipped	Q.	Ans.	Correct / Skipped	Q.	Ans.	Correct / Skipped
1	D	67.5 % / 1.45 %	17	B	41.6 % / 1.99 %	33	A	42.99 % / 1.01 %	49	B	45.47 % / 1.05 %	65	A	51.53 % / 1.76 %
2	B	11.59 % / 3.18 %	18	B	59.35 % / 1.05 %	34	C	82.44 % / 0.0 %	50	B	85.1 % / 0.0 %	66	A	53.61 % / 1.19 %
3	B	24.43 % / 3.19 %	19	A	66.68 % / 1.77 %	35	D	88.68 % / 0.0 %	51	C	80.81 % / 0.0 %	67	A	44.33 % / 1.73 %
4	C	47.15 % / 1.39 %	20	C	89.43 % / 0.0 %	36	C	21.11 % / 4.79 %	52	C	40.34 % / 1.76 %	68	C	69.03 % / 1.03 %
5	D	61.41 % / 1.68 %	21	A	79.53 % / 0.0 %	37	A	29.85 % / 4.85 %	53	B	82.4 % / 0.0 %	69	A	65.49 % / 1.02 %
6	B	65.68 % / 1.37 %	22	B	43.12 % / 1.96 %	38	B	53.98 % / 1.02 %	54	A	46.11 % / 1.35 %	70	B	48.05 % / 1.2 %
7	C	44.16 % / 1.3 %	23	A	53.11 % / 1.17 %	39	C	21.18 % / 4.4 %	55	B	40.0 % / 1.85 %	71	D	88.88 % / 0.0 %
8	A	76.2 % / 0.0 %	24	B	69.57 % / 1.6 %	40	B	53.95 % / 1.83 %	56	C	64.89 % / 1.53 %	72	D	54.06 % / 1.38 %
9	C	82.35 % / 0.0 %	25	C	87.92 % / 0.0 %	41	B	86.19 % / 0.0 %	57	D	62.62 % / 1.3 %	73	D	51.38 % / 1.04 %
10	A	49.78 % / 1.43 %	26	A	52.69 % / 1.19 %	42	C	89.47 % / 0.0 %	58	B	58.66 % / 1.67 %	74	A	20.45 % / 4.36 %
11	B	76.6 % / 0.0 %	27	A	64.76 % / 1.16 %	43	D	85.64 % / 0.0 %	59	A	62.62 % / 1.56 %	75	A	81.66 % / 0.0 %
12	B	24.58 % / 3.98 %	28	A	45.74 % / 1.82 %	44	B	69.22 % / 1.32 %	60	B	88.25 % / 0.0 %	76	C	79.36 % / 0.0 %
13	B	87.72 % / 0.0 %	29	B	45.07 % / 1.54 %	45	A	56.84 % / 1.38 %	61	D	66.29 % / 1.42 %	77	C	51.75 % / 1.83 %
14	D	82.23 % / 0.0 %	30	B	56.15 % / 1.2 %	46	B	19.06 % / 4.81 %	62	D	54.3 % / 1.6 %	78	C	52.21 % / 1.41 %
15	C	88.02 % / 0.0 %	31	B	88.64 % / 0.0 %	47	B	78.4 % / 0.0 %	63	A	43.13 % / 1.06 %	79	D	61.57 % / 1.31 %
16	A	58.19 % / 1.48 %	32	D	62.79 % / 1.81 %	48	C	66.12 % / 1.0 %	64	C	84.94 % / 0.0 %	80	B	49.67 % / 1.57 %

Q.	Ans.	Correct / Skipped
81	C	64.57 %
		1.79 %
82	C	49.98 %
		1.18 %
83	A	43.75 %
		1.65 %
84	B	62.41 %
		1.58 %

Q.	Ans.	Correct / Skipped
85	B	77.95 %
		0.0 %
86	C	45.86 %
		1.38 %
87	D	69.77 %
		1.06 %
88	B	50.89 %
		1.65 %

Q.	Ans.	Correct / Skipped
89	A	40.74 %
		1.16 %
90	C	84.42 %
		0.0 %
91	A	60.14 %
		1.39 %
92	A	67.07 %
		1.69 %

Q.	Ans.	Correct / Skipped
93	B	81.29 %
		0.0 %
94	C	45.12 %
		1.86 %
95	D	76.75 %
		0.0 %
96	A	17.87 %
		3.42 %

Q.	Ans.	Correct / Skipped
97	B	83.38 %
		0.0 %
98	C	80.39 %
		0.0 %
99	D	79.52 %
		0.0 %
100	B	64.54 %
		1.85 %

Performance Analysis

Avg. Score (%)	50.0%
Toppers Score (%)	57.0%
Your Score	

General Awareness

Q.1 In which of the following regions Passage Exercise between India and Russia was conducted in January 2022?

A. Red Sea   **B.** Arabian Sea

C. South China Sea   **D.** Mediterranean Sea

Q.2 As on March 2018, which of the following is the India's fastest supercomputer?

[Super TET Paper - I, 2019]

A. Summit   **B.** Sierra   **C.** Mihir   **D.** Pratyush

Q.3 Where has the only Genome Sequencing Lab in the Bihar started?

[Delhi Forest Guard, 2021]

A. Patna   **B.** Darbhanga

C. Gaya   **D.** Vaishali

Q.4 IKF Finance, backed by Motilal Oswal Private Equity, has entered into a co-lending partnership with which bank in March 2022?

A. Bank of India

B. ICICI Bank

C. Union Bank of India

D. Central Bank of India

Q.5 For the first time in its 100-year-old history, Dehradun's Rashtriya Indian Military College (RIMC) will induct girls. How many girls cadets are set to join Rashtriya Indian Military College in July 2022?

A. 3   **B.** 5   **C.** 7   **D.** 9

Q.6 Which of the following department has released an Approach Paper for the Draft National Policy for the Medical Devices, 2022 on its website for consultation?

A. Department of Pharmaceuticals

B. Department of Biotechnology

C. Department of Science & Technology

D. Department of Scientific & Industrial Research

Q.7 Who has been appointed as the new brand ambassadors for My11Circle, fantasy sports platform, in March 2022?

A. Shubman Gill and Shreyas Iyer

B. Devdutt Padikkal and Mayank Agarwal

C. Shreyas Iyer and Ruturaj Gaikwad

D. Shubman Gill and Ruturaj Gaikwad

Q.8 The sequence of living organisms in a community, in which one organism consumes another with the transfer of food energy, is known as:

A. Food chain   **B.** Food web

C. Ecosystem   **D.** Biosphere

Q.9 'Bachpan Bachao Andolan' was initiated by:

A. Jawaharlal Nehru   **B.** Kailash Satyarthi

C. Malala Yousafzai   **D.** Benazir Bhutto

Q.10 Which one of the following age groups is eligible for enrolment under 'Sarva Shiksha Abhiyan'?

A. 5-15 years   **B.** 6-15 years

C. 5-14 years   **D.** 6-14 years

Q.11 Punch mark coin of ancient India is developed by which of the following metals?

A. Silver   **B.** Gold   **C.** Bronze   **D.** Tin

Q.12 Which of the following computer language is used for Artificial Intelligence?

A. FORTRAN   **B.** C

C. PROLOG   **D.** COBOL

Q.13 NBA is world famous league of which sport?

A. Baseball   **B.** Basketball

C. Motor Car Racing   **D.** Badminton

Q.14 Rafael Nadal, who is a tennis player belongs to which of the following country?

A. The US   **B.** Switzerland

C. Germany   **D.** Spain

Q.15 Which of the following acts was amended after the Bhopal gas tragedy?

A. Factories Act, 1948

B. Mines Act, 1952

C. Plantation Labour Act, 1951

D. None of the above

Q.16 Which organization has made a declaration on Fundamental Principles and Rights at Workplace as one of the components of 'Decent Work'?

A. First National Commission on Labour

B. Indian Labour Conference

C. International Labour Organization

D. Sachar Committee on Worker's Participation

Q.17 When was the first Factories Act passed in India?

A. 1881   **B.** 1891   **C.** 1911   **D.** 1948

Q.18 When was the GSLV used in India for the first time?

A. 1980   **B.** 1987   **C.** 1994   **D.** 2001

Q.19 To generate employment in rural areas, a programme named SFURTI was launched all over the country. By which ministry is this programme governed?

A. Ministry of Tourism

B. Ministry of Human Resource Development

C. Ministry of Micro, Small and Medium Enterprises

D. Ministry of Information and Communication Technology

Q.20 Which of the following pairs is mismatched?

A. Fossil fuel burning - Release of carbon dioxide
B. Nuclear power plant - Radioactive waste
C. Aeroplanes - Aerosols
D. Solar energy - Greenhouse effect

Q.21 The Indian National Calendar is based on:

A. Christian era
B. Saka era
C. Vikram era
D. Hijri era

Q.22 Who among the following is NOT one of the players to be inducted into the ICC Cricket Hall of Fame?

A. Sachin Tendulkar
B. Anil Kumble
C. Mahendra Singh Dhoni
D. Kapil Dev

Q.23 The national song of India was composed by:

A. Iqbal
B. Rabindranath Tagore
C. Jai Shankar Prasad
D. Bankim Chandra Chatterjee

Q.24 Who among the following introduced the printing press in India?

A. Mughals
B. Nizams
C. Britishers
D. Portuguese

Q.25 The excessive richness of nutrients in a lake or some other body of water, frequently due to run-off from the land, is called:

A. Eutrophication
B. Biological magnification
C. Nitrification
D. Hypoxia

Q.26 What are the main features of the charter act 1833?

A. Complete abolition even in terms of Tea and China trade.
B. Governor-General of Bengal was designated as Governor-General of India.
C. Bombay and Madras were deprived of their power to legislate.
D. All of the above

Q.27 Which dynasty built the temple of Khajuraho?

A. Mauryan dynasty
B. Chandela dynasty
C. Shunga dynasty
D. Gupta dynasty

Q.28 Pt Ravi Shankar is a renowned:

A. Table player
B. Sitarist
C. Violinists
D. Sarangi player

Q.29 The Reserve Bank of India provides:

A. All currencies, except hundred-rupee notes
B. All notes, except one-rupee notes
C. All currencies, except the twenty-rupee note
D. All currencies, except the ten-rupee note

Q.30 Sattriya is a classical Indian dance which is originated in its eastern state of ______________.

A. Nagaland
B. Meghalaya
C. Arunachal Pradesh
D. Assam

Q.31 Which of the following are agencies of social change in education?

(a) Family
(b) School
(c) National Army
(d) National Calamity

A. (a) and (b)
B. (b) and (c)
C. (c) and (d)
D. (d) and (a)

Q.32 Which of the following parts in the Indian Constitution is justiciable?

A. Fundamental Rights
B. Fundamental Duties
C. Preamble
D. Directive Principles of State Policy

Q.33 Which layer of the Earth's atmosphere protects it from the harmful UV radiation of the Sun?

A. Stratosphere
B. Ozonosphere
C. Troposphere
D. Ionosphere

Q.34 Which of the following concepts is emphasized by Swami Vivekananda?

A. Integral education
B. Man making education
C. Education for harmony
D. Citizenship education

Q.35 Which of the following causes the lowest carbon dioxide emission?

A. Solar energy
B. Hydroelectric energy
C. Wind energy
D. Nuclear energy

Q.36 The scientific study of old age is called:

A. Anthropology
B. Genetics
C. Gerontology
D. Genealogy

Q.37 Who among the following is associated with the radical approach to industrial relations?

A. Mahatma Gandhi
B. John T. Dunlop
C. Karl Marx
D. Allan Flanders

Q.38 Where are India's two operational Satellite Launch Pads located?

A. Rajkot
B. Jalandhar
C. Mumbai
D. Sriharikota

Q.39 What do the five interlinked rings in the Olympic flag represent?

A. Oceans
B. Sports
C. Mountains
D. Continents

Q.40 Which of the following Amendments brought the GST into existence?

A. 99th Amendment Act
B. 100th Amendment Act

C. 101st Amendment Act
D. 123rd Amendment Act

English Proficiency

Q.41 Direction: The sentence is divided into four parts. Find out which part has an error and mark it as your answer. If there is no error, mark 'No error' as your answer.
The members of the family(A) / who live next to our home (B) / is adorable. (C) / No error (D)

A. (A)   **B.** (B)   **C.** (C)   **D.** (D)

Q.42 Direction: A sentence/a part of the sentence is underlined. Four alternatives are given to the underlined part which will improve the sentence. Choose the correct alternative and click the button corresponding to it. In case no improvement is needed, click the button corresponding to "No improvement".
He is a fast bowler of repute, but his yesterday's performance was not up to the mark.

A. Performance for yesterday
B. Yesterday performance
C. Performances for yesterday
D. No improvement

Q.43 Direction: Select the correct active/passive form of the given sentence.
What did you buy?

A. What was bought by you?
B. What has brought by you?
C. What has been bought by you?
D. What has been brought by you?

Q.44 Direction: Look at the underlined part of the sentence. Below the sentence, three possible substitutions are given for the underlined part. If one of the possible substitutions is better than the underlined part, indicate it as your answer. If none of the substitutions improves the sentence, indicate (D) as your answer.
He said that he would not believe it even if he saw it with his own eyes.

A. Will not
B. Could not
C. Had not
D. No improvement needed

Q.45 Direction: Select the most appropriate synonym of the given word.
REMORSE

A. Affection   **B.** Indifference
C. Regret   **D.** Reproach

Q.46 Direction: Select the most appropriate ANTONYM of the given word.
CONSPICUOUS

A. Distinct   **B.** Obscure
C. Noticeable   **D.** Apparent

Q.47 Direction: Select the appropriate synonym of the given word.
TIMID

A. Willful   **B.** Shy   **C.** Kind   **D.** Strong

Q.48 Direction: Find the odd one out.

A. Shiny   **B.** Smooth   **C.** Burnish   **D.** Ordinary

Q.49 Direction: Find the odd one out.

A. Potion   **B.** Meal
C. Beverage   **D.** Drink

Q.50 Direction: Select the most appropriate ANTONYM of the given word.
BENEVOLENT

A. Generous   **B.** Friendly
C. Stingy   **D.** Liberal

Q.51 Direction: In the following question, one part of the sentence may have an error. Find out which part of the sentence has an error and click the button corresponding to it. If the sentence is free from error, click the "No error" option.
Do you (A)/ mind me (B)/ smoking a pipe. (C)/ No error (D)

A. (A)   **B.** (B)   **C.** (C)   **D.** (D)

Q.52 Direction: The given sentence has four underlined words or phrases, marked as (1), (2), (3) and (4). Identify the one underlined word or phrase that must be changed in order for the sentence to be correct.
(1) Theological view of human development sometimes (2) differ from (3) an anthropological (4) perspective.

A. (1)   **B.** (2)   **C.** (3)   **D.** (4)

Ques (53-57):Direction: Read the paragraph and answer the question.

Adolescence is a period of rapid growth and development bridging childhood and adulthood. Practicing healthy eating behaviour is one of the most important factors to meet the nutritional needs of adolescents. Proper eating behaviours that are learned in early life are maintained in adulthood thus reducing the risk of major chronic disease. Physical and psychological changes occurring during this period usually significantly influence their dietary behaviours. As teens become more independent, they make more of their own food choices. However, being influenced by a massive amount of factors (biological, social, physical, economic, psychological beliefs and knowledge about food) and changing of lifestyle may affect their dietary choices and eating behaviour, thus making them fail to adhere to healthy eating practices. Peer pressure in colleges leads adolescents to eat non-nutritional foods like pizzas and burgers. Due to irregular college schedules, intake of caffeinated drinks increases and water intake reduces. Poor nutrition can lead to reduced concentration in studies, low stamina, depression or poor posture.

Q.53 As per the author, how does dietary behavior in adolescence affect health in adulthood?

A. Major chronic diseases are transferred from the early stages to adulthood

B. The seed of ill health in adulthood is sown by diet in the early stages

C. Dietary habits of adolescence are carried out in adulthood

D. Dietary habits are maintained throughout life

Q.54 What is the meaning of dietary behavior?

A. Taking different types of diets

B. Taking caffeinated drinks

C. Knowledge of different types of diets

D. Making choices about diet

Q.55 The author marks adolescence as bridging childhood and adulthood because it is a:

A. Period of independence in making dietary choices

B. Period of physical and psychological changes

C. Period of changing lifestyle

D. Period of peer pressure

Q.56 Reduced concentration in studies is because of:

A. Nature of Adolescent period

B. Not bring able to meet nutritional needs

C. Influence of factors like biological and psychological

D. Eating of foods like pizzas and burgers

Q.57 Unhealthy dietary habits mean:

A. Eating pizzas and burgers

B. Caffeinated drinks

C. Poor nutritional diet

D. Drinking less water

Ques (58-59):Direction: Read the given sentence to find out whether there is any grammatical or idiomatic error in it. The error, if any, will be in one part of the sentence. The letter denoting that part is the answer. If there is no error, the answer is (d). Ignore the errors of punctuation, if any.

Q.58 Supposing if (a) it rains (b) what shall (c) we do? No error (d)

A. (a) **B.** (b) **C.** (c) **D.** (d)

Q.59 The directors must be able to (a) operate automatically and reach (b) important decisions on their own. (c) No error (d)

A. (a) **B.** (b) **C.** (c) **D.** (d)

Q.60 Direction: In the following, the question choose the word which best expresses the meaning of the given word.

Embezzle

A. Misappropriate **B.** Balance

C. Remunerate **D.** Clear

Q.61 Direction: Read the given sentence to find out whether there is any grammatical or idiomatic error in it. The error, if any, will be in one part of the sentence. The letter denoting that part is the answer. If there is no error, the answer is (d). Ignore the errors of punctuation, if any.

It will be a severe hardship (a) and loss to our town's citizens (b) if the museum close on Saturdays. (c) No error (d)

A. (a) **B.** (b) **C.** (c) **D.** (d)

Q.62 Direction: Choose the appropriate word from the given options and fill in the blank.

The treatises of Nicolai and Lichtenberg were written to _____ his theory.

A. Refuse **B.** Repress **C.** Refute **D.** Subdue

Q.63 Direction: From the given alternatives, choose the correct antonym of the following word.

Facsimile

A. Mail **B.** Original

C. Reproduce **D.** Real

Q.64 Direction: Choose the best option to fill in the blanks.

Hume is not content with reducing the _______ of a causal connection to the experience of frequent conjunction. He proceeds to argue that such an experience does not _______ the expectation of similar conjunctions in the future.

A. Instance, rationalise

B. Evidence, justify

C. Boundaries, preclude

D. Validity, extend

Q.65 Direction: Select the option that expresses the given sentence in indirect speech.

Amir asked me, "Why didn't you answer the phone?"

A. Amir asked me why I didn't answer the phone.

B. Amir asked me why I haven't answered the phone.

C. Amir asked me why I hadn't answered the phone.

D. Amir asked me why I answered the phone.

Ques (66-70):Direction: Answer the given question based on the following passage.

Cultural contrasts are exciting for tourists. They pay to experience them. But for those who have to live and work in a foreign culture, the contrasts can be difficult, confusing, and painful. Differences are hard to live with.

Not everybody believes that cultural differences matter. 'We are all human beings,' an Iowan businessman declared at a meeting on cross-cultural business interacts, 'Japanese, Americans, or Germans, underneath we are all just the same. We cry the same tears, we smile the same smiles, and we bleed the same blood.' He, like so many others, believes that in the face of love and profit people are all the same.

Sameness was also on the mind of the American student when she walked into an Amsterdam shop to ask the way to the Anne Frank house. Still shocked she later told how the woman in the shop had refused to answer. She had suggested she buy a map! According to the student, such a rude response was unheard of in the US.

This student had failed to recognize that not all people are the same. Some people consider an American who demands directions in a loud voice rude. Likewise, Japanese and German business people may not appreciate 'Just call me John', 'a deal is a deal', 'get to the point', 'I am what I am', or any other expression that the Iowan businessman customarily uses. Not recognizing such differences can cost dearly, in emotional energy, and possibly lost deals.

There is a need to focus on the differences that exist between the people of Europe and the US. It offers the transnationals two metaphors as an aid for coping with those differences, namely the citadel for European society with its firm roots in tradition, and the caravan for the less established and more fluid society of the United States. It can well be predicted that people who see the transatlantic contrasts through these metaphors will avoid much confusion, pain, and, who knows, some cost. Here is a sample.

A few years ago an American sales team made a presentation to the manufacturing team of an Italian tractor company. The Americans had prepared themselves thoroughly. They came right to the point, provided illustrations with slides, had anticipated all conceivable questions about their products, and could counter all objections. Afterward, the Americans congratulated each other on a job well done. They did not, however, get the sales contract.

An executive who is familiar with cross-cultural business dealings attended the meeting. He noted: 'The Americans came to the point too quickly. They alienated the Italians with the style of their presentation. The Italians operate in a business environment where personal relations are crucial; they want to get to know the people they deal with. The Americans would have done better to take the Italians out for a long business conversation over lunch with good food and wine.'

Misunderstandings like this one are all too common. One would expect that, with the increasing internationalization of politics and business, sensitivity to cultural differences would grow, and that at the same time such differences would become less pronounced. Yet neither expectation is fulfilled. Cultural differences are real and pervasive, and we have learned that frequent contact does not guarantee mutual understanding. (Excerpted from The Caravan and The Citadel by Arjo Klamer)

Q.66 What, according to the passage, excites tourists?

A. Cultural homogeneity

B. Cultural contrasts

C. Cross-cultural business

D. Foreign culture

Q.67 What, according to the writer, should be the people's approach towards others' culture in general?

A. It should be one of tolerance.

B. It should be one of sensitivity.

C. It should be one of judgement.

D. It should be one of isolation.

Q.68 Which of the following sums up the essence of the passage?

A. Cultural differences do not matter as all human beings are the same underneath.

B. Cultural differences can be taken care of by making some minor adjustments.

C. Cultural differences are the real issue and overlooking them could prove costly.

D. Caravan and citadel are the metaphors that describe US and European cultures.

Q.69 Which of the following can **definitely not** be inferred from the passage?

A. Cultural differences do exist between the people of Europe and US and they show this in their conduct.

B. Basic human elements are the same with all people irrespective of where they reside.

C. Those who proceed with the notion that sameness permeates through all could be in for shock.

D. It is not necessary to highlight on cultural differences while formulating business policies.

Q.70 Why does the author use the metaphors of 'citadel' and 'caravan' and what purpose do they serve?

A. These metaphors draw out the cultural contrast between the people of Europe and US and drive home the underlying idea.

B. These metaphors are used to give sample of how the cultural contrasts are demonstrated to explain the matter.

C. 'Citadel' refers to the cultural attitudes of the Europeans while 'caravan' refers to the cultural attitudes of the Americans.

D. The basic difference that exists between the Europeans and Americans is best brought out by these metaphors.

Maths and Logical Reasoning

Q.71 Direction: Study the following information carefully and answer the question given below.

There are six persons A, B, C, D, E, and F. C is the sister of F. B is the brother of E's husband. D is the father of A and the grandfather of F. There are two fathers, three brothers, and a mother in the group.

How many male members are there in the group?

A. One   **B.** Two   **C.** Three   **D.** Four

Q.72 In a ratio, which equals to $9:8$. If the antecedent is 72, what is its consequent?

A. 81   **B.** 64   **C.** 72   **D.** 49

Q.73 The population of a town is 7000. If the number of males increases by 8% and the number of females increases by 5%, the population will be 7470. Find the number of males and females.

A. Males - 4170, Females - 2830

B. Males - 4000, Females - 3000

C. Males - 4200, Females - 2800

D. Males - 3000, Females - 4000

Q.74

Direction: Study the given graph and answer the question that follows.

The graph below indicates the production target and production achieved (in units) with the number of defects produced for a company during $1987-90$.

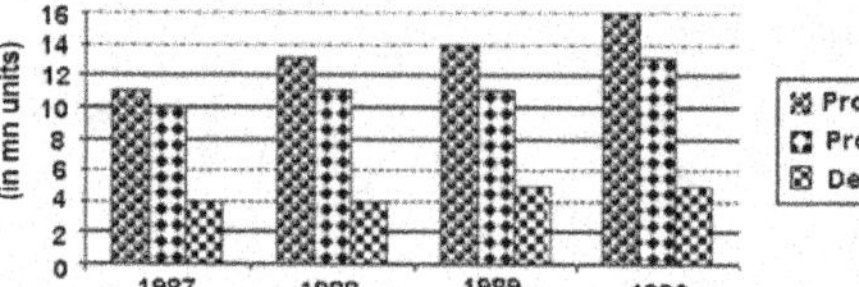

Net production is defined as production achieved with less defects. In which year is the largest change in net production was in the year.

A. 1987 − 88   **B.** 1988 − 89
C. 1989 − 90   **D.** All are equal

Q.75 Find the missing number in the following sequence:

$8,4,12,6,18,9,?$

A. 27   **B.** 29   **C.** 28   **D.** 30

Q.76 Direction: Study the following information carefully and answer the question that follows.

Six people A, B, C, D, E, and F are sitting on the ground in a hexagonal shape. All the sides of the hexagon so formed are of the same length. A is not adjacent to B or C; D is not adjacent to C or E; B and C are adjacent, and F is in the middle of D and C.

Who is at the same distance from D as E is from D?

A. B   **B.** C   **C.** A   **D.** F

Q.77 Area of a circle having radius $7\ cm$ is equal to the area of a rectangle. If breadth of the rectangle is $14\ cm$, Find the length of the rectangle:

A. 17 cm **B.** 11 cm **C.** 13 cm **D.** 15 cm

Q.78 A man travels 30 km at speed of 10 km/h and the next 40 km at 20 km/h and thereafter travels 60 km at 30 km/h. His average speed is:

A. 31.6 kmph   **B.** 25.6 kmph
C. 19.6 kmph   **D.** 18.6 kmph

Q.79 In the following question, a number series is given with missing of one term. Choose the correct alternative that will continue the same pattern and replace the question mark (?) in the given series.

$122,170,226,290,?$

A. 289   **B.** 362   **C.** 290   **D.** 325

Q.80 Three natural numbers are in the ratio $2:3:4$. If sum of the squares of the extremes is 180, then the middle number is

A. 6   **B.** 12   **C.** 15   **D.** 9

Q.81 Direction: Six faces of a cube have been marked with numbers $1,2,3,4,5$ and 6. The surfaces of the cube have been unfolded and this unfolded position of the cube has been shown in four different figures $(A),(B),(C)$ and (D). Choose the figure that will be formed when the cube is unfolded.

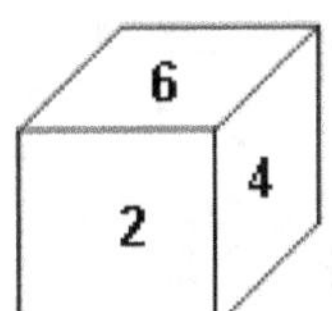 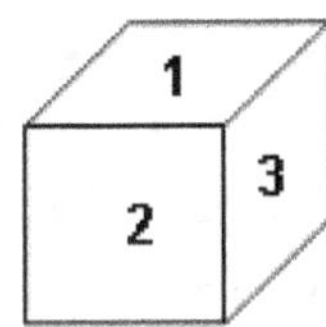 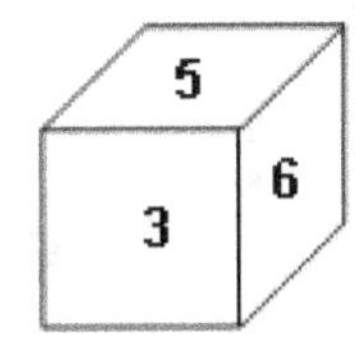

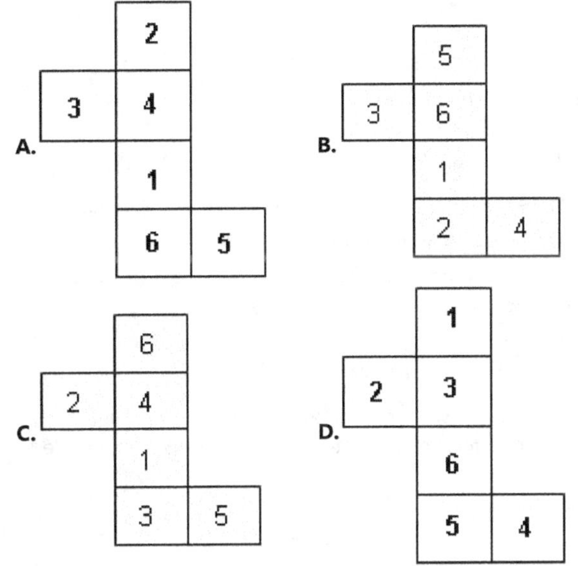

Q.82 If $+$ means $\div$, $\times$ means $-$, $-$ means $\times$ and $\div$ means $+$, then $38 + 19 - 16 \times 17 \div 3 =?$

A. 16   **B.** 19   **C.** 18   **D.** 12

Q.83 Direction: Read the given statements and conclusions carefully. Assuming that the information given in the statements is true, even if it appears to be at variance with commonly known facts, decide which of the given conclusion logically follows(s) from the statements.

Statements:

All Books are Cats

Some Cats are Dogs

Conclusions:

I. Some Books are Dogs

II. No Cats are Books

A. Only conclusion II follow

B. Both conclusions I and II follow

C. Only conclusion I follow

D. Neither conclusions I nor II follow

Q.84 Point B is 75 m to the south of Point A. Point C is 27 m to the East of Point B. Point D is 30 m to the North of Point C. Point E is 54 m to the West of Point D. Point F is 45 m to the North of Point E. What is the distance between A and F and which direction is F with respect to A?

A. 27 m, West   **B.** 27 m, East
C. 54 m, West   **D.** 54 m, East

Q.85 A person sold two shirts each for 440 rupees. On one he gained 10% and on the other he lost 60%. What is the overall profit or loss percentage?

A. 51.33%   **B.** 33.33%   **C.** 41.33%   **D.** 42.33%

Q.86 In ΔXYZ, O is the in-center and ∠Y = 52°. Then, what is the measure of ∠XOZ?

A. 116°   **B.** 126°   **C.** 134°   **D.** 129°

Q.87 Which of the given options will replace the question mark (?) in the following series?

AOZ, BOY, COX, DOW, ?

A. EOX   **B.** FPY   **C.** EVO   **D.** EOV

Q.88 Find out the median of values of this set 11.1, 12.1, 11.5, 11.9, and 12.3.

A. 11.1   **B.** 11.5   **C.** 11.9   **D.** 12.1

Q.89 The perimeter of a square is equivalent to twice the perimeter of a rectangle whose length is $8\ cm$ and breadth is $7\ cm$. Find out the circumference of a semicircle which has a diameter equivalent to the side of the square.

A. $23.57\ cm$ **B.** $47.47\ cm$

C. $42.46\ cm$ **D.** $38.57\ cm$

Q.90 Find the amount at compound interest on Rs. 1000 at 20% per annum for nine months if the interest is compounded quarterly.

A. Rs. 1160   **B.** Rs. 1157.625

C. Rs. 1200   **D.** Rs. 1100.625

Q.91 Direction: Read the following information carefully and answer the question given below it.

A, B, C, D, E, F, and G purchased TVs of different brands viz. Onida, Samsung, MI, LG, Texla, Panasonic, and Sony on seven different days of a week starting from Monday, but not necessarily in the same order. MI TV was not purchased by F. G purchased TV before C. D did not purchase MI or Panasonic TV. A purchased TV on Wednesday. Panasonic TV was purchased by one of the friends on Saturday. Samsung TV was purchased by one of the friends on Monday. G did not purchase Samsung TV. C purchased Sony TV. Onida TV was purchased by one of the friends a day before LG TV was purchased. E purchased Texla TV three days after C.

Who purchased Panasonic TV?

A. A   **B.** B   **C.** E   **D.** F

Q.92 In the numbers between 250 and 400 how many numbers are divisible by 7?

A. 22   **B.** 25   **C.** 35   **D.** 15

Q.93 Based on the relation between the first two words, find out the missing word.

Garbha : Gujarat :: Dumhal : ?

A. Punjab

B. Uttar Pradesh

C. West Bengal

D. Jammu and Kashmir

Q.94

Direction: Study the graph and answer the question that follows.

Production of Groundnut (in 1000 Tonnes)

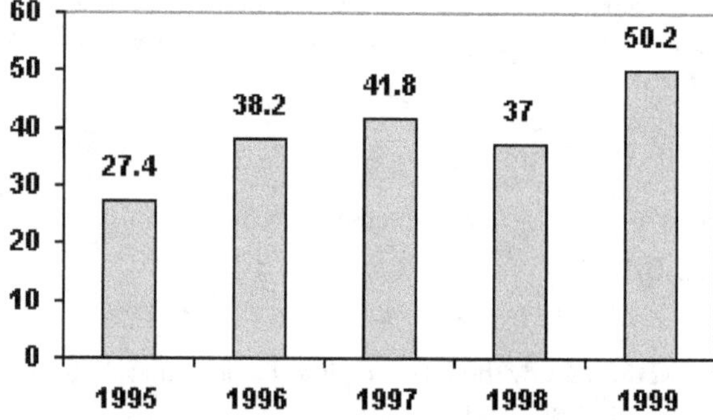

Among the given production figures, the one closest to the average production per year is away from the average production figure over the given years by:

A. 0.72 tonnes   **B.** 720 tonnes

C. 72 tonnes   **D.** None of these

Q.95 Three of the four following number pairs are alike in a certain way, and one is different. Pick up the odd one from the given alternatives.

A. 39 - 28   **B.** 43 - 32   **C.** 57 - 45   **D.** 78 - 67

Q.96 If $\dfrac{\cos^2\theta}{\cot^2\theta-\cos^2\theta}=3, 0°<\theta<90°$, then the value of $\tan\theta + \sin\theta$ is:

A. $\dfrac{\sqrt{3}}{2}$ **B.** $\dfrac{6\sqrt{3}}{7}$ **C.** $\sqrt{3}$ **D.** $\dfrac{3\sqrt{3}}{2}$

Q.97

Select the option that is related to the third term in the same way as the second term is related to the first term.

JMP : HON :: ADG : ?

A. JKM   **B.** ZGF   **C.** YFE   **D.** CBI

Q.98 In a committee, 50 people speak French, 20 speak Spanish and 10 speak both Spanish and French. How many speak at least one of the two languages?

A. 55   **B.** 50   **C.** 70   **D.** 60

Q.99 How many triangles are there in the following figure?

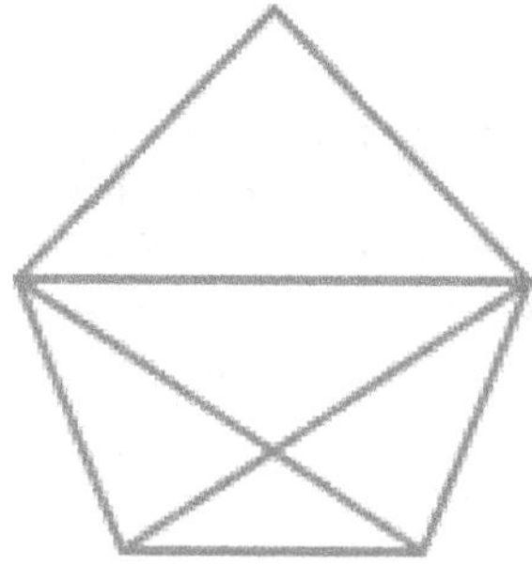

A. 15   **B.** 12   **C.** 9   **D.** 18

Q.100 Rohit is seventeenth from the left end of a row of 29 boys and Karan is seventeenth from the right end of the same row. How many boys are there between the two in the row?

A. 3   **B.** 4

C. 5   **D.** Data inadequate

// Smart Answer Sheet //

Correct Indicates percentage of students who answered questions correctly.

Skipped Indicates percentage of students who skipped questions.

Q.	Ans.	Correct / Skipped
1	B	54.73 % / 1.18 %
2	D	49.97 % / 1.54 %
3	A	43.47 % / 1.72 %
4	A	29.87 % / 3.92 %
5	B	66.66 % / 1.83 %
6	A	32.2 % / 4.25 %
7	D	52.81 % / 1.44 %
8	A	81.62 % / 0.0 %
9	B	49.07 % / 1.91 %
10	D	42.67 % / 1.51 %
11	A	61.33 % / 1.82 %
12	C	50.24 % / 1.69 %
13	B	88.51 % / 0.0 %
14	D	62.02 % / 1.25 %
15	A	84.8 % / 0.0 %
16	C	63.79 % / 1.57 %

Q.	Ans.	Correct / Skipped
17	A	61.95 % / 1.83 %
18	D	18.68 % / 4.88 %
19	C	22.56 % / 4.07 %
20	D	30.58 % / 3.55 %
21	B	63.74 % / 1.27 %
22	C	69.11 % / 1.8 %
23	D	79.36 % / 0.0 %
24	D	56.92 % / 1.5 %
25	A	66.31 % / 1.44 %
26	D	24.23 % / 4.7 %
27	B	46.94 % / 1.66 %
28	B	85.41 % / 0.0 %
29	B	78.12 % / 0.0 %
30	D	11.25 % / 3.77 %
31	A	69.88 % / 1.4 %
32	A	85.58 % / 0.0 %

Q.	Ans.	Correct / Skipped
33	A	42.45 % / 1.16 %
34	B	54.14 % / 1.24 %
35	B	89.38 % / 0.0 %
36	C	76.69 % / 0.0 %
37	C	29.19 % / 3.1 %
38	D	82.65 % / 0.0 %
39	D	76.95 % / 0.0 %
40	C	50.52 % / 1.31 %
41	C	78.44 % / 0.0 %
42	D	41.59 % / 1.59 %
43	A	79.05 % / 0.0 %
44	D	69.17 % / 1.86 %
45	C	49.4 % / 1.89 %
46	B	51.26 % / 1.69 %
47	B	57.78 % / 1.28 %
48	D	49.06 % / 1.55 %

Q.	Ans.	Correct / Skipped
49	B	83.24 % / 0.0 %
50	C	59.17 % / 1.3 %
51	B	68.47 % / 1.28 %
52	B	50.83 % / 1.18 %
53	B	55.64 % / 1.78 %
54	A	68.81 % / 1.49 %
55	B	50.71 % / 1.92 %
56	B	66.96 % / 1.04 %
57	A	47.03 % / 1.23 %
58	A	41.06 % / 1.83 %
59	B	15.14 % / 4.22 %
60	A	43.51 % / 1.92 %
61	C	87.34 % / 0.0 %
62	C	60.95 % / 1.01 %
63	B	82.11 % / 0.0 %
64	B	11.25 % / 4.43 %

Q.	Ans.	Correct / Skipped
65	C	57.58 % / 1.75 %
66	B	59.27 % / 1.31 %
67	B	30.76 % / 4.03 %
68	C	67.97 % / 1.41 %
69	D	26.74 % / 4.22 %
70	A	11.05 % / 4.41 %
71	D	88.49 % / 0.0 %
72	B	85.47 % / 0.0 %
73	B	45.49 % / 1.05 %
74	C	66.57 % / 1.98 %
75	A	46.04 % / 1.94 %
76	B	62.82 % / 1.84 %
77	B	64.68 % / 1.98 %
78	D	40.83 % / 1.21 %
79	B	81.3 % / 0.0 %
80	D	49.61 % / 1.08 %

Q.	Ans.	Correct	
		Skipped	
81	C	80.45 %	
		0.0 %	
82	C	63.51 %	
		1.39 %	
83	D	58.3 %	
		1.57 %	
84	A	11.69 %	
		4.44 %	

Q.	Ans.	Correct	
		Skipped	
85	C	61.58 %	
		1.03 %	
86	A	49.91 %	
		1.0 %	
87	D	89.37 %	
		0.0 %	
88	C	86.35 %	
		0.0 %	

Q.	Ans.	Correct	
		Skipped	
89	D	62.04 %	
		1.1 %	
90	B	64.59 %	
		1.72 %	
91	D	29.62 %	
		3.42 %	
92	A	41.86 %	
		1.16 %	

Q.	Ans.	Correct	
		Skipped	
93	D	87.33 %	
		0.0 %	
94	B	50.33 %	
		1.06 %	
95	C	65.94 %	
		1.44 %	
96	D	61.92 %	
		1.74 %	

Q.	Ans.	Correct	
		Skipped	
97	C	55.61 %	
		1.35 %	
98	D	58.78 %	
		1.15 %	
99	C	43.43 %	
		1.63 %	
100	A	76.76 %	
		0.0 %	

Performance Analysis

Avg. Score (%)	**44.0%**
Toppers Score (%)	**55.0%**
Your Score	

General Awareness

Q.1 The Prime Minister released a commemorative coin of Rs 100 denomination, to honour which personality?
A. Vijaya Raje Scindia
B. Syama Prasad Mukherjee
C. Deendayal Upadhyaya
D. M. S. Golwalkar

Q.2 Which institution released the 'Women and girls left behind: Glaring gaps in pandemic responses' report?
[Delhi Forest Guard, 2021]

A. World Economic Forum
B. World Bank
C. UN Women
D. NITI Aayog

Q.3 India's rank in Human Development Index, 2018 is:
[Super TET Paper - I, 2019]

A. 128th   B. 129th   C. 130th   D. 131st

Q.4 How many hi-tech libraries will be built in the villages of Haryana?
A. 500   B. 700   C. 900   D. 1000

Q.5 First cyber police station of Haryana was established in?
A. Panchkula   B. Ambala
C. Gurugram   D. Karnal

Q.6 The winner of US Open Tennis Tournament, 2018 (Women's Singles) was:
[Delhi Forest Guard, 2020], [Super TET Paper - I, 2019]

A. Caroline Wozniacki   B. Simona Halep
C. Naomi Osaka   D. Serena Williams

Q.7 The Centre is set to launch a doorstep distribution drive for the Pradhan Mantri Fasal Beema Yojana (PMFBY). It will deliver crop insurance policies to the farmers under which of the following in all the implementing states?
A. Meri Policy Mere Hath
B. Meri Sahayata Mere Dwar
C. Mera Gaon, Meri Yojna
D. Meri Madad, Mere Ghar

Q.8 RESPOND program, recently in news is related to which of the following organization?
A. NASA   B. ISRO
C. JAXA   D. NITI Aayog

Q.9 Jhora folk dance belongs to which state?
A. Uttarakhand   B. Karnataka
C. Assam   D. Rajasthan

Q.10 Who was the founder of the autonomous kingdom of Awadh in 1722?
A. Saadat Ali Khan   B. Safdar Jung
C. Shuja-ud-daula   D. None of these

Q.11 Which of the following Article of the Indian Constitution guarantees complete equality of men and women?
A. Article 14   B. Article 21
C. Article 18   D. Article 15

Q.12 The acronym UDHR stands for:
A. Universal Declaration on Human Resources
B. Universal Development of Human Resources
C. Universal Declaration of Human Rights
D. United Nations Development Fund for Health and Rehabilitation

Q.13 In a pond ecosystem, the BOD increases due to:
A. A Photosynthetic activity of algae
B. High density of aquatic macrophytes
C. High density of fish
D. Increase in the population of bacteria

Q.14 Which article comes under the Attorney General of India?
A. Article 148   B. Article 165
C. Article 280   D. Article 76

Q.15 What is the study of the interaction between living organisms and the environment called?
A. Ecology   B. Phytogeography
C. Psychology   D. Mycology

Q.16 The launch vehicle of Mars Orbiter Mission was __________.
A. PSLV C-45   B. PSLV C-42
C. PSLV C-25   D. PSLV C-46

Q.17 The trapping of the long wavelength radiation leads to more heating and a higher resultant temperature.
Which phenomenon is being talked about in this line?
A. Whirlwinds
B. Ozone layer depletion
C. Greenhouse effect
D. Energy crisis

Q.18 Kalamkari painting is related to which state?
A. Karnataka   B. Uttar Pradesh
C. Manipur   D. Andhra Pradesh

Q.19 Which female athlete is nicknamed as 'Dhing Express' after her village's name?
A. Hima Das   B. Mary Kom
C. M R Poovamma   D. Sarita Gayakwad

Q.20 Secularism means __________.

A.   The State is to give patronage to any one religion.

B.   Respect all religions without favoring any one religion.

C.   Lacking religious emotion, doctrines, and practices.

D.   To impose any particular religion upon the rest of the people.

Q.21 What is the minimum permissible age for employment in any factory or mine?

A. 14 years   B. 16 years

C. 18 years   D. None of these

Q.22 Who suggested for the first time that India's national dress should have combined elements of Hindus and Muslims?

A.   Rabindranath Tagore

B.   Mahatma Gandhi

C.   Subhash Chandra Bose

D.   Dadabhai Naoroji

Q.23 With which one of the following games is the Hopman Cup associated?

A. Badminton   B. Tennis

C. Hockey   D. Football

Q.24 Factors affecting population change are:

A.   Births, Migration, and Deaths

B.   Births and Deaths only

C.   Births, Deaths, and Marriage

D.   Births, Deaths and Life expectancy

Q.25 _______ won the Nobel prize for her discovery of radioactivity and became the first women who won the Noble Prize.

A.   Donna Strickland

B.   Nadia Murad

C.   Maria Goeppert Mayer

D.   Marie Curie

Q.26 What is social mobility associated with?

A.   Upliftment in the same stratum

B.   Upliftment in the upper stratum

C.   Change in the stratification

D.   Consistency in the stratification

Q.27 In India who directly controls the "Monetary Policy"?

A.   Finance Department of India

B.   Reserve Bank of India

C.   State Bank of India

D.   Prime Minister of India

Q.28 The Council of Ministers during the time of Shivaji Maharaj was known as:

A. Agraharam   B. Navaratnas

C. Ashta Diggajas   D. Ashta Pradhan

Q.29 With which of the following sports is the term 'twiddle' associated?

A. Hockey   B. Rugby

C. Table Tennis   D. Cricket

Q.30 Which of the following is not related to the first independence movement of 1857?

A.   Begum Hazrat Mahal

B.   Kunwar Singh

C.   Udham Singh

D.   Maulawi Ahamadulla

Q.31 Arrange the following in sequential order to describe complete socialization. Use the Roman Numbers given as codes.

I. Man to society, Man to country

II. Man to Relatives, Man to Friends

III. Man to Mankind, Man to Universe

IV. Man to self, Man to family

A. III, I, II, and IV   B. IV, I, III, and II

C. II, III, I, and IV   D. IV, II, I, and III

Q.32 The book 'Gita Govinda' was written by:

A. Banabhatta   B. Kalidas

C. Jayadev   D. None of these

Q.33 India's first-ever gold medal at the Youth Olympics was won by _______.

A. Vicky Batta   B. Jeremy Lalrinnunga

C. Sneha Soren   D. Vicky Bhatia

Q.34 Which of the following is a Non-Constitutional body of India?

A.   Finance Commission

B.   Election Commission

C.   Union Public Service Commission

D.   NITI Aayog

Q.35 Which of the following is not a method of water conservation?

A.   Prevention of water pollution

B.   Chlorination of water

C.   Rainwater harvesting

D.   Maintaining the water cycle

Q.36 Rukmini Devi Arundale was a reputed dancer and choreographer in which form of dancing?

A. Opera   B. Lavani

C. Bharatnatyam   D. Dandiya

Q.37 Which of the following statements is false about the 'President' of India?

A.   Dr. Rajendra Prasad had been the President of India from Jan. 26, 1950, to May 13, 1962.

B.   Shri Ramnath Kovind is the 14th President of India.

C.   K.R. Narayanan and Ram Nath Kovind were the two Presidents so far who belong to the Scheduled Castes.

D.   The candidate for Presidentship requires 25 persons to propose the nomination and another 25 persons to second the proposal.

Q.38 Indian athlete Vikas Gowda is associated with:

A. Wrestling   B. Sprint

C. Discus throw   D. Archery

Q.39 Who is regarded as the founder of scientific socialism?

A. Max Muller   **B.** Lenin

C. Karl Marx   **D.** None of these

Q.40 Who among the following invented the Barometer?

A. Evangelista Torricelli

B. Benjamin Franklin

C. John J Loud

D. None of the above

English Proficiency

Ques (41-42):Direction: In the following question, a sentence is given in Direct/Indirect speech. Out of the four alternatives choose the one which best expresses the sentence in Indirect/Direct Speech.

Q.41 "Come out from where you are hiding." shouted the police at the suspect.

A. The police shouted at the suspect to come out from where he was hiding.

B. The police shouted at the suspect to come out from where he is hiding.

C. The police shouts at the suspect to come out from where he was hiding.

D. The police shouts at the suspect to come out from where he is hiding.

Q.42 She said to him, "Consult a doctor."

A. She suggested him to consult a doctor.

B. She wanted him to consult a doctor.

C. She ordered him to consult a doctor.

D. She told him to consult a doctor.

Ques (43-45):Direction: A sentence has been given in Active/Passive Voice. Out of the four alternatives suggested, select the one which best expresses the same sentence in Passive/Active Voice.

Q.43 Mary kept her schedule meticulously.

A. Mary's schedule was being kept.

B. Schedule was been kept by Mary.

C. Mary's schedule was kept meticulously by her.

D. Schedule was being kept

Q.44 Did Mrs.Green recognize you in your costume?

A. Was you recognized in your costume by Mrs.Green?

B. Had you been recognized in your costume by Mrs.Green?

C. Were you recognized in your costume by Mrs.Green?

D. Was you being recognized in your costume by Mrs.Green?

Q.45 The fire engulfed the warehouse.

A. The warehouse was engulfed in the fire.

B. The warehouse had been engulfed by the fire.

C. The warehouse got engulfed in the fire.

D. The warehouse was engulfed by the fire.

Q.46 Direction: Select the word that is antonymous to the given word.

PRUDENT

A. Irremediable   **B.** Indeterminable

C. Indiscreet   **D.** Irresolute

Ques (47-51):Direction: Read the following text and answer questions.

Sixty percent of rural India lives in utter poverty with no electricity. Rural India uses 180 million tonnes of fuel every year for cooking, creating indoor pollution and health hazards. The WHO estimates 1.5 million deaths per year are caused by pollution from chulha smoke. Making available locally grown clean and renewable cooking and lighting fuel can improve the quality of rural life. Liquid fuels are far superior to solid fuels for cooking because of their clean-burning and higher energy. Ethanol is one the best as it is an excellent substitute for kerosene and burns better with no unpleasant smell. Its burning power is almost as clean as that of LPG.

Ethanol can be produced from any sugary material and is presently produced the world over from sugarcane and corn. However, as the ethanol economy grows, there is a need to produce it from a crop that uses much less water than sugarcane and also produces food. Sorghum (Jowar) is one such crop whose stem is sweet like sugarcane. Its earhead produces grains that can be used for making bread. Its sweet stem has nearly the same amount of sugar and hence the juice can be fermented and used for ethanol production. The left-over stem after juice extraction, together with leaves is excellent fodder for animals. So from the same price of land one can get food, fuel, and fodder. Besides, sweet sorghum (Jowar) uses nearly fifty percent less water than sugarcane to produce the same amount of sugar. It is a four-month crop so farmers can grow two crops per year from the same piece of land. Also, the energy output ratio from sweet sorghum is very positive.

Q.47 The purpose of the paragraph is to bring out:

A. Problems of rural poor

B. The limitations of sugar cane

C. Benefits of sorghum (Jowar)

D. Remedies for pollutant energy

Q.48 The most suitable heading for the paragraph will be:

A. Go for Ethanol

B. Alternate Fuels

C. Solid Fuels Vs. Liquid Fuels

D. Efficient Fuels

Q.49 As per the authors, who are the rural poor?

A. Who do not have any electricity

B. Who use solid fuel for cooking

C. Who live with pollution and health hazards

D. Who do not use cooking gas

Q.50 As per the author which can be an easy source of energy:

A. The fuel that does not give an unpleasant smell

B. The fuel that can be used alternate to kerosene

C. The fuel that can be produced from crops

D. The fuel that can be locally produced

Q.51 The nature of the paragraph is:

A. Analytical   **B.** Critical

C. Conceptual   **D.** Comprehensive

Q.52 Direction: In the following question, the given sentence has four parts marked as P, Q, R, and S. Choose the part of the sentence with the error and mark it as your answer. If there is no error, mark 'S' as your answer.

Can you tell me (P)/ the name of the person (Q)/ whom wrote the book? (R)/ No error (S)

A. P   **B.** Q   **C.** R   **D.** S

Ques (53-54):Direction: Identify the most appropriate word after the verb (in bold italics) in the following sentence so that the combination of the verb and the word becomes the proper phrasal verb.

Q.53 These hat boxes are used for storing toys in the drawing-room. They *double* ____ decoration as well.

A. of   **B.** to   **C.** as   **D.** on

Q.54 Be careful not to *drag* ____ your old arguments in the discussion.

A. up   **B.** off   **C.** across   **D.** of

Ques (55-56):Direction: Select the word that is synonymous with the given word.

Q.55 CONTEMPT

A. Respect   **B.** Affection
C. Esteem   **D.** Hatred

Q.56 TRANSITION

A. Change   **B.** End
C. Introduction   **D.** Stagnation

Q.57 Direction: In the following sentence, four words/phrases have been underlined. Choose the word/phrase that is not appropriate according to the standard written English and mark the answer accordingly.

(1) Next week we will /(2) study more about /(3) universe and /(4) our solar system.

A. (1)   **B.** (2)   **C.** (3)   **D.** (4)

Q.58 Direction: Read the sentence carefully to find out whether there is any grammatical error in it. The error, if any, will be in one part of the sentence. Select the option of that part as your answer. If there is no error, mark option (D).

(A) Supposing if you (B) are arrested (C) what will you do? (D) No error

A. (A)   **B.** (B)   **C.** (C)   **D.** (D)

Q.59 Direction: Rewrite the sentence by replacing the underlined word with a noun.

She is a very intelligent person.

A. Her intelligence is great.
B. She is an intelligent person.
C. She is a person of great intelligence.
D. None of the above

Ques (60-61):Direction: Fill in the blanks in the following sentences with the help of options that follow.

Q.60 Sharman will not eat food unless he ______ accompanied by her.

A. will be   **B.** is
C. shall be   **D.** should be

Q.61 He said that he ____ in the USA for seven years before he returned.

A. have lived   **B.** had lived
C. has lived   **D.** can have lived

Q.62 Direction: In the following sentence, there are two blank spaces. Below the sentence is given pairs of words. Find out which pair of words can be used to fill in the blanks in the sentence in the same sequence to make the sentence meaningful and complete.

As the train reached full speed, the ______ of speeding wheels ______ Peter's ears.

A.   cacophony, filled
B.   music, satiated
C.   disharmony, satisfied
D.   consonance, spread

Q.63 Direction: In the following, the question choose the word which best expresses the meaning of the given word.

INDICT

A. Condemn   **B.** Reprimand
C. Accuse   **D.** Allege

Q.64 Direction: In the following sentence, there are two blank spaces. Below the sentence is given pairs of words. Find out which pair of words can be used to fill in the blanks in the sentence in the same sequence to make the sentence meaningful and complete.

The year 1903 proved most ______ and in a few years, all traces of the ______ drought of 1902 passed away.

A.   Ample, Unsuccessful
B.   Free, Injurious
C.   Bountiful, Disastrous
D.   Generous, Untoward

Q.65 Direction: Choose the correct opposites of the given word.

Bucolic

A. Reserved   **B.** Rustic
C. Cheerful   **D.** Urban

Ques (66-70):Direction: Answer the question based on the following passage.

"I think Indian firms have achieved the highest levels of efficiency in the world software outsourcing industry. Some researchers have assumed that Indian firms use the same programming languages and techniques as Chinese firms but have benefited from their familiarity with English, the language used to write software code. However, if this were true, then one would expect software vendors in Hong Kong, where most people speak English, to perform not worse than Indian vendors do. However, this is obviously not the case.

Other researchers link high Indian productivity to higher levels of human resource investment per engineer. But a historical perspective leads to a different conclusion. When the two top Indian vendors matched and then doubled Chinese productivity levels in the mid-eighties, human resource investment per employee was comparable to that of Chinese vendors. Furthermore, by the late eighties, the number of fixed assets required to develop one software package was roughly equivalent in India and in China. Since human resource investment was not higher in India, it had to be other factors that led to higher productivity.

A more fruitful explanation may lie with the Indian strategic approach in outsourcing. Indian software vendors did not simply seek outsourced contracts more effectively: they made an aggressive strategy in outsourcing. For instance, most software firms of India were initially set up to outsource the contract in western countries, such as the United States. On contrary, most Chinese firms seem to position their business in China, a promising yet under-developed market. However, rampant piracy in China took almost 90 percent of the potential market, making it impossible for most Chinese firms to obtain sufficient compensation for the investment in development and research, let alone thrive in a competitive environment.

Q.66 Which of the following statements can be inferred about the business strategy of India?

I. It advocates clemency and that is why they endorse actual physical contact with the developed world.

II. A stress on quality rather than quantity proves to be their trump card.

III. A strong posturing towards seeking overseas business helped Indian vendors stay competitive.

A. III   **B.** II   **C.** I   **D.** I and II

Q.67 Which of the following statements concerning the productivity levels of engineers can be inferred from the passage?

A. Before the 1980s, the productivity levels of the top Indian software firms were exceeded by those of Chinese software firms.

B. The official language of a country has a large effect on the productivity levels of its software developers.

C. During the mid-1980s, Indian software vendors surpassed the efficiency levels of their Chinese counterparts.

D. The greater the number of engineers a software firm has, the higher a firm's productivity level.

Q.68 According to the passage, which of the following statements is true about Indian software developers?

A. Their productivity levels did not equal those of Chinese software engineers until the late eighties.

B. Their high-efficiency levels were a direct result of English language familiarity.

C. They developed component-specific software.

D. They built products to meet the outsourcing requirements of the western orders.

Q.69 The primary purpose of the passage is to:

A. Contrast possible outcomes of a type of business strategy.

B. Emphasize careful orientation of a business strategy to beat the competition.

C. illustrate various ways in which a type of business strategy could fail to enhance revenues.

D. Trace the general problems of a company to a certain type of business strategy.

Q.70 Which of the following statements best describes the organization of the first paragraph?

A. A thesis is presented and supporting examples are provided.

B. Opposing views are presented, classified, and then reconciled.

C. A fact is stated, and an explanation is advanced, and then refuted.

D. A theory is proposed, considered, and then amended.

Maths and Logical Reasoning

Q.71 The average of the ages of a group of 45 men is 30 years if 5 men join the group, the average of the ages of 50 men becomes 33 years. Then the average of the ages of those 5 men joined later (in years) is:

A. 55 years   **B.** 60 years   **C.** 65 years   **D.** 45 years

Q.72 Find the next term of the given series.

5, 7, 11, 19, 35, ___

A. 47   **B.** 57   **C.** 67   **D.** 77

Q.73 Direction: On the basis of the numbers given below, answer the following question.

856   754   348   718   177

If all the digits are rearranged within the numbers in decreasing order, which of the following numbers will be the second-lowest?

A. 856   **B.** 754   **C.** 348   **D.** 177

Q.74 If sin A - cos A = 0, then the value of $\sin^4 A + \cos^4 A$ is:

[HTET PGT - Computer Science, 2018]

A. 0   **B.** 1   **C.** $\frac{1}{2}$ **D.** 2

Q.75 Direction: Find the missing number in the series.

3, 10, 101, ?

A. 10101   **B.** 10201   **C.** 10202   **D.** 11012

Q.76 The average of 45 numbers is 32. If two numbers 30 and 45 are excluded, then the approximate average of the remaining numbers will be:

A. 30.6   **B.** 29.7   **C.** 31.7   **D.** 30.7

Q.77 In the figure, chords AB and CD of a circle intersect externally at P. If AB = 4 cm, CD = 11 cm, and PD = 15 cm, then the length of PB is:

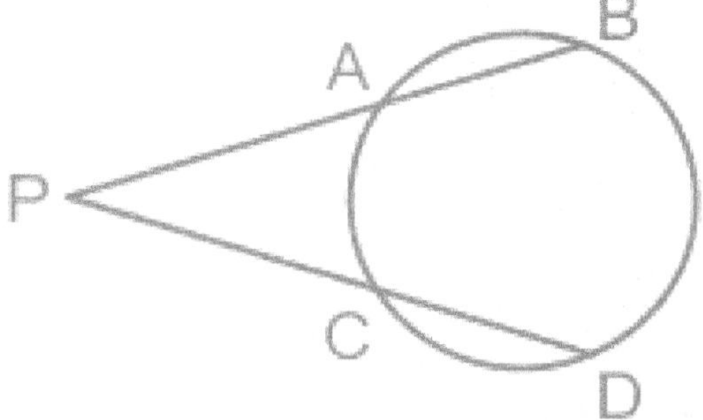

A. 10 cm   **B.** 12 cm   **C.** 8 cm   **D.** 14 cm

Q.78 Direction: Select the letter-cluster that is related to the third letter-cluster in the same way as the second letter-cluster is related to the first letter-cluster.

ZKR : BNV :: OHC : ?

A. OLG   **B.** RKF   **C.** QKR   **D.** QKG

Q.79 If $2\sec^2\theta + \tan^2\theta = 17$ then find the value of $\cot\theta$.

A. $\sqrt{5}$ **B.** $\frac{1}{\sqrt{5}}$ **C.** $\sqrt{3}$ **D.** $\frac{1}{\sqrt{3}}$

Q.80 In the given figure, what is the value of x?

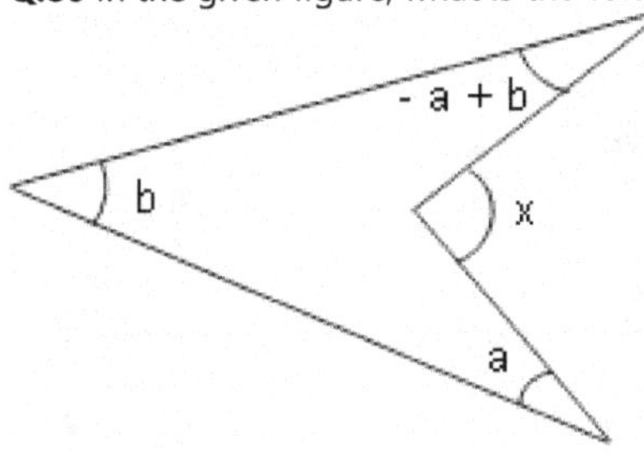

A. 2a + b   **B.** a - b   **C.** a + b   **D.** 2b

Q.81 Direction: The question is based on the following figures of the same dice.

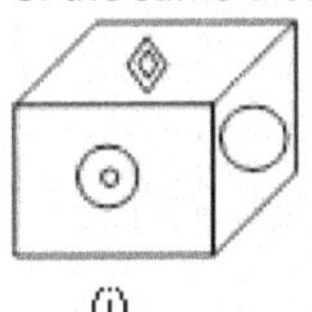 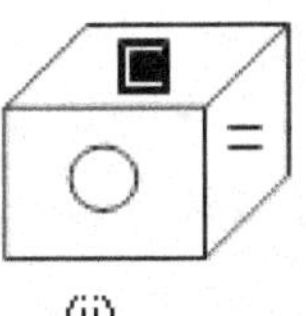 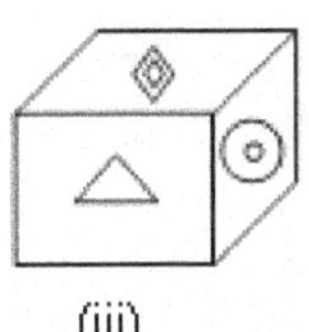

(i)   (ii)   (iii)

The symbol that appears at the bottom in figure (ii) is:

A. ◈

B. △

C. ◎

D. Either △ or ◈

Q.82 Direction: Study the given bar graph and answer the following question accordingly.

The bar graph shows the number of students from all three departments.

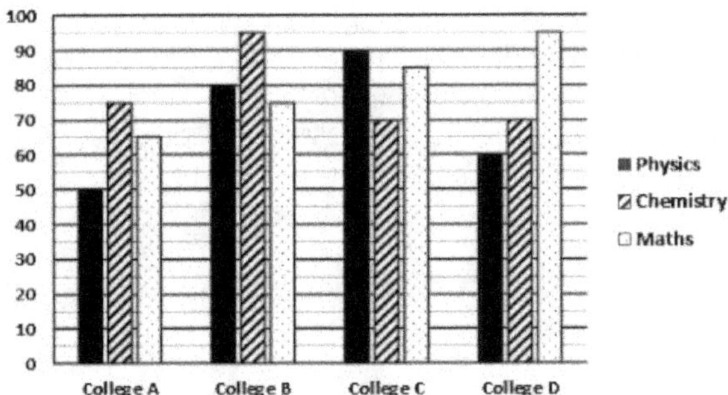

Find the total number of students from the chemistry department from all four colleges.

A. 210   **B.** 410   **C.** 320   **D.** 310

Q.83 Direction: In the question, below are given few statements followed by a few conclusions. You have to take the given statements to be true even if they seem to be at variance with the commonly known facts and then decide which of the given conclusion logically follows from the given statements, disregarding commonly known facts.

Statements:

No pen is page.

All page is paper.

No paper is white.

Conclusions:

I. Some paper is a page.

II. Some white is not paper.

A.   Only conclusion I follows

B.   Only conclusion II follows

C.   Both conclusion I and conclusion II follows

D.   Either conclusion I or conclusion II follows

Q.84 Consider the following statements and answer the question given below.

(a) P is the brother of Q.

(b) R is the daughter of Q.

(c) S is the sister of P.

(d) T is the brother of R.

Who is the uncle of T?

A. P   **B.** R   **C.** S   **D.** Q

Q.85 Direction: Study the following data carefully and answer the questions accordingly.

Eight persons A, B, C, D, E, F, G, and H are sitting at a circular table facing the center but not necessarily in the same order. F sits to the immediate right of H. D does not sit third to the left of H. C sits three places away from B. G sits third to the right of A, who is not an immediate neighbor of D and B. H sits opposite to E. D sits three places away from C.

How many persons are sitting between B and H when counted from the left of H?

A. One   **B.** Four   **C.** Three   **D.** Two

Q.86 Direction: Study the following pie chart and answer the questions based on it.

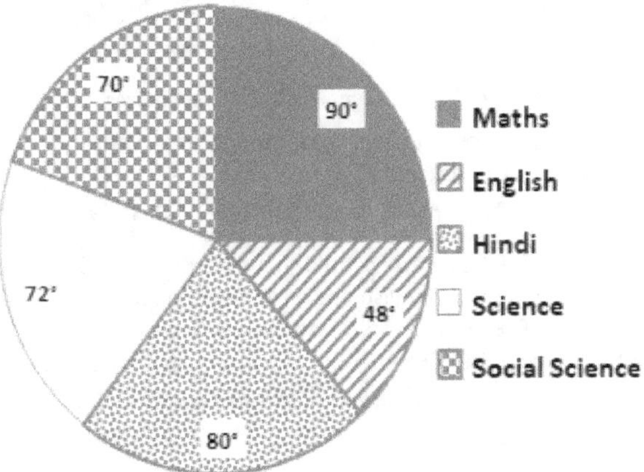

In which subject 100 marks have been obtained?

A. Hindi   **B.** Science

C. English   **D.** Mathematics

Q.87 Some students are lined up in a queue, in which Ashish stands 15th from the left and Sachin is 7th from the right. If they interchange their positions, then Sachin would be 15th from the right. How many students are there in the queue?

A. 21   **B.** 22
C. 29   **D.** None of these

Q.88 ΔABC and ΔPQR are similar to each other. If the ratio of the area of ΔABC and ΔPQR is 1 : 16, and the length of side AC is 28 cm, then find the length of PR.

A. 156 cm   **B.** 96 cm   **C.** 100 cm   **D.** 112 cm

Q.89 The value of $\dfrac{\cos^2 60° + 4\sec^2 30° - \tan^2 45°}{\sin^2 30° + \cos^2 30°}$.

[Territorial Army Officer, 2017]

A. $\dfrac{64}{\sqrt{3}}$ **B.** $\dfrac{55}{12}$ **C.** $\dfrac{67}{12}$ **D.** $\dfrac{67}{10}$

Q.90 How many straight lines are there in the figure given below?

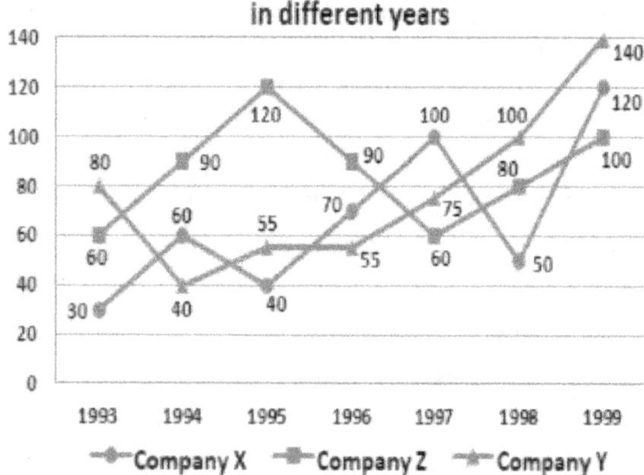

A. 16   **B.** 17   **C.** 18   **D.** 19

Q.91 Direction: Study the following line graph and answer the questions.

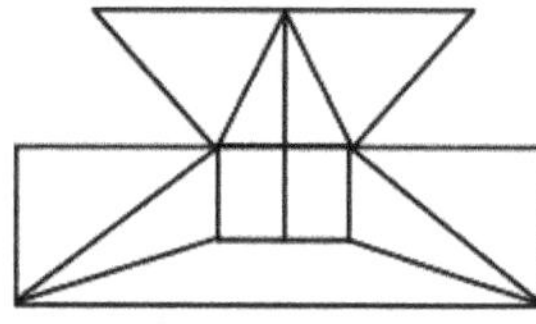

In which of the following years, total exports of the three companies were in maximum?

A. 1996   **B.** 1998   **C.** 1994   **D.** 1999

Q.92 A survey of a city represented that 45%, 30% and 60% of the people read Hindi, English and Urdu newspapers, respectively, 30% of the people read exactly two of the three newspapers, and 3% of the people don't read any newspaper. What percentage of people read all three newspapers?

A. 6%   **B.** 4%   **C.** 5%   **D.** 30%

Q.93 Direction: Answer the given question based on the following data.

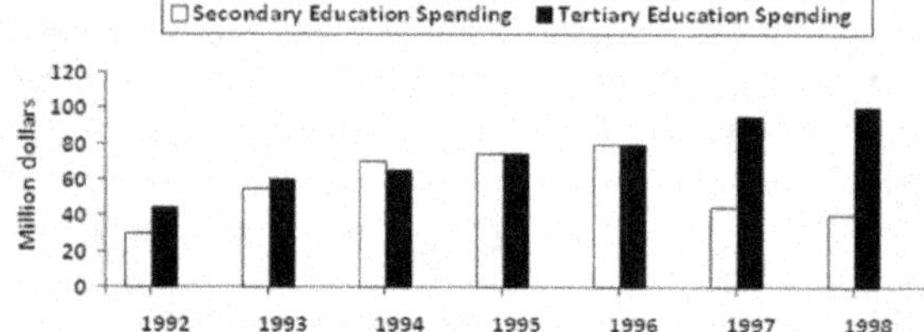

In which year did country X spend approximately \$30 million on secondary education?

A. 1992   **B.** 1994   **C.** 1995   **D.** 1996

Q.94 If 30% of A is added to 40% of B, then the answer is 80% of B. What percentage of A is B?

A. 100%   **B.** 72%   **C.** 70%   **D.** 75%

Q.95 A book-shelf contains 2 English, 3 Hindi, and 4 Sanskrit books. If two books are picked at random, then what is the probability that either all are Sanskrit or all are English books?

A. $\dfrac{12}{36}$ **B.** $\dfrac{7}{36}$ **C.** $\dfrac{15}{36}$ **D.** $\dfrac{11}{36}$

Q.96 Direction: Three of the following four numbers are alike in a certain way and one is different. Pick the number that is different from the rest.

A. 122   **B.** 190   **C.** 142   **D.** 193

Q.97 Which of the following options will replace the question mark (?) in the given series?

$CG,\ GH,\ LJ,\ RM,\ ?$

A. ZR **B.** YR **C.** ZQ **D.** YQ

Q.98 Six friends are sitting around a circular dining table facing towards the center of the table. Patrick is between Bob and Nanny. Alice is between Clark and Frank. Clark is to the immediate left of Bob. Who is to the immediate right of Bob?

A. Patrick   **B.** Frank   **C.** Nanny   **D.** Clark

Q.99 0.25 part of $A = 0.5$ part of $B = 0.75$ part of C, which of the following represents $A : B : C$?

A. $6:3:2$ **B.** $3:2:6$ **C.** $6:2:3$ **D.** $2:3:4$

Q.100 For a certain article, the ratio of the cost price to the selling price is $4:5$. What is the profit percentage?

A. 10%   **B.** 20%   **C.** 25%   **D.** 30%

// Smart Answer Sheet //

Correct Indicates percentage of students who answered questions correctly.

Skipped Indicates percentage of students who skipped questions.

Q.	Ans.	Correct / Skipped
1	A	51.72 % / 1.71 %
2	C	57.04 % / 1.55 %
3	C	48.37 % / 1.8 %
4	D	50.8 % / 1.89 %
5	C	54.53 % / 1.16 %
6	C	42.32 % / 1.37 %
7	A	79.41 % / 0.0 %
8	B	32.24 % / 3.33 %
9	A	50.28 % / 1.53 %
10	A	58.56 % / 1.24 %
11	A	81.08 % / 0.0 %
12	C	66.0 % / 1.27 %
13	D	64.59 % / 1.15 %
14	D	43.68 % / 1.32 %
15	A	87.61 % / 0.0 %
16	C	66.55 % / 1.49 %
17	C	67.15 % / 1.19 %
18	D	62.43 % / 1.14 %
19	A	85.46 % / 0.0 %
20	B	78.74 % / 0.0 %
21	A	82.46 % / 0.0 %
22	A	69.11 % / 1.95 %
23	B	52.99 % / 1.18 %
24	A	76.7 % / 0.0 %
25	D	82.99 % / 0.0 %
26	C	54.09 % / 1.5 %
27	B	59.82 % / 1.52 %
28	D	41.26 % / 1.1 %
29	C	22.45 % / 4.39 %
30	C	76.89 % / 0.0 %
31	D	26.93 % / 4.69 %
32	C	40.24 % / 1.36 %
33	B	69.72 % / 1.91 %
34	D	86.35 % / 0.0 %
35	B	84.68 % / 0.0 %
36	C	69.6 % / 1.98 %
37	D	12.75 % / 3.46 %
38	C	44.67 % / 1.96 %
39	C	66.31 % / 1.32 %
40	A	40.04 % / 1.18 %
41	A	60.12 % / 1.49 %
42	A	81.26 % / 0.0 %
43	C	78.3 % / 0.0 %
44	C	83.13 % / 0.0 %
45	A	87.92 % / 0.0 %
46	C	65.09 % / 1.17 %
47	D	67.75 % / 1.44 %
48	A	60.96 % / 1.15 %
49	A	53.81 % / 1.55 %
50	D	49.32 % / 1.59 %
51	A	54.62 % / 1.51 %
52	C	63.51 % / 1.97 %
53	C	61.8 % / 1.92 %
54	A	82.94 % / 0.0 %
55	D	83.71 % / 0.0 %
56	A	82.31 % / 0.0 %
57	C	89.99 % / 0.0 %
58	A	56.87 % / 1.17 %
59	C	77.32 % / 0.0 %
60	B	89.09 % / 0.0 %
61	B	86.82 % / 0.0 %
62	A	57.86 % / 1.55 %
63	C	58.29 % / 1.68 %
64	C	61.27 % / 1.63 %
65	D	32.44 % / 3.1 %
66	A	17.87 % / 3.35 %
67	C	24.13 % / 4.87 %
68	D	51.38 % / 1.91 %
69	B	58.63 % / 1.7 %
70	C	44.46 % / 1.55 %
71	B	51.79 % / 1.07 %
72	C	86.51 % / 0.0 %
73	D	61.47 % / 1.41 %
74	C	61.15 % / 1.69 %
75	C	65.74 % / 1.15 %
76	C	66.96 % / 1.63 %
77	A	58.96 % / 1.36 %
78	D	78.9 % / 0.0 %
79	B	83.22 % / 0.0 %
80	D	57.32 % / 1.7 %

Q.	Ans.	Correct / Skipped
81	C	56.49 %
		1.79 %
82	D	48.12 %
		1.59 %
83	C	66.09 %
		1.86 %
84	A	49.67 %
		1.24 %

Q.	Ans.	Correct / Skipped
85	D	23.37 %
		3.89 %
86	A	55.3 %
		1.03 %
87	C	42.47 %
		1.43 %
88	D	44.12 %
		1.37 %

Q.	Ans.	Correct / Skipped
89	B	66.35 %
		1.93 %
90	B	48.6 %
		1.49 %
91	D	62.89 %
		1.97 %
92	B	23.45 %
		3.29 %

Q.	Ans.	Correct / Skipped
93	A	88.13 %
		0.0 %
94	D	45.58 %
		1.57 %
95	B	68.97 %
		1.82 %
96	D	57.14 %
		1.08 %

Q.	Ans.	Correct / Skipped
97	D	77.33 %
		0.0 %
98	A	65.85 %
		1.92 %
99	A	53.52 %
		1.77 %
100	C	81.93 %
		0.0 %

Performance Analysis

Avg. Score (%)	50.0%
Toppers Score (%)	64.0%
Your Score	

General Awareness

Q.1 In which of the following fields, the Nobel Prize, 2018 has not been announced?

[Super TET Paper - I, 2019]

A. Medical

B. Literature

C. Physics

D. Chemistry

Q.2 In which state, was India's first pure green hydrogen plant commissioned in April 2022?

A. Assam

B. Karnataka

C. Gujarat

D. Punjab

Q.3 Who presided over the historic 1916 Lucknow Session of Congress?

A. Ambica Charan Majumdar

B. Madan Mohan Malviya

C. Subash Chandra Bose

D. Annie Besant

Q.4 Sherwani, a very popular attire in South Asia came from:

A. Syria

B. West Asia

C. Egypt

D. Central Asia

Q.5 'Swayamsidha' is a scheme launched by the Government of India to help?

A. Women only

B. School children only

C. Health workers only

D. None of the above

Q.6 Which of the following components is not recycled in nature?

A. Nitrogen   **B.** Water   **C.** Sodium   **D.** Carbon

Q.7 Which of the following bodies has been empowered to decide on the priority of work to be taken up under MGNREGA?

A. Gram Panchayat

B. Gram Sabha

C. Zila Parishad

D. State Government

Q.8 Which amendment of the Indian Constitution has abolished the nomination of Anglo-Indians to the Lok Sabha and Legislative Assemblies?

A. 101th Amendment Act

B. 102nd Amendment Act

C. 103rd Amendment Act

D. 104th Amendment Act

Q.9 Who called the Preamble as Political Horoscope of the Indian Constitution?

A. Thakurdas Bhargava

B. N. A. Palkhi Wala

C. K. M. Munshi

D. Jawahar Lal Nehru

Q.10 Which of the following articles contain provisions to regulate the organization of subordinate courts?

A. Articles 233 to 237

B. Articles 211 to 222

C. Articles 200 to 210

D. Articles 181 to 200

Q.11 Which rural schemes were merged with Swarna Jayanti Gram Swarozgar Yojana?

A. NREP and RLEGP

B. TRYSEM and MNP

C. IRDP and TRYSEM

D. DPAP and IRDP

Q.12 The Bijauliya Movement is related to the agrarian struggle in the current state of __?

A. Kerala

B. Assam

C. Odisha

D. Rajasthan

Q.13 Which among the following was/were the consequences of the Third Battle of Panipat?

1. Decentralization of Maratha's Power

2. Consolidation of East India Company in north-western India

3. Attack of Nadir Shah

Select the correct option from the codes given below:

A. Only 1

B. Only 1 & 2

C. Only 1 & 3

D. 1, 2 & 3

Q.14 What is the initial corpus of the National Infrastructure investment fund(NIIF)?

A. Rs 20,000 crores

B. Rs 30,000 crores

C. Rs 40,000 crores

D. Rs 50,000 crores

Q.15 Who among the following was the founder of 'Arya Samaj'?

A. Ram Mohan Roy

B. Dayanand Saraswati

C. Swami Vivekanand

D. None of these

Q.16 With which of the following subjects does the Stockholm Convention deal?

A. Ozone depletion

B. Marine pollution

C. Organic pollutants

D. Genetic pollution

Q.17 The biological treatment of wastewater makes use of-

A. aerobic bacteria and fungi

B. anaerobic bacteria and algae

C. aerobic and anaerobic bacteria

D. anaerobic bacteria and eucalyptus leaves

Q.18 NATO planned to set up a new space center in which country?

A. Norway

B. Germany

C. Denmark

D. India

Q.19 'SAPTA' is related to

A. Environment   **B.** Education
C. Security   **D.** Trade

Q.20 Consider the following:
1. Temple complex at Pattadakal
2. Group of Monuments at Hampi
3. Badami Cave Temples
Which among the above is/are World Heritage Sites?
A. 1 & 2   **B.** 1, 2 & 3   **C.** 1 & 3   **D.** 2 & 3

Q.21 The main cause of mismanagement of natural resources is
_________.

A. Individuals not using the three R's
B. The conversion of land for food crops
C. A large increase in population
D. A great demand for hydrocarbons

Q.22 NHAI signed a pact to share expertise for the betterment of highways with which IIT?
A. IIT Delhi   **B.** IIT Kanpur
C. IIT Jodhpur   **D.** IIT Lucknow

Q.23 The ozone protects the Earth from:
A. UV rays   **B.** X-rays
C. Gamma rays   **D.** Infrared rays

Q.24 Who among the following started the Kheda Satyagraha?
A. Raja Ram Mohan Roy
B. Mahatma Gandhi
C. Gopal Krishna Gokhale
D. Surendra Nath Banerjee

Q.25 Shishu, Kishor and Tarun are the schemes of-
A. Regional Rural Banks (RRB)
B. Micro Units Development and Refinance Agency Ltd. (MUDRA)
C. Small Industries Development Bank of India (SIDBI)
D. Industrial Development Bank of India (IDBI)

Q.26 The aim of Prime Minister Rozgar Yojana (PMRY) is to create self-employment opportunities for educated unemployed youth in rural areas and-
A. Big towns   **B.** Small towns
C. Urban towns   **D.** Big cities

Q.27 Which agency estimates the national income of India?
A. Reserve Bank of India
B. Planning Commission
C. Ministry of Finance
D. Central Statistical Organisation

Q.28 World Heritage Day is observed on which date?
A. 28 January   **B.** 18 April
C. 22 May   **D.** 21 June

Q.29 'Great Indian Bustard, Asian Elephant and Bengal Florican' have been classified as which category under the UN's Convention on Conservation of Migratory Species?

A. Endangered migratory species
B. Migratory species conserved through Agreements
C. Critically Endangered Species
D. Vulnerable Species

Q.30 Which of the following are the objectives behind the specification of the regional languages in the Eighth Schedule?
1. The members of these languages are to be given representation in the Official Language Commission.
2. The forms, style and expression of these languages are to be used for the enrichment of the Hindi language.
Select the correct option from the codes given below:
A. Only 1   **B.** Only 2
C. Both 1 & 2   **D.** Neither 1 & 2

Q.31 Which technology company has launched the 'Women Will' web platform in India?
A. Amazon   **B.** Google
C. Microsoft   **D.** IBM

Q.32 What is the name of the certification system that allows people who have been vaccinated against Covid-19 to access certain facilities?
A. Covid Shield   **B.** Vaccine Passport
C. Vaccine Drive   **D.** Covid Protect

Q.33 In India, the scheme of workers' education operates at-
A. National level   **B.** Regional level
C. Unit/Village level   **D.** All of the above

Q.34 Which sport's competition is known as "SaarLorLux Open"?
A. Tennis   **B.** Badminton
C. Golf   **D.** Hockey

Q.35 Who became the top scorer of the 2018 FIBA Women's Basketball World Cup?
A. Liz Cambage   **B.** Diana Taurasi
C. Sue Bird   **D.** Breanna Stewart

Q.36 Which professional boxer is nicknamed the "Kid Dynamite"?
A. Muhammad Ali   **B.** Mike Tyson
C. Joe Frazier   **D.** James Toney

Q.37 Which among the following articles helped the Madarsas in India to remain out of the purview of the Right to Education Act?
A. Article 26   **B.** Article 27
C. Article 28   **D.** Article 30

Q.38 Which ruler was successful in annexing the Lichchavis of Vaisali?
A. Ashoka
B. Ajatshatru
C. Kalasoka
D. Chandragupta Maurya

Q.39 Consider the following:
1. Rhizobium

2. Azotobacter

3. Blue-Green Algae

Which of the above are used as biofertilizers?

A. 1 & 2 Only   **B.** 2 & 3 Only

C. 1 & 3 Only   **D.** 1, 2 & 3

Q.40 Which of the following is/are part of India's external debt?

1. External Commercial Borrowings

2. NRI Deposits

3. Inward Remittances

Select the correct option from the codes given below:

A. Only 1 & 2   **B.** Only 2 & 3

C. Only 1 & 3   **D.** 1, 2 & 3

English Proficiency

Q.41 Direction: Choose the best option to fill in the blank.

Our country is a spiritual country, theirs _____ religious.

A. is   **B.** are   **C.** also   **D.** have

Q.42 Direction: In the following question, choose the word which best fills the blank from the four options given.

Leisure should be utilized not in ______ away the time saved, but in engaging in some pleasurable activity.

A. Idling   **B.** Wishing   **C.** Running   **D.** Sending

Q.43 Direction: Select the correct passive form of the given sentence.

The fierce storm wrecked the ship.

A. The ship was being wrecked by the fierce storm.

B. The storm is wrecked by the fierce ship.

C. The ship has been wrecked by the fierce storm.

D. The ship was wrecked by the fierce storm.

Q.44 Direction: In the following question, choose the word which best fills the blank from the four options given.

The imperfections and ______ edges remind us that our lives are works in progress.

A. low   **B.** high   **C.** rough   **D.** dry

Q.45 Direction: Select the correct passive form of the given sentence.

Who has broken the chair?

A. By whom has the chair been broken?

B. By whom was the chair been broken?

C. By whom had the chair been broken?

D. By whom is the chair been broken?

Q.46 Direction: Select the word/phrase that is antonymous to the word given in capital letters.

LUNACY

A. Desiccation   **B.** Sagacity

C. Veracity   **D.** Revocation

Q.47 Direction: Select the correct passive form of the given sentence.

Harsh has applied for leave.

A. Leave had been applied by Harsh.

B. Leave was applied by Harsh.

C. Leave has been applied for by Harsh.

D. Leave is applied for by Harsh.

Q.48 Pick the odd one out.

A. Cub   **B.** Kitten   **C.** Fowl   **D.** Calf

Q.49 Pick the odd one out.

A. Genuine   **B.** Bogus

C. Farce   **D.** Superficial

Q.50 Pick the odd one out.

A. Trivial   **B.** Lofty

C. Petty   **D.** Frivolous

Q.51 Direction: Out of the four alternatives, choose the one which can be substituted for the given words.

A member of middle class

A. Bureaucrat   **B.** Bourgeois

C. Bigot   **D.** Credulous

Ques (52-56):Direction: Read the passage given below carefully and then answer the following questions.

Russia ________ (1) its space satellite Arktika-M on Sunday on a mission to monitor the climate and environment in the Arctic amid a push by the Kremlin to expand the country's activities in the region.

The Arctic has ________(2) more than twice as fast as the global average over the last three decades and Moscow is seeking to develop the energy-rich region, investing in the Northern Sea Route for shipping across its long northern flank as ice melts.

The satellite ________ (3) reached its intended orbit after being launched from Kazakhstan's Baikonur cosmodrome by a Soyuz rocket, Dmitry Rogozin, the head of Russia's Roscosmos space agency, said in a post on Twitter.

Russia plans to send up a second satellite in 2023 and, combined, the two will offer round-the-clock, all-weather ________ (4) of the Arctic Ocean and the surface of the Earth, Roscosmos said.

"There is also an element of data nationalism that is feeding into all this. Countries, especially those that see themselves as ________(5) powers, want to be able to rely on their own satellites and data to inform their activities, whether commercial or military in nature," she said.

Q.52 Which of the following is the most appropriate option for blank 1?

A. crashed   **B.** taxied   **C.** sprung   **D.** launched

Q.53 Which of the following is the most appropriate option for blank 2?

A. frozen   **B.** grappled

C. stagnated   **D.** warmed

Q.54 Which of the following is the most appropriate option for blank 3?

A. randomly   **B.** mistakenly
C. successfully   **D.** unsuccessfully

Q.55 Which of the following is the most appropriate option for blank 4?

A. Morphing   **B.** Monitoring
C. Altering   **D.** Suffocating

Q.56 Which of the following is the most appropriate option for blank 5?

A. space   **B.** rocket   **C.** flying   **D.** NASA

Q.57 In the following question choose the word which best expresses the meaning of the given word.
CORPULENT

A. Lean   **B.** Gaunt
C. Emaciated   **D.** Obese

Ques (58-61):Direction: In the following question, out of the four alternatives, select the alternative which will improve the underlined part of the sentence. In case no improvement is needed, select "No improvement".

Q.58 Each of the students of this class **has to submit their** assignment before the end of this month.

A. has to submit his   **B.** have to submit his
C. have to submit their   **D.** No improvement

Q.59 Acclaimed Punjabi singer Sardool Sikander **has passed away at** Fortis hospital in Mohali in Punjab on Wednesday.

A. had passed away at   **B.** passed away at
C. passes away at   **D.** No improvement

Q.60 The trip to Ladakh seemed to be very expensive so **I did not went there** with my friends.

A. I haven't gone there   **B.** I do not go there
C. I did not go there   **D.** No improvement

Q.61 Although he is working in this organization for the last two years, he hasn't done anything remarkable.

A. Although he had been working
B. Although he was working
C. Although he has been working
D. No improvement

Q.62 Direction: Choose the best option to fill in the blank.
The accused _________ that he had met the deceased before.

A. remarked   **B.** alleged
C. exclaimed   **D.** denied

Q.63 Direction: Choose the option which is opposite to the given word.
Tepid

A. Passionate   **B.** Grandiose
C. Carefree   **D.** Faintly reminiscent

Q.64 Direction: Choose the best option to fill in the blank.
However, the group's long-term strategy is to _____ on core business sectors connected with infrastructure and energy.

A. attend   **B.** breed
C. develop   **D.** concentrate

Q.65 Direction: In the following question, out of the four alternatives, select the alternative which will improve the underlined part of the sentence. In case no improvement is needed, select "No improvement".

They built a wall to avoid soil **being washed away**.

A. to be washed away   **B.** been washed away
C. be washed away   **D.** No improvement

Ques (66-70):Direction: Read the following passage carefully and answer the question that follows:

Progress in life depends a good deal on crossing one threshold after another. Some time ago, a man watched his little nephew trying to write his name. It was hard work, very hard work. The little boy had arrived at an effort threshold. Today, he writes his name with comparative ease. No new threshold confronts him. This is the way with all. Conquer one difficulty, a new difficulty appears or should appear. Some people make the mistake of steering clear of thresholds. They avoid anything that requires genuine thinking and the use of energy. They prefer to stay in a rut where thresholds are not met. Probably they have been at their job a number of years; things are easy for them. They make no effort to seek out new obstacles to overcome. Real progress stops under such circumstances.

Some middle-aged and elderly people greatly enrich their lives by continuing to cross thresholds. One man went into an entirely new business when he was past middle-age and made a success of it. De Morgan did not start to write novels until he was past sixty. Psychologists have discovered that man can continue to learn throughout life and it is undoubtedly better to try and fail than not to try at all. Here, one can be placed in the category of the Swiss mountaineer of whom it was said that he died climbing. When a new difficulty rises to obstruct your path, do not complain. Accept the challenge. Determine to cross this threshold as you have crossed numerous other thresholds in your past life. In the world of the poet, do not rest. Strive to pass from dream to grander dream.

Q.66 What does progress in life depend upon?
A. Slowing down after crossing a threshold
B. Overcoming one difficulty after another
C. Seeking out new work with sincerity
D. Showing spirit of service and cooperation

Q.67 When did De Morgan start to write novels?
A. When he was a student.
B. When he was 60 years old.
C. When he was below the age of 60 years.
D. When he was above the age of 60 years.

Q.68 What does 'he died climbing' signify?
A. The mountaineer strove hard till the last moment of life.
B. The mountaineer climbed the hill and then died.
C. The mountaineer died before getting at the top.
D. The mountaineer died when he was climbing the hill.

Q.69 What does 'to pass from dream to grander dream' mean?
A. Seeing one dream after another
B. Always having greater and greater aspirations in life

C. Making plan after plan

D. Seeing one good dream and then hoping for a better dream

Q.70 How can you accomplish the most difficult of tasks?
A. By mobilising all possible resources
B. By sticking to hard work
C. By doing it bit by bit and persevering in the effort
D. By getting other people to do your work for you

Maths and Logical Reasoning

Q.71 The number 111111111111 is divisible by-
A. 9 and 11
B. 5 and 11
C. 5 and 9
D. 3 and 11

Q.72 In the triangle below, if $AC = BD$, what is the length of AD?

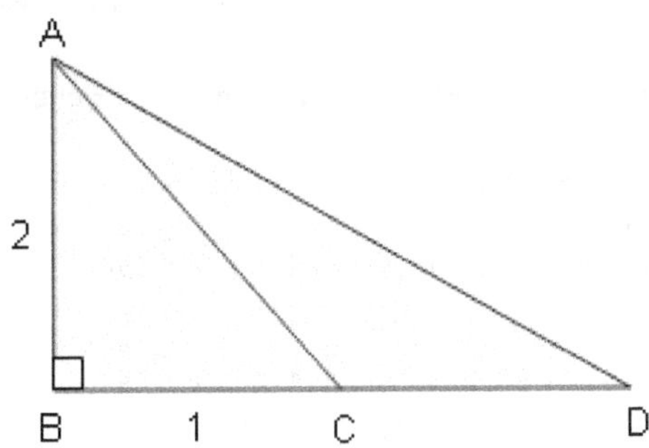

A. 3
B. $\sqrt{5}$
C. $\sqrt{3}$
D. None of these

Q.73 A man buys 1000 items at $\$3$ each. He sells 700 of them at $\$4.50$ each and the rest at $\$2.50$ each. Find his average profit per item sold.
A. $\$0.90$
B. $\$1$
C. $\$1.285$
D. $\$1.50$

Q.74 A company employed 600 men and 400 women and the average wage was $\$2.55$ per day. If a woman gets $\$0.5$ less than a man, then what will be their daily wages?
A. Man $\$2.95$, woman $\$2.45$.
B. Man $\$.75$, woman $\$3.25$
C. Man $\$2.75$, woman $\$2.25$
D. Man $\$3.25$, woman $\$2.75$

Q.75 A 100 m long wire is cut into two pieces such that one piece is one and a half times longer than the other piece. What is the length of the shorter piece?
A. 20 m
B. 40 m
C. 33 m
D. 60 m

Q.76 Robin and Robert have some money in the ratio of $4 : 3$. Robin gives Rs. p to Robert. Now, they have equal amounts of money. Robert spends Rs. q out of the money he has. Now, the ratio becomes $4 : 3$. Find the ratio p: q?
A. $1 : 1$
B. $1 : 2$
C. $2 : 3$
D. $4 : 7$

Q.77 The maximum marks in a test were 1000. A scored 10% less than B, B scored 25% more than C, and C scored 20% less than D. If A scored 720 marks, then what percentage marks did D score?
A. 90%
B. 85%
C. 80%
D. 78%

Q.78 A sum of money is to be distributed among A, B, C, D in the proportion of $5 : 2 : 4 : 3$. If C gets Rs. 1000 more than D, what is B's share?
A. Rs. 2000
B. Rs. 1500
C. Rs. 500
D. Rs. 3000

Q.79 Direction: Read the following passage carefully and answer the question.

In the recruitment process of teachers, there appear $15,000$ candidates, out of which 450 candidates have prior experience in working in rural area government schools only. 25% of the total number of candidates have experience in teaching in private schools only in rural areas. 12% of the total number of candidates have experience in teaching in private schools only in urban areas. 2% of the total number of candidates have experience in teaching in government schools only in urban areas. 3600 candidates have experience in teaching in both private and government schools in urban areas only and 600 candidates have experience in teaching in both government and private schools in rural areas only. The remaining candidates have no experience in teaching.

How many candidates have experience in teaching in urban areas?
A. 3600
B. 4200
C. 5700
D. 6800

Q.80 Direction: Study the graphs carefully to answer the following question.

A total number of children in 6 different schools and the percentage of girls among them:

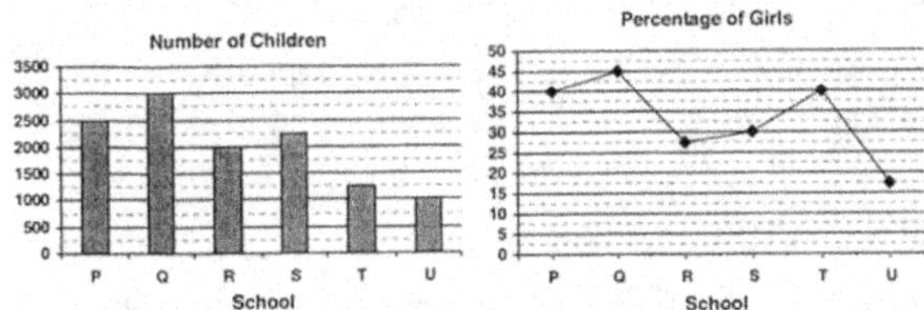

What is the total percentage of boys in schools R and U?
A. 78.55%
B. 77.59%
C. 76.28%
D. 75.83%

Q.81 Which of the following has the most number of divisors?
A. 99
B. 101
C. 176
D. 182

Q.82 Choose the option that will come into the place of the question mark (?).
$12 : 156 :: ?$
A. 10 : 101
B. 15 : 340
C. 10 : 110
D. 7 : 50

Q.83 In the following question, select the correct word from the given alternatives.

ADF : EHJ : : PQT : ?

A. QVW   **B.** TUX   **C.** TVX   **D.** URY

Q.84 Janta Airline has a free luggage allowance for its passengers. If any passenger carries excess luggage, it is charged at a constant rate per kg. The total luggage charge paid by Ravind Jekriwal and Pranas Shubhan is Rs. 1100. If both Ravind and Pranas had carried luggage twice the weight than they actually did, their luggage charges would have been Rs. 2000 and Rs. 1000 respectively. What was the charge levied on Ravind's luggage?

A. Rs. 900   **B.** Rs. 880
C. Rs. 800   **D.** None of these

Q.85 Find the smallest number that leaves a remainder of 4 on division by 5, 5 on division by 6, 6 on division by 7, 7 on division by 8, and 8 on division by 9?

A. 5435   **B.** 4980   **C.** 2519   **D.** 2577

Q.86 Direction: The below Bar Graph shows the sales of different brands of TYRE.

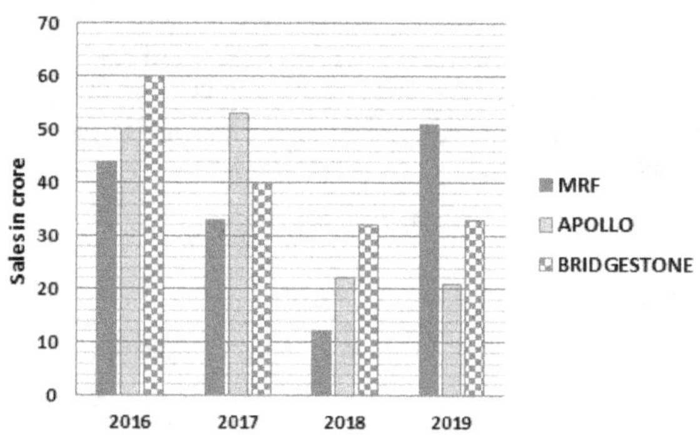

What is the average of sales of the tyre in the year 2019?

A. 40 Cr   **B.** 50 Cr.   **C.** 35 Cr.   **D.** 44 Cr.

Q.87 Direction: In the following question, various terms of a number series are given with one term missing as shown by (?). Choose the missing term out of the given alternatives.

12, 18, 27, 40.5, ?

A. 58.75   **B.** 64.25   **C.** 60.75   **D.** 72.5

Q.88 Direction: Read the following information and answer the question given below.

'P - Q' means 'P is the husband of Q'.

'P + Q' means 'P is the daughter of Q'.

'P × Q' means 'P is the mother of Q'.

Which of the following is false for R × L × M - N?

A.   M is the son of L.
B.   L is the mother-in-law of N.
C.   M is the husband of N.
D.   N is the daughter L.

Q.89 Direction: In the following question, various terms of a number series are given with one term missing as shown by (?). Choose the missing term out of the given alternatives.

10, 3, 17, 8, ?, 18, 31

A. 24   **B.** 14   **C.** 10   **D.** 20

Q.90 Direction: Read the following passage carefully and answer the question.

Twelve people are sitting in two parallel rows such that each row has six people. A, B, C, D, E, and F are sitting in the first row and P, Q, R, S, T, and U are sitting in the second row. People in the first row are sitting facing towards south and people in the second row are sitting facing towards north. They are sitting in such a manner that each member of the first row is facing another member in the second row.

U is sitting third to the right of S. S is facing F and F is not sitting at any of the extreme ends of the row. D is sitting third to the right of C. R is sitting facing towards C. The person sitting facing towards E is sitting third to the right of P. B and P are not sitting at any of the extreme ends of the row. T is not an immediate neighbor of U, and A is not an immediate neighbor of C.

Four of the following five are alike in a certain way based on their positions as given in the passage and so form a group. Which of the following does not belong to that group?

A. D   **B.** S   **C.** U   **D.** T

Q.91 Direction: Study the three different orientations of a cube given below and answer the question that follows.

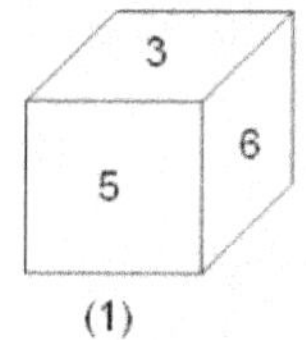
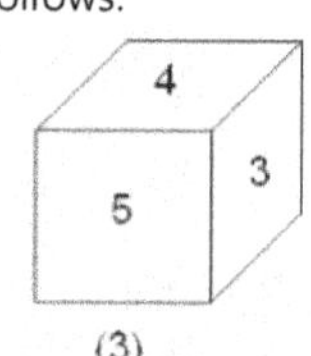

Which of the following numbers appears on the face opposite the one having 2?

A. 1   **B.** 4   **C.** 5   **D.** 3

Q.92 Direction: In the following question, various terms of a number series are given with one term missing as shown by (?). Choose the missing term out of the given alternatives.

5, 17, 53, ?, 485

A. 161   **B.** 157   **C.** 163   **D.** 159

Q.93 Direction: Study the following information carefully and answer the question given below.

Six people A, B, C, D, E, and F are sitting on the ground in a hexagonal shape. All the sides of the hexagon so formed are of the same length. A is not adjacent to B or C; D is not adjacent to C or E; B and C are adjacent, and F is in the middle of D and C.

Which of the following is not a correct neighboring pair?

A. A and F   **B.** D and F   **C.** B and E   **D.** C and F

Q.94 Direction: Read the following information and answer the given question.

(1) A, B, C, D, E, and F are six members of a family. Each is in a different profession - Doctor, Lawyer, Teacher, Engineer, Nurse, Manager.

(2) Each of them remains at home on a different day of the week from Monday to Saturday.

(3) The lawyer in the family remains at home on Thursday.

(4) C remains at home on Tuesday.

(5) A the Doctor does not remain at home either on Saturday or on Wednesday.

(6) D is neither the Doctor nor the Teacher and remains at home on Friday.

(7) B is the Engineer and E is the Manager.

Which of the following combinations is correct?

A.   Lawyer - Tuesday
B.   Teacher - Wednesday
C.   Doctor - Monday
D.   Doctor - Friday

Q.95 Direction: Study the following information carefully and answer the question given below.

A, B, C, D, E, F, G and H are sitting in a straight line equidistant from each other (but not necessarily in the same order). Some of them are facing south, while some are facing north (Note: Facing the same direction means if one is facing north, then the other also faces north and vice-versa. Facing the opposite directions means if one is facing north, then the other faces south and vice-versa). F is the immediate neighbour of E and B. B is not facing the same direction as F and G. C is not an immediate neighbour of A or H but faces the same direction as A and H. H is not an immediate neighbour of G. G is second to the left of E, who is facing south. D is fourth to the right of H and both are facing opposite directions.

What is the position of C with respect to D?

A. Second to the left   **B.** Second to the right
C. Third to the left   **D.** Fourth to the right

Q.96 Direction: Find the missing term.

nd, iy, dt, yo, tj,?

A. mp   **B.** nq   **C.** of   **D.** oe

Q.97 Direction: Find the missing term.

HUA, GTZ, FSY, ERX,?

A. DWQ   **B.** DQW   **C.** WDQ   **D.** WQD

Ques (98-99):Direction: Based on the table below answer the following questions:

The table given below shows the percentage distribution of the total expenditures of a company Zeta Interactive Services under various expense heads during 2003.

Infrastructure	20
Transport	12.5
Advertisement	15
Taxes	10
R & D	5
Salaries	20
Interest on Loans	17.5

Q.98 If the interest on the loan amounted to Rs. 2.45 crores, then the total amount of expenditure on advertisement taxes and research and development of Zeta Interactive Services is

A. Rs. 7 crores

B. Rs. 5.4 crores

C. Rs. 4.2 crores

D. Rs. 3 crores

A. A   **B.** C   **C.** B   **D.** D

Q.99 If the expenditure of Zeta Interactive Services on advertisement is 2.10 crores then the difference between the expenditure on transport and taxes is?

A. Rs. 1.25 crores

B. Rs. 95 lakhs

C. Rs. 65 lakhs

D. Rs. 35 lakhs

A. A   **B.** C   **C.** D   **D.** B

Q.100 How many triangles are there in the following figure?

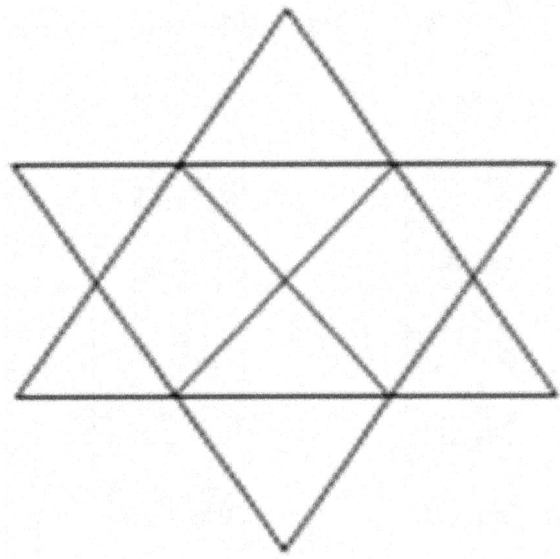

A. 10   **B.** 12   **C.** 14   **D.** 15

// Smart Answer Sheet //

Correct — Indicates percentage of students who answered questions correctly.

Skipped — Indicates percentage of students who skipped questions.

Q.	Ans.	Correct / Skipped	Q.	Ans.	Correct / Skipped	Q.	Ans.	Correct / Skipped	Q.	Ans.	Correct / Skipped	Q.	Ans.	Correct / Skipped
1	B	40.19 % / 1.74 %	17	C	51.36 % / 1.68 %	33	D	25.03 % / 4.68 %	49	A	64.54 % / 1.32 %	65	D	54.68 % / 1.03 %
2	A	66.09 % / 2.0 %	18	B	53.12 % / 1.39 %	34	B	59.35 % / 1.07 %	50	B	67.8 % / 1.84 %	66	B	12.9 % / 3.16 %
3	A	63.18 % / 1.15 %	19	D	49.08 % / 1.44 %	35	A	49.44 % / 1.52 %	51	B	31.19 % / 4.26 %	67	D	30.28 % / 3.71 %
4	D	44.82 % / 1.98 %	20	A	40.4 % / 1.69 %	36	B	51.0 % / 1.46 %	52	D	10.02 % / 4.1 %	68	A	10.74 % / 3.14 %
5	A	40.23 % / 1.59 %	21	C	46.53 % / 1.27 %	37	D	63.91 % / 1.81 %	53	D	47.6 % / 1.91 %	69	B	18.14 % / 3.62 %
6	C	42.38 % / 1.79 %	22	C	65.69 % / 1.35 %	38	B	58.65 % / 1.55 %	54	C	41.89 % / 1.47 %	70	A	20.27 % / 4.41 %
7	A	62.56 % / 1.67 %	23	A	81.63 % / 0.0 %	39	D	65.85 % / 1.96 %	55	B	40.17 % / 1.44 %	71	D	69.45 % / 1.58 %
8	D	68.52 % / 1.12 %	24	B	51.35 % / 1.02 %	40	A	62.7 % / 1.47 %	56	A	21.1 % / 4.75 %	72	A	68.82 % / 1.25 %
9	C	54.74 % / 1.42 %	25	B	48.6 % / 1.92 %	41	A	85.54 % / 0.0 %	57	D	60.35 % / 1.07 %	73	A	55.13 % / 1.44 %
10	A	54.81 % / 1.74 %	26	B	56.08 % / 1.67 %	42	A	50.34 % / 1.8 %	58	A	44.83 % / 1.73 %	74	C	12.55 % / 4.31 %
11	A	57.95 % / 1.53 %	27	D	64.6 % / 1.02 %	43	D	49.46 % / 1.92 %	59	B	69.81 % / 1.61 %	75	B	69.17 % / 1.45 %
12	D	10.72 % / 4.61 %	28	B	47.84 % / 1.19 %	44	C	50.59 % / 1.34 %	60	C	58.17 % / 1.1 %	76	D	59.38 % / 1.3 %
13	A	62.08 % / 1.35 %	29	A	49.91 % / 1.01 %	45	A	50.99 % / 1.41 %	61	C	55.91 % / 1.24 %	77	C	57.44 % / 1.89 %
14	C	47.05 % / 1.6 %	30	C	64.34 % / 1.01 %	46	B	59.68 % / 1.91 %	62	D	49.83 % / 1.46 %	78	A	77.13 % / 0.0 %
15	B	48.23 % / 1.23 %	31	B	24.74 % / 3.01 %	47	C	52.55 % / 1.03 %	63	A	44.27 % / 1.25 %	79	C	32.71 % / 4.18 %
16	C	62.77 % / 1.53 %	32	B	43.31 % / 1.07 %	48	C	51.35 % / 1.77 %	64	D	42.98 % / 1.69 %	80	D	46.62 % / 1.66 %

Q.	Ans.	Correct		Q.	Ans.	Correct		Q.	Ans.	Correct		Q.	Ans.	Correct		Q.	Ans.	Correct
		Skipped				Skipped				Skipped				Skipped				Skipped
81	C	78.08 %		85	C	58.8 %		89	A	45.63 %		93	A	68.74 %		97	B	46.82 %
		0.0 %				1.26 %				1.18 %				1.79 %				1.69 %
82	C	77.45 %		86	C	50.75 %		90	B	15.24 %		94	C	11.33 %		98	B	41.09 %
		0.0 %				1.75 %				3.11 %				4.24 %				1.41 %
83	B	57.33 %		87	C	47.55 %		91	C	85.46 %		95	A	54.35 %		99	C	41.71 %
		1.82 %				1.33 %				0.0 %				1.78 %				1.88 %
84	C	27.92 %		88	D	48.08 %		92	A	56.19 %		96	D	28.39 %		100	C	49.84 %
		4.76 %				1.59 %				1.31 %				3.1 %				1.42 %

Performance Analysis

Avg. Score (%)	45.0%
Toppers Score (%)	70.0%
Your Score	

General Awareness

Q.1 Who has won the Best Male actor award in the International Indian Film Academy Awards 2022 held in Abu Dhabi?

A. Salman Khan **B.** Shah Rukh Khan

C. Vicky Kaushal **D.** Varun Dhawan

Q.2 Which bank has signed an MoU with the Central Board of Direct Taxes (CBDT) and Central Board of Indirect Taxes and Customs (CBIC) for tax collection?

A. Kotak Mahindra Bank

B. Dhanlaxmi Bank

C. Federal Bank

D. DCB Bank

Q.3 Abhijit Sen, who passed away on August 29, 2022, was related to which field?

A. Geography **B.** Psychology

C. Biology **D.** Economics

Q.4 Who has been appointed as a director in the Prime Minister's Office (PMO) in August 2022?

A. Shweta Singh

B. Ravi Kumar

C. Ruchi Mishra

D. Anoop Kumar Pathak

Q.5 Which country's organisation in June 2022 signed an MoU with Bharat Electronics Limited (BEL) for the Supply of Airborne Defense Suite for Indian Air Force (IAF) helicopters?

A. Japan

B. United States of America

C. Belarus

D. France

Q.6 Queen Naikidevi is remembered as the woman who defeated ________ in 1178 CE.

A. Muhammad bin Tughlag

B. Mumhammad al-Baqir

C. Al-Salih Muhammad

D. Muhammad Ghori

Q.7 'Rauf' is a folk dance associated with the state of ________.

A. Haryana

B. Punjab

C. Rajasthan

D. Jammu and Kashmir

Q.8 Which of the following rivers makes Dhuandhar Waterfall?

A. Tapti **B.** Subarnarekha

C. Narmada **D.** Betwa

Q.9 The famous festival of 'Tsokum Samai' is celebrated by the people of which state to invoke blessings for a rich harvest?

A. Mizoram **B.** Assam

C. Meghalaya **D.** Nagaland

Q.10 The Maharana Pratap Sagar reservoir on the rivers Beas in Himachal Pradesh is also known as ________.

A. Pong Dam **B.** Ukai Dam

C. Dharoi Da **D.** Tehri Dam

Q.11 Article ________ of the Constitution of India states that the Judge of a High Court shall be appointed by the President with consultation of the Chief Justice of India and the Governor of the state.

A. 21 **B.** 201 **C.** 217 **D.** 72

Q.12 Acid rain is caused because of the pollution of the environment by:

A. carbon dioxide and nitrogen

B. carbon dioxide and carbon monoxide

C. nitrous oxide and sulphur dioxide

D. nitrogen and sulphur dioxide

Q.13 The term 'Eagle' is used in which of the following sports?

A. Golf **B.** Football **C.** Polo **D.** Chess

Q.14 When is the World Fisheries Day celebrated every year?

A. 19th November **B.** 20th November

C. 21st November **D.** 22nd November

Q.15 Which of the following states does NOT share a border with Bangladesh?

A. Meghalaya **B.** Manipur

C. Tripura **D.** Mizoram

Q.16 The Battle of Chausa was fought between Humayun and Sher Shah Suri on 26 June in the year ______.

A. 1729 **B.** 1539 **C.** 1639 **D.** 1440

Q.17 Who became the first England batsman who scores 200 in the 100th Test against India?

A. Ben Stokes **B.** Eoin Morgan

C. Joe Root **D.** Jos Buttler

Q.18 The Treaty of Sagauli was signed between the British and the ______.

A. Gurkhas **B.** Nawab of Bengal

C. Nawab of Awadh **D.** Marathas

Q.19 Which of the following measures is **not** adopted by the Reserve Bank of India for controlling credit?

A. Open Market Operations

B. Cash Reserve Ratio

C. Statutory Liquidity Ratio

D. Cash Deposit Ratio

Q.20 Who was the Governor General of India during the first Anglo-Sikh War?

A. Lord Cornwallis   **B.** Lord Hardinge

C. Lord Dalhousie   **D.** Lord Canning

Q.21 The world's longest railway platform is in:

A. Storvik, Sweden   **B.** New York, USA

C. Gorakhpur, India   **D.** Canberra, Australia

Q.22 Swadeshi Movement started in India during ________.

A. Anti-Bengal Partition agitation

B. The first non-co-operation movement of 1919-22

C. The Champaran Satyagraha of Gandhi

D. The protest against Rowlatt Act

Q.23 Which of the following is NOT a federal feature of the Indian Constitution?

A. Flexibility of Constitution

B. Supremacy of Constitution

C. Written Constitution

D. Bicameralism

Q.24 Article 35A was incorporated into the Constitution of India in ________ by an order of then president Rajendra Prasad on the advice of the Jawaharlal Nehru Cabinet.

A. 1956   **B.** 1959   **C.** 1954   **D.** 1950

Q.25 Which of the following schedules of the Indian Constitution deals with the administration and control of scheduled areas and scheduled tribes?

A. Fifth Schedule   **B.** Second Schedule

C. Eighth Schedule   **D.** Tenth Schedule

Q.26 Which of the following is used to draw the attention of Lok Sabha on a matter of public importance?

A. Privilege Motion

B. Adjournment Motion

C. No Confidence Motion

D. Censure Motion

Q.27 Tulsi Award is given in which field:

A. Poetry   **B.** Literature

C. Music   **D.** Folk arts

Q.28 Alzheimer's Day is observed on:

A. 21st September   **B.** 21st October

C. 21st November   **D.** 21st December

Q.29 Who was the first Indian woman to win an Olympic medal?

[MP Jail Prahari, 2018]

A. Karnam Malleswari   **B.** Sakshi Malik

C. P.V. Sindhu   **D.** Saina Nehwal

Q.30 Nuclear family refers to:

A. any family born after 1950

B. family includes parents and their children

C. entire family including children, their parents and grandparents

D. only husband and wife

Q.31 Which of the following acts prevent Child Marriage?

A. Child Marriage Act, 2006

B. The National Policy for Children, 1974

C. Child Labor (Prohibition & Regulation) Act was enacted in 1986

D. All of the above

Q.32 The first incident of the Revolt of 1857 was noticed in the:

A. 19th Native Infantry at Arrah

B. 19th Native Infantry at Berhampur

C. 19th Native Infantry at Meerut

D. 19th Native Infantry at Delhi

Q.33 The rearing of Earthworms is associated with which of the following?

A. Vermiculture   **B.** Sericulture

C. Aquaculture   **D.** Agriculture

Q.34 When is the World Humanitarian Day observed?

A. 17 August   **B.** 18 August

C. 19 August   **D.** 20 August

Q.35 Subroto Cup and Santosh Trophy are related to which sport?

A. Cricket   **B.** Football   **C.** Hockey   **D.** Bridge

Q.36 Match the list-1 and list-2 and select the correct answer using the codes given below the lists.

List-1	List-2
A) Mandamus	1) "By what warrant or authority"
B) Habeas Corpus	2) "We Command"
C) Quo Warranto	3) "To be certified"
D) Certiorari	4) "To produce the body of"

A. A-2, B-3, C-4, D-1   **B.** A-2, B-4, C-3, D-1

C. A-1, B-4, C-2, D-3   **D.** A-2, B-4, C-1, D-3

Q.37 How many languages have been listed in 8th schedule of Indian constitution?

A. 18   **B.** 22   **C.** 15   **D.** 14

Q.38 Which of the following is a tertiary economic activity?

A. Weaving   **B.** Farming   **C.** Trading   **D.** Hunting

Q.39 A situation where the expenditure of the government exceeds its revenue is called ______.

A. Default Revenue   **B.** Budget Deficit

C. Default Financing   **D.** Deficit Revenue

Q.40 One of the essential conditions of "perfect competition" is:

A. product differentiation

B. multiplicity of prices for identical products of a one time

C. many sellers and a few buyers

D. same price for same things at one time

English Proficiency

Ques (41-45):Direction: In the following passage, some words have been deleted. Fill in the blanks with the help of the alternatives given. Select the most appropriate option for each number.

What does the word scout mean? During a war, a soldier is chosen to go________ (1) of an army in order to ________ (2) out where the enemy is. He then _______(3) back to the commander all the _______(4) he has gathered about the________ (5). Such a soldier is known as a scout.

Q.41 Select the most appropriate option to fill in the blank No. 1.

A. behind   **B.** before   **C.** ahead   **D.** after

Q.42 Select the most appropriate option to fill in the blank No. 2.

A. call   **B.** bring   **C.** carry   **D.** find

Q.43 Select the most appropriate option to fill in the blank No. 3.

A. sends   **B.** tells   **C.** carries   **D.** reports

Q.44 Select the most appropriate option to fill in the blank No. 4.

A. information   **B.** news
C. messages   **D.** communications

Q.45 Select the most appropriate option to fill in the blank No. 5.

A. commanders   **B.** army
C. soldiers   **D.** enemy

Q.46 Direction: Choose the word from the options which is opposite in meaning to the given word.

Rash

A. Harmful   **B.** Cautious   **C.** Foolish   **D.** Tactless

Ques (47-48):Direction: Select the synonym of the given word.

Q.47 MASSIVE

A. Huge   **B.** Strong   **C.** Solid   **D.** Thick

Q.48 AMPLIFY

A. Satisfy   **B.** Electrify   **C.** Supply   **D.** Magnify

Ques (49-50):Direction: Select the antonym of the given word.

Q.49 ADVERSITY

A. Misfortune   **B.** Casualty
C. Calamity   **D.** Prosperity

Q.50 VANITY

A. Humility   **B.** Timidity   **C.** Dignity   **D.** Pride

Q.51 Direction: Select the most appropriate word to fill in the blank.

The assistant in the library picked up the books from the tables and put _____ back on the shelves.

A. its   **B.** them   **C.** it   **D.** they

Q.52 Direction: Fill in the blank with the correct option.

All three friends decided to keep the secret _______ themselves.

A. between   **B.** amongst   **C.** among   **D.** to

Q.53 Direction: Identify the segment in the sentence, which contains the grammatical error.

Why she was angry with her son?

A. Why   **B.** angry with
C. her son   **D.** she was

Q.54 Direction: Select the most appropriate word after the verb (in bold) in the following sentence so that the combination of the verb and the supplied word becomes the proper phrasal verb.

Kamal **dotes** _____ Katreena Kaif. He is just crazy for her.

A. on   **B.** in   **C.** at   **D.** of

Q.55 Direction: Select the most appropriate option to substitute the underlined segment in the given sentence. If there is no need to substitute it, select No substitution required.

The cause of the disaster has not yet known but an enquiry has been set up to find out what happened.

A. have not yet been known

B. was not yet known

C. is not yet known

D. No substitution required

Q.56 Direction: Fill in the blank with the correct option.

He is simply biding his ______ until the prices go down.

A. time   **B.** activity
C. wherewithal   **D.** wait

Ques (57-59):Direction: A sentence has been divided into three parts. Identify the part containing an error. If there is no error, then mark option (D) as your answer.

Q.57 Rahul as well as(A)/ his friends/ (B) were present.(C)/ No error(D)

A. A   **B.** B   **C.** C   **D.** D

Q.58 Neither of the (A)/ two girls (B)/ are beautiful. (C)/ No error(D)

A. A   **B.** B   **C.** C   **D.** D

Q.59 Many a girl (A)/ at the party (B)/ were crying.(C)/ No error

A. A   **B.** B   **C.** C   **D.** D

Ques (60-61):Direction: In the following question, a sentence is given in Direct/Indirect speech. Out of the four alternatives choose the one which best expresses the sentence in Indirect/Direct Speech.

Q.60 The Inspector said to Nalin, "Were you living under a rock or something?"

A. The Inspector told Nalin if he was living under a rock or something.

B. The Inspector enquired of Nalin if he were living under a rock or something.

C. The Inspector asked Nalin if he had been living under a rock.

D. The Inspector asked Nalin whether he had lived under a rock.

Q.61 "You can't bathe in this sea," he said to me, "it's very rough."

A. He said that I can't bathe in this sea because it's very rough.

B. He said that you couldn't bathe in that sea if it was very rough.

C. He said that I couldn't bathe in that sea as it was very rough.

D. He said that you can't bathe in this sea since it was very rough.

Ques (62-63):Direction: In the following question, a sentence has been given in Active/Passive Voice. Out of the four alternatives suggested, select the one which best expresses the same sentence in Passive/Active Voice.

Q.62 Politicians have always been perceived by people as corrupt and degraded villains.

A. People have continuously been perceiving politicians as corrupt.

B. Politicians are corrupt as noticed by people.

C. People have always perceived politicians as corrupt and degraded villains.

D. Perceptions by people regard politicians as corrupt and degraded.

Q.63 People have ignored the role of women in national development.

A. The role of women in national development is being ignored.

B. The national development in the role of women has been ignored.

C. The role of women in national development will be ignored.

D. The role of women in national development has been ignored.

Q.64 Direction: In the following sentence, there are two blank spaces. Below the sentence, there are four pairs of words given in the options (A), (B), (C), and (D). Find out which pair of words can be used to fill in the blanks in the sentence in the same sequence to make the sentence meaningful and complete.

Success in parenthood is _______ ,and _______ only after a lifetime of battle and worry.

A. vital, rejuvenating

B. delusive, eternalises

C. symbolic, commemorates

D. uncertain, apparent

Q.65 Direction: Select the most appropriate option to substitute the underlined segment in the given sentence. If there is no need to substitute it, select No substitution required.

Thirteen miners <u>were trapped inside a coal mine</u> due to flooding from a nearby river yesterday

A. were trapped into a coal mine

B. trapped inside a coal mine

C. have been trapped inside a coal mine

D. No substitution required

Ques (66-70):Direction: Read the passage and answer the question that follows.

Our thinking about the dimensions of emotional intelligence (EI) and their accompanying competencies has evolved and streamlined as new data has been analyzed. Readers familiar with earlier versions of the emotional intelligence model will notice some changes here. Where we formerly listed five domains of EI, we now have simplified the model into four domains: self-awareness, self-management, social awareness, and relationship management with eighteen competencies instead of the original twenty-five. For instance, an EI domain would be social awareness; a competency in that domain would be empathy or service. The result is an EI model that more clearly links specific clusters of competencies to the underlying brain dynamics that drive them. Recent findings of emotions and the brain make clearer the neurological basis of these competencies. This lets us sketch their dynamics more thoroughly while providing practical guidelines for building leadership skills. These EI competencies are not innate talents but learned abilities, each of which has a unique contribution to making leaders more resonant, and therefore more effective. Guided by the neurology underlying EI framework, we can make a sharp distinction between what works and what does not when it comes to learning the art of leadership.

The basic argument, in a nutshell, is that primal leadership operates better through emotionally intelligent leaders who create resonance. Underlying that proposition is the theory of performance, one that surfaces the link between the neurology of the four fundamentals of emotional intelligence and the EI competencies that build on these fundamentals. These EI competencies are in turn the building blocks of the modes of leadership that foster resonance in the group. Interestingly, no leader we have ever encountered, no matter how outstanding, has strengths across the board in every one of the many EI competencies. Highly effective leaders typically exhibit a critical mass of strength in half a dozen or so EI competencies. Moreover, there is no fixed formula for great leadership: There are many paths to excellence and super leaders can possess very different personal styles. Still, we find that effective leaders typically demonstrate strengths in at least one competence from each of the four fundamental areas of emotional intelligence.

Q.66 Based on the new data, which of the following conclusions can be drawn about the new model of emotional intelligence?

A. The new simplified model of EI has five domains with eighteen competencies instead of the original twenty-five competencies.

B. Twenty-five competencies go to make four domains of emotional intelligence, while the earlier model had five domains with eighteen competencies.

C. Formerly, five domains of EI were listed, but the new simplified model has four domains with eighteen competencies instead of the original twenty-five competencies.

D. While formerly five domains of EI were listed with twenty-five competencies, the new model has also five domains but with eighteen competencies.

Q.67 Which of the following are domains of emotional intelligence according to the new research?

A. Self-awareness, self-control, social awareness, and relationship management

B. Relationship management, self-management, self-control, and self-awareness

C. Self-management, social awareness, social control, and relationship management

D. Relationship management, self-management, social awareness, and self-awareness

Q.68 What inference can be made regarding the relationship between leadership and emotional intelligence from the passage?

A. Successful leaders have their own style of leadership, along with high emotional intelligence.

B. There is no clear relationship between successful leadership and emotional intelligence.

C. All successful leaders possess at least one competency in each domain of emotional intelligence.

D. None of the above

Q.69 The passage talks about the relationship between leadership, emotional intelligence and neurology. Which of the following statements represents a valid relationship between the three?

A. Because emotional intelligence has a neural base, the skills to be successful leaders cannot be learned.

B. The linkage between emotional intelligence and neurology indicates that leadership skills are not entirely innate and can be learned.

C. Both (A) and (B) are correct.

D. Both (A) and (B) are incorrect.

Q.70 'These EI competencies are in turn the building blocks of the modes of leadership that foster resonance in the group'. Which of the following reflect(s) the spirit of the statement as per the passage?

A. The leader's and group's aspirations match with each other.

B. There is no dissonance among group members.

C. Group members follow the leader.

D. All of the above

Maths and Logical Reasoning

Q.71 The selling price of a wooden table is Rs. 2600. It is sold at a profit of 30%. If 10% of the total amount is deducted as tax, then what will be the net profit?

A. Rs. 792   **B.** Rs. 720   **C.** Rs. 340   **D.** Rs. 504

Q.72 In a group of 1000 people, 750 people can speak Hindi and 400 people can speak English. In the group, all the people speak at least one out of the two languages. How many people can speak only Hindi?

A. 600   **B.** 500   **C.** 650   **D.** 700

Q.73 In the following question, select the related letters from the given alternatives.

AVENGER : VEZMIVT :: CAPTAIN : ?

A. KZXGMRZ   **B.** KZYHMRZ

C. KZXHNRZ   **D.** None of these

Q.74 What is the probability that a leap year, selected at random, will contain 53 Sundays?

A. $\frac{52}{365}$ **B.** $\frac{52}{366}$ **C.** $\frac{2}{7}$ **D.** $\frac{5}{7}$

Q.75 Four numbers have been given, out of which three are alike in some manner and one is different. Select the one that is different.

A. 486   **B.** 531   **C.** 442   **D.** 627

Q.76 Which of the following options will replace the question mark (?) in the given series?

Z15A, W13C, ?, Q9G, N7I

A. T12F   **B.** R11F   **C.** T11E   **D.** R13D

Q.77 What value should come in the place of the question mark(?) in the given number series?

6, 8, 14, 26, 46, ?, 118

A. 70   **B.** 65   **C.** 53   **D.** 76

Q.78

Direction: Study the given pie chart, and answer the question.

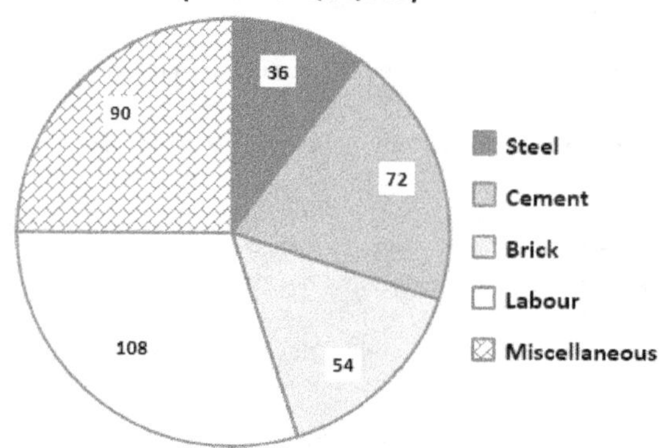

In the given pie chart, what is the ratio of the total expenditure on steel, cement, and bricks to the total expenditure on labour and miscellaneous expenses?

A. 3 : 7   **B.** 3 : 5   **C.** 4 : 5   **D.** 9 : 11

Q.79 Direction: Study the given histogram chart, and answer the question.

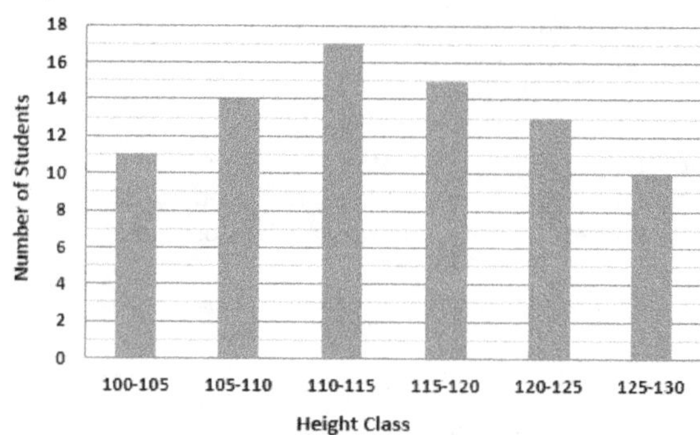

In the given histogram, what is the mean height of all students correct to one decimal place?

A. 116.8 cm   **B.** 114.7 cm   **C.** 116.2 cm   **D.** 115.6 cm

Q.80 PA and PB are two tangents to a circle with center O, from a point P outside the circle. A and B are points on the circle. If $\angle APB = 40°$, then $\angle OAB$ equal to:

A. 40°   **B.** 20°   **C.** 50°   **D.** 25°

Q.81 Direction: The temperature (in°F) in a region during a week is shown in the histogram.

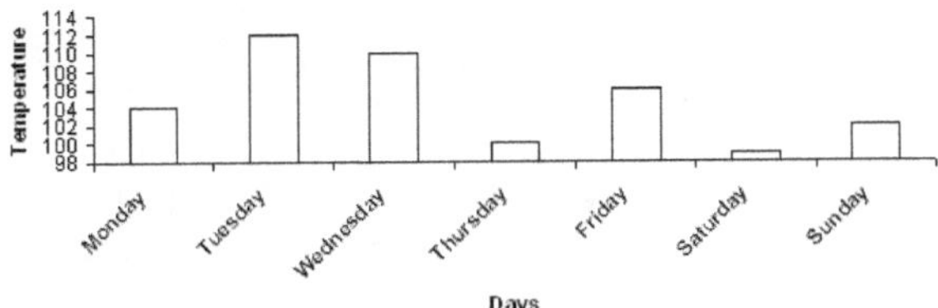

Find the difference between the maximum and the minimum temperature recorded during the week.

A. 13 °F **B.** 15 °F **C.** 16 °F **D.** 18 °F

Q.82 In $\triangle ABC, BY$ and CX are median drawn on AC and AB, respectively. Medians BY and CX intersects at $90°$ at point O. If $BY = 12\ cm$ and $CX = 9\ cm$, then, what is the area of $\triangle XYO$ (in sq. cm)?

A. 12 sq. cm **B.** 10 sq. cm
C. 6 sq. cm **D.** 8 sq. cm

Q.83 Direction: Read the following information and answer the question given below.

A, B and C are three students from Don School, while P, Q and R are three students from Elite School. Q is more intelligent than R, but less intelligent than the Don School student who is more intelligent than A. The same Don School student is less intelligent than P, but more intelligent than C.

Who is the most intelligent amongst all of them?

A. B
B. P
C. R
D. Cannot be determined

Q.84 The value of $\left[\dfrac{\sin^2 24° + \sin^2 66°}{\cos^2 24° + \cos^2 66°} + \sin^2 61° + \cos 61° \sin 29°\right]$ is equal to:

A. 2 **B.** 3 **C.** 1 **D.** 0

Q.85 In the given triangle ABC, BC is parallel to PQ. Find the value of x.

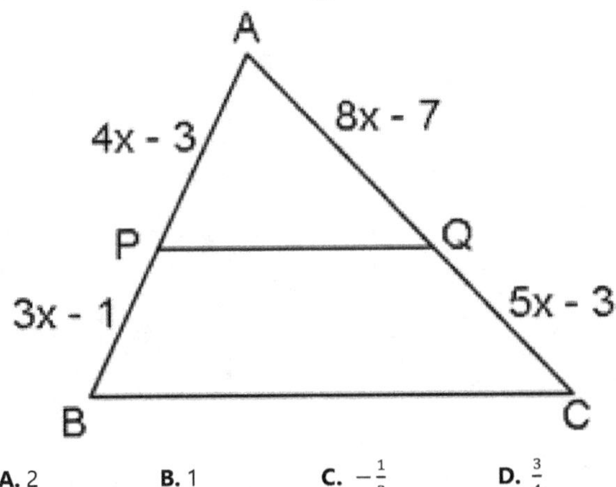

A. 2 **B.** 1 **C.** $-\dfrac{1}{2}$ **D.** $\dfrac{3}{4}$

Q.86 ABCD is a cyclic quadrilateral such that AB is the diameter of the circle circumscribing it and angle ADC = 140°. Then angle BAC is equal to:

A. 75° **B.** 50° **C.** 55° **D.** 40°

Q.87 Direction: Read the following information to answer the given question.

A, B, C, D, E, F, and G are standing in a line. G is just to the right of D and just to the left of B. A is just to the right of C. A and D have one person between them. E and B have two persons between them. D and F have two persons between them.

Who is at the extreme right?

A. B **B.** E **C.** F **D.** G

Q.88 If a train runs at 60 km/h, it reaches its destination 15 minutes late. But, if it runs at 80 km/h, it is late by 7 minutes only. The right time for the train to cover its journey is:

A. 18 minutes **B.** 17 minutes
C. 20 minutes **D.** 21 minutes

Q.89 If $a, b, c, d,$ and e are five consecutive odd numbers, then find their average in terms of a.

A. $5a + 20$ **B.** $5a + 10$ **C.** $a + 4$ **D.** $a + 3$

Q.90 A bag contains 25 cents, 10 cents, and 5 cent coins in the ratio $1 : 2 : 3$. If the total value of these is $\$36$, then what is the number of 25 cent coins?

A. 40 **B.** 45 **C.** 50 **D.** 60

Q.91 A series is given with one term missing. Select the correct alternative from the given ones that will complete the series.

3, 10, 41, 206, ?, 8660

A. 4237 **B.** 1000 **C.** 1200 **D.** 1237

Q.92 Direction: The figure (X) given on the left-hand side is folded to form a cube. From the given alternatives (a), (b), (c) and (d), the cube(s) that are similar to the cube formed is/are:

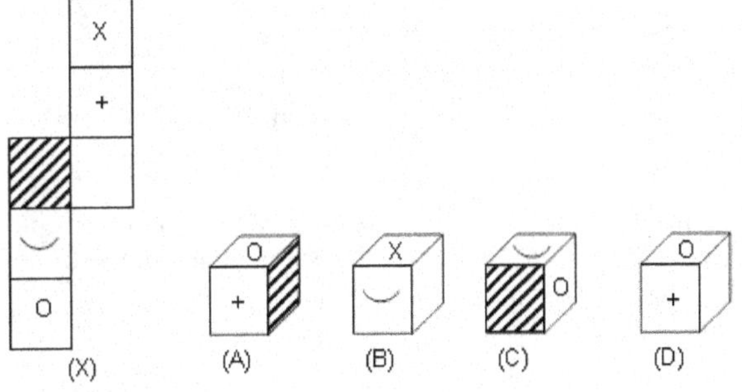

A. A and B only **B.** C and D only
C. D only **D.** B and D only

Q.93 Four letter clusters have been given, out of which three are alike in some manner, while one is different. Select the odd letter cluster.

A. CEG **B.** UWY **C.** ACF **D.** GIK

Q.94 Direction: Answer the given question based on the following data.

FEDERAL SPENDING ON SECONDARY AND TERTIARY EDUCATION IN COUNTRY X, 1992-1998

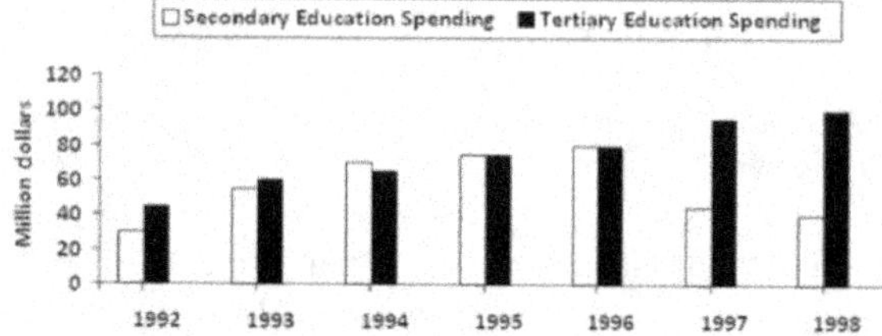

In which year was the total amount spent on both secondary and tertiary education by country X approximately $135 million?

A. 1993   **B.** 1994   **C.** 1995   **D.** 1996

Q.95 If the length of each side of a regular hexagon is 8 inches, then what is the area of the hexagon?

A.   148.14 sq. inches   **B.**   159.07 sq. inches
C.   166.27 sq. inches   **D.**   187.04 sq. inches

Q.96 Mr. Vijender spends 10% of his income on charity, 15% of the remaining on household and saves 50% of the remaining in a bank. Finally, he is left with Rs. 38,250. What is his total income?

A. Rs. 14,630.60   **B.** Rs. 1,54,080
C. Rs. 1,00,000   **D.** Rs. 1,20,000

Q.97 The marks of a group of 7 students in a class are $25, 56, 76, 87, 96, 34,$ and 65. How many students got more marks than the average marks for the group?

A. 5   **B.** 7   **C.** 3   **D.** 4

Q.98 Select the related number from the given alternatives.
4183 : 4096 : : 5267 : ?

A. 6700   **B.** 8000   **C.** 7683   **D.** 4000

Q.99 If 6 man working 8 hours a day can finish a work in 12 days, how many days will it take for 4 man working 8 hours a day to finish the same work?

A. 22   **B.** 15   **C.** 12   **D.** 18

Q.100 Tim is Tara's brother. Tara tells her friend Tanya that she has as many sisters as brothers. What is the total number of brothers and sisters in the family?

A.   1 brother and 2 sisters
B.   1 brother and 1 sister
C.   2 brothers and 1 sister
D.   2 brothers and 2 sisters

// Smart Answer Sheet //

Correct — Indicates percentage of students who answered questions correctly.

Skipped — Indicates percentage of students who skipped questions.

Q.	Ans.	Correct / Skipped
1	C	67.0 % / 1.82 %
2	B	46.62 % / 1.49 %
3	D	85.16 % / 0.0 %
4	A	77.13 % / 0.0 %
5	C	44.0 % / 1.5 %
6	D	51.72 % / 1.1 %
7	D	81.28 % / 0.0 %
8	C	48.42 % / 1.94 %
9	D	22.48 % / 4.83 %
10	A	64.69 % / 1.86 %
11	C	45.74 % / 1.83 %
12	C	85.82 % / 0.0 %
13	A	45.53 % / 1.03 %
14	C	82.06 % / 0.0 %
15	B	53.65 % / 1.22 %
16	B	28.51 % / 4.07 %
17	C	89.91 % / 0.0 %
18	A	47.61 % / 1.4 %
19	D	61.22 % / 1.09 %
20	B	80.92 % / 0.0 %
21	C	82.6 % / 0.0 %
22	A	79.61 % / 0.0 %
23	A	65.78 % / 1.69 %
24	C	49.36 % / 1.84 %
25	A	63.77 % / 1.91 %
26	B	57.32 % / 1.07 %
27	D	65.7 % / 1.85 %
28	A	46.73 % / 1.32 %
29	A	63.08 % / 1.04 %
30	B	81.19 % / 0.0 %
31	A	40.27 % / 1.79 %
32	B	63.63 % / 1.57 %
33	A	84.03 % / 0.0 %
34	C	46.0 % / 1.36 %
35	B	67.07 % / 1.78 %
36	D	24.85 % / 4.95 %
37	B	81.06 % / 0.0 %
38	C	82.07 % / 0.0 %
39	B	78.27 % / 0.0 %
40	D	56.8 % / 1.34 %
41	C	47.96 % / 1.59 %
42	D	62.02 % / 1.58 %
43	D	53.54 % / 1.6 %
44	A	58.32 % / 1.3 %
45	D	86.13 % / 0.0 %
46	B	87.08 % / 0.0 %
47	A	83.94 % / 0.0 %
48	D	68.86 % / 1.68 %
49	D	68.19 % / 1.33 %
50	A	88.24 % / 0.0 %
51	B	84.48 % / 0.0 %
52	C	79.8 % / 0.0 %
53	D	54.67 % / 1.74 %
54	A	46.09 % / 1.57 %
55	C	40.1 % / 1.56 %
56	A	55.06 % / 1.94 %
57	C	62.3 % / 1.88 %
58	C	82.61 % / 0.0 %
59	C	45.78 % / 1.18 %
60	C	63.77 % / 1.19 %
61	C	77.0 % / 0.0 %
62	C	78.21 % / 0.0 %
63	D	44.63 % / 1.44 %
64	D	41.82 % / 1.44 %
65	D	25.78 % / 3.03 %
66	C	47.93 % / 1.77 %
67	D	49.08 % / 1.83 %
68	C	42.59 % / 1.81 %
69	B	69.43 % / 1.45 %
70	D	31.59 % / 4.81 %
71	C	45.77 % / 1.84 %
72	A	43.8 % / 1.52 %
73	A	50.85 % / 1.61 %
74	C	69.15 % / 1.49 %
75	C	78.7 % / 0.0 %
76	C	41.22 % / 1.26 %
77	D	47.75 % / 1.68 %
78	D	43.32 % / 1.91 %
79	B	42.97 % / 1.85 %
80	B	26.96 % / 3.02 %

Q.	Ans.	Correct		Q.	Ans.	Correct		Q.	Ans.	Correct		Q.	Ans.	Correct		Q.	Ans.	Correct
		Skipped				Skipped				Skipped				Skipped				Skipped
81	A	89.38 %		85	B	63.53 %		89	C	51.85 %		93	C	58.95 %		97	D	87.86 %
		0.0 %				1.14 %				1.7 %				1.99 %				0.0 %
82	C	59.51 %		86	B	67.15 %		90	D	58.35 %		94	B	76.93 %		98	B	51.06 %
		1.01 %				1.25 %				1.22 %				0.0 %				1.49 %
83	B	56.49 %		87	C	78.51 %		91	D	62.9 %		95	C	63.6 %		99	D	57.76 %
		1.99 %				0.0 %				1.78 %				1.56 %				1.12 %
84	A	67.02 %		88	B	83.66 %		92	C	61.02 %		96	C	44.24 %		100	A	54.65 %
		1.68 %				0.0 %				1.71 %				1.55 %				1.9 %

Performance Analysis

Avg. Score (%)	66.0%
Toppers Score (%)	67.0%
Your Score	

General Awareness

Q.1 Who among the following was the chief economic advisor to the Government of India as of August 2020?

[SSC MTS, 2021]

A. Krishnamurthy Subramanian
B. Ajay Bhushan Pandey
C. Atanu Chakraborty
D. Rajeev Kumar

Q.2 Which Indian Higher Educational Institution has developed a seed ball named 'BEEG'?

A. IIT Madras
B. IIT Kanpur
C. BITS
D. None of these

Q.3 Who is the head of the Labour Ministry's commission, which recommended a basic living wage?

A. Santosh Kumar Gangwar
B. C V Ananda Bose
C. Apurva Chandra
D. Alok Kumar Mathur

Q.4 When 'India Water Week' 2019 was celebrated?

[Haryana Primary Teacher (PRT), 2020]

A. 15 January to 21 January
B. 22 March to 26 March
C. 2 October to 8 October
D. 24 September to 28 September

Q.5 Where was the first Regional Toys Fair held in May 2022?

A. Varanasi
B. Bengaluru
C. Kanchipuram
D. Kolkata

Q.6 Who assassinated W.C. Rand, the Plague Commissioner of Pune in 1897?

A. Ganesh Savarkar
B. Chapekar Brothers
C. Vasudev Balwant Phadke
D. Chiplunkar Brothers

Q.7 The World Bank has sanctioned USD 350 million to which state to implement the Systems Reform Endeavours for Transformed Health Achievement?

A. Gujarat
B. Maharashtra
C. Rajasthan
D. Uttar Pradesh

Q.8 The Moplah Rebellion in 1921 in Malabar was Muslim Peasants Rabellion against:

A. Muslim Land Holders
B. The British Government Authority
C. The non-tribal outsiders
D. Hindu Land Holders

Q.9 The standard of living in a country is represented by its

A. Per capita income
B. National income
C. Poverty ratio
D. None of these

Q.10 The term 'net shot' is associated with

A. Badminton
B. Tennis
C. Table tennis
D. Volleyball

Q.11 Who was admired as a tempestuous Hindu in 1893 in the World Parliament of Religious in Chicago?

A. Swami Dayanand Sarshawati
B. Rabindra Nath Tagore
C. Gautam Budha
D. Swami Vivekanand

Q.12 When was the World Day of Remembrance for Road Traffic Victims observed in 2019?

A. 16th November
B. 17th November
C. 18th November
D. None of the above

Q.13 The National Stock Exchange has terminated the broking license of which company and declared it as 'Defaulter'?

A. Karvy Stock Broking Ltd
B. Zerodha
C. Angel Broking
D. CAMS

Q.14 Global dimming, observed for several decades after 1950s, is thought to have been caused by

A. Methane
B. Particulate matter
C. CFCs
D. Carbon dioxide

Q.15 Which of the following fall under the category of greenhouse gases?

1. Water vapour
2. Nitrous oxide
3. Ozone

A. 1 and 2
B. 2 and 3
C. 1 and 3
D. All 1, 2 and 3

Q.16 When is the International Day of Peace observed every year globally?

A. 21st September
B. 22nd September
C. 23rd September
D. 24th September

Q.17 The amount of carbon dioxide in the atmosphere has increased in recent years. Environmentalists suggest that this change is a direct result of

A. Overcutting of forests and increased use of fossil fuels
B. Dumping of inorganic material into lakes and rivers
C. Improper storage of solid and nuclear waste
D. Use of herbicides and toxic substances such as asbestos and DDT

Q.18 Which of the following is not the goal adopted by UNDP under the UN Millennium Declaration?

A. Eradication of extreme poverty and hunger
B. Universal primary education
C. Combating HIV/AIDS
D. Global trade authority

Q.19 Which among the following is the birth place of Buddha?

A. Sarnath
B. Kushinagar
C. Lumbini
D. None of these

Q.20 Nagoba Jatara, a tribal festival is celebrated in which Indian state/ UT?

A. Madhya Pradesh
B. Assam
C. Telangana
D. Meghalaya

Q.21 What is the motto of Indian Renewable Energy Development Agency?

A. Energy For Ever
B. Energy For All
C. Energy Clean and Green
D. Reduce, Reuse, Renew

Q.22 With which of the following sport is 'clean and jerk' associated?

A. Weightlifting
B. Hockey
C. Judo
D. Taekwondo

Q.23 Which of the following Sections of the Indian Penal Code is associated with LGBT rights in India?

A. Section 227
B. Section 377
C. Section 733
D. Section 387

Q.24 Which 'Five Year Plan' was the main attention given to the weaker sections of the society?

A. Fifth
B. Third
C. Second
D. None of these

Q.25 Which nation was hosted the 11ᵗʰ BRICS Summit 2019?

A. Brazil
B. China
C. South Africa
D. Russia

Q.26 Which radiation enters the Earth on depletion of ozone layer of the atmosphere?

A. Ultraviolet radiation
B. Infrared radiation
C. Beta radiation
D. Gamma radiation

Q.27 Who among the following became the first ever Indian woman to be signed by the World Wrestling Entertainment (WWE)?

A. Kavita Devi
B. Geeta Phogat
C. Sakshi Malik
D. Indu Ojha

Q.28 Who among the following has won Booker Prize 2019?

A. Margaret Atwood
B. Nilima Riddhi
C. Jennifer Williamson
D. Pedro Roberto

Q.29 Ram V. Sutar designed the world's tallest statue 'Statue of Unity' in Gujarat. He hails from

A. Maharashtra
B. Gujarat
C. Madhya Pradesh
D. Rajasthan

Q.30 To which of the following causes is the 'Vande Matram Scheme' devoted?

A. Establishing girls' schools in districts having low female literacy rate
B. Providing insurance security to people living below poverty line
C. Providing free checkup and counselling to expectant and nursing mothers
D. Arranging finance for schemes related to tourism

Q.31 The temple 'Angkor Wat' is in

A. Cambodia
B. India
C. Vietnam
D. None of these

Q.32 The permanent memory built into a computer is called:

A. RAM
B. Floppy
C. CPU
D. ROM

Q.33 'Dandiya' is a popular dance of

A. Punjab
B. Gujarat
C. Tamil Nadu
D. Maharashtra

Q.34 "Clavicle" in the human body is a _______?

A. Collar bone
B. Rib
C. Upper limb bone
D. Lower limb bone

Q.35 International Labour Day is celebrated on

A. May 1
B. July 14
C. September 22
D. August 2

Q.36 Many scientists believe that greenhouse effect is predominantly the result of

A. Using chemical fertilizers to increase crop production
B. Testing nuclear weapons in violation of the Nuclear Test Ban Treaty
C. Using large amounts of gasoline, oil and coal in developed nations
D. Overgrazing on land

Q.37 Soda water contains

A. Carbonic acid
B. Sulphuric acid
C. Carbon dioxide
D. Nitrous acid

Q.38 Human Development Report for each year at global level is published by

A. WTO
B. World Bank
C. UNDP
D. IMF

Q.39 Which of the following pollutants is/are dangerous for Taj Mahal?

A. Sulphur dioxide
B. Carbon dioxide
C. Carbon monoxide
D. All of these

Q.40 The first session of Lok Sabha was held in which among the following years?

A. 1950
B. 1951
C. 1952
D. 1953

English Proficiency

Q.41 Direction: There is some relationship between the words of the pair given on the left of the sign (: :). The same relationship exists between the words on the right of the sign;

one word is missing from the second-word pair. Choose the missing word from the given alternatives.

Safe : Secure : : Protect : ____

A. Persevere
B. Sure
C. Guard
D. Lock

Q.42 Direction: Identify the correct idiom or phrase to complete the sentence.

I am trying to ________ of how to drive a car.

A. grasp
B. make a grasp
C. get a grasp
D. find a grasp

Q.43 Direction: In the following question, out of the four given alternatives, select the one which is opposite in the meaning of the given word.

Degenerate

A. Corrupt
B. Mean
C. Worsen
D. Moral

Q.44 Direction: Fill in the blank.

The Minister flew ________ the flooded areas in a helicopter.

A. about
B. in
C. over
D. along

Q.45 Direction: Identify the correct idiom or phrase to complete the sentence.

The slum areas should be as scarce in the city as _________.

A. cow's teeth
B. crow's teeth
C. sow's teeth
D. hen's teeth

Q.46 Direction: Select the word that is antonymous to the given word.

COMMISERATE

A. Miserable
B. Condone
C. Persecute
D. Pity

Q.47 Direction: Fill in the blank.

His name has become a synonym ______ evil.

A. of
B. for
C. to
D. with

Q.48 Direction: Pick the odd one out.

A. Vertigo
B. Giddy
C. Dizzy
D. Awake

Q.49 Direction: Pick the odd one out.

A. Assumption
B. Hypothesis
C. Tentative
D. Evidence

Q.50 Direction: Pick the odd one out.

A. Love
B. Romance
C. Sibling
D. Woo

Q.51 Direction: Replace the underlined word with the noun:
The two shades are slightly <u>different</u>.

A. The two shades differ slightly
B. There is a slight difference between the two shades
C. The two shades differ
D. None of the above

Q.52 Direction: Choose the correct preposition and fill in the blank.

The teacher warned him ________ being careless with his work.

A. towards
B. of
C. in
D. against

Q.53 Direction: Fill in the blank.

A poor man, ________ I knew, nursed the orphan.

A. who
B. whom
C. that
D. which

Ques (54-57):Direction: Read the given passage carefully and select the best answer to each question out of the four given alternatives.

Ruskin Bond is an Indian author of British descent. India's most adored writer Ruskin Bond was born in Kasauli. Bond spent his early childhood in Jamnagar and Shimla. At the age of ten, Ruskin went to live at his grandmother's house in Dehradun after his father's death that year from jaundice. Ruskin was raised by his mother and stepfather. He did his schooling from Bishop Cotton School in Shimla, from where he graduated in 1950 after winning several writing competitions in the school including the Irwin Divinity Prize and the Hailey Literature Prize. He wrote one of his first short stories, 'Untouchable', at the age of sixteen in 1951. He moved to London and worked in a photo studio while searching for a publisher. After getting it published, Bond used the advance money to pay the sea passage to Bombay and settle in Dehradun. Since 1963 he has lived as a freelance writer in Mussorie, a town in the Himalayan foothills in Uttarakhand, and lives with his adoptive family in Landour, Mussoorie's Ivy Cottage, which has been his house since 1980. About what he likes the most about his life, he said, "That I have been able to write for so long. I started at the age of 16 or 17 and I am still writing. If I were not a professional writer who was getting published I would still write." In his essay, "On being an Indian", he explains his Indian identity, "Race did not make me one. Religion did not make me one. But history did. And in the long run, it's history that counts".

Q.54 In 1980, Ruskin Bond settled in Mussorie, what do you think was his age by then?

A. 29
B. 39
C. 45
D. Cannot be determined, on the basis of information given in the passage

Q.55 According to Ruskin Bond, why is he an Indian?

A. Because his parents have always lived in India
B. Because he has a history with India
C. Because he owns a house in India
D. Because he was raised by his step-father, an Indian Hindu

Q.56 What did Bond do with his first advance payment?

A. He flew to his dream destination
B. He bought a house Ivy Cottage in Mussoorie
C. He went back to India from London
D. He started working for children's literature

Q.57 Why is Ruskin Bond happy about his life?

A. Because he has finally settled in India
B. Because has adopted a family and it is very loving
C. Because he is successful
D. Because he has been able to write for so long

Q.58 Direction: Read the given sentence to find out whether there is any grammatical or idiomatic error in it. The error, if any, will be in one part of the sentence. The number of that part is the answer. If there is no error, the answer is (d). (Ignore the errors of punctuation, if any.)

Before giving the exam, (a) the participant must first (b) register as a nurse. (c) No error (d)

A. (a)   **B.** (b)   **C.** (c)   **D.** (d)

Q.59 Direction: Read the given sentence to find out whether there is any grammatical or idiomatic error in it. The error, if any, will be in one part of the sentence. The number of that part is the answer. If there is no error, the answer is (d). (Ignore the errors of punctuation, if any.)

Ecuador is a country (a) that is positioning himself (b) as a strong ecotourism destination. (c) No error (d)

A. (a)   **B.** (b)   **C.** (c)   **D.** (d)

Ques (60-61):Direction: In the following question, some parts of the sentence may have errors. Find out which part of the sentence has an error and select the appropriate option. If a sentence is free from error, select 'No Error'.

Q.60 Many a man have (1)/ come to India from Canada (2)/ to live here permanently. (3)/ No error (4)

A. 1   **B.** 2   **C.** 3   **D.** 4

Q.61 Our cricket team (1)/ comprises of (2)/ eleven skilled players. (3)/ No error (4)

A. 1   **B.** 2   **C.** 3   **D.** 4

Q.62 Direction: In the following question, out of the four given alternatives, select the one which best expresses the meaning of the given word.

Concise

A. Sympathetic   **B.** Redundant
C. Abridged   **D.** Expensive

Ques (63-64):Direction: In the following question, out of the four given alternatives, select the one which is opposite in meaning of the given word.

Q.63 MINION
A. Master   **B.** Follower   **C.** Gigantic   **D.** Sizeable

Q.64 Intolerance
A. Hatred   **B.** Justness   **C.** Partial   **D.** Madness

Q.65 Direction: Find a similar relation between the words given in any of the options.

Manager : Office ::
A. Doctor : Patient   **B.** Curator : Museum
C. Bank : Account   **D.** Fruit : Seed

Ques (66-70):Direction: Answer the question based on the following passage.

The Germans were formerly the best fighting men and the most warlike nation of Europe. Germans have bled and conquered on countless battlefields in every part of the world. In striking contrast to this military attitude, they have today become a peace-loving nation. The change springs first from the reverses the Germans suffered in the two world wars, but also in part from the good-natured character of the German people, which finds intense satisfaction in doctrinaire disputations and partisanship but dislikes pushing things to an extreme. It is connected with another characteristic of German nature. Our aim is to be just, and we strangely imagine that all other nations with whom we exchange relations share this aim. We are always ready to consider the peaceful assurances of foreign diplomacy. We obstinately resist the view that the political world is only ruled by interests and never from ideal aims of philanthropy. Justice, Goethe says aptly, is a quality and a phantom of the Germans.

We are always inclined to assume that disputes between States can find a peaceful solution on the basis of justice without clearly realizing what international justice is. An additional cause of the love of peace, besides those which are rooted in the very soul of the German people, is the wish not to be disturbed in commercial life. The Germans are born businessmen, more than any others in the world. Notwithstanding the reverses in the none-too-distant past, we have made marvelous progress, and our young industries challenge competition with all the great industrial states. German merchants traverse every quarter of the globe. Under these conditions, our national wealth has increased with rapid strides. Our trade and our industries - owners no less than employees - do not want this development to be interrupted. They believe that peace is an essential condition of commerce.

Q.66 What is the main purpose of the passage?
A. To highlight the transformation of Germany from a war mongering and military oriented country to a commercial hub
B. To showcase the 'philanthropic' leanings of the Germans
C. To elucidate the causes of change in the temperament of Germans from warring people to excessively peace loving people
D. To discuss Germany's evolution as a truly commercial hub

Q.67 Why does the author use the phrase "without clearly realizing what international justice is", in the context of German people?
A. Germans have a warped notion of international justice, which is not shared by other political powers
B. Germans have a mistaken belief that their ideas of peace and justice are shared by the international community
C. Unhealthy competition among European powers has clouded their sense of justice
D. Conflicting thoughts debar the conduct of peaceful diplomacy

Q.68 Which of the following is not a quality of the Germans as per the passage?
A. Non-partisan bearing
B. Aim to be just to all
C. Inclination toward their own foreign diplomacy
D. Business instinct

Q.69 All are the causes helpful for maintaining peace by Germans except
A. Their philanthropic optimism
B. The spirit to resolve argumentation

C. Disbelief in the notion that the world is governed by self interest

D. The will to establish communal justice and peace as an omnipresent feature globally

Q.70 Which of the following statements will the author most likely agree with?

A. The Germans are a fiercely antagonistic people.

B. The World Wars were but an aberration in the otherwise illustrious history of Germany.

C. The German share the world view about solving their disputes through military means.

D. The will to succeed in international business gets only a second priority in German psyche.

Maths and Logical Reasoning

Q.71 If $\tan^2 45° - \cos^2 30° = x\sin45°\cos45°$, then $x =$

A. 2   **B.** -2   **C.** $-\frac{1}{2}$ **D.** $\frac{1}{2}$

Q.72 If $\sec\theta + \tan\theta = x$, then $\sec\theta =?$

A. $\frac{x^2+1}{x}$ **B.** $\frac{x^2+1}{2x}$ **C.** $\frac{x^2-1}{2x}$ **D.** $\frac{x^2-1}{x}$

Q.73 A man on tour travels the first $120\ km$ at $60\ km/hr$ and the next $120\ km$ at $75\ km/hr$. Find the average speed for the first $240\ km$ of the tour.

A. $66km/hr$ **B.** $60km/hr$

C. $66.67km/hr$ **D.** $67.5km/hr$

Q.74 Write the value of $\cos1°\cos2°\cos3°………\cos179°\cos180°.$

A. 0   **B.** 5   **C.** 8   **D.** 3

Q.75 Direction: Complete the series.

CFL, EIK, GLJ, IOI, ____

A. KRH   **B.** KRJ   **C.** JRH   **D.** KQH

Q.76 In the figure given below, if ∠EBC – ∠ACF = 5° and ∠DAB – ∠ACF = 25°, find the value of x.

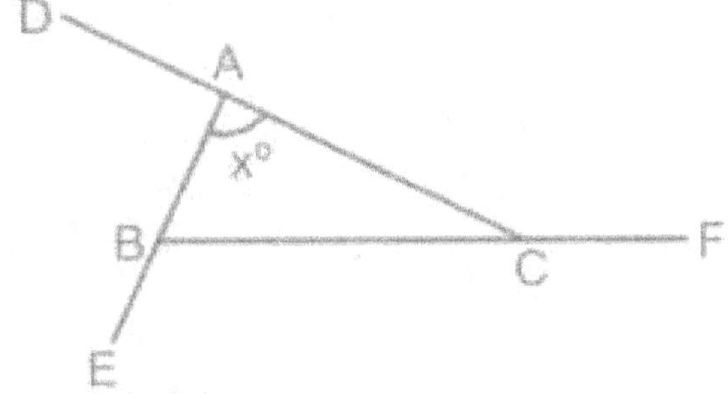

A. 20°   **B.** 30°   **C.** 45°   **D.** 60°

Q.77 Out of three positive numbers, the ratio of the first and the second numbers is $3:4$ that of the second and the third number is $5:6$ if the product of the second and the third number is 4320. What is the sum of the three numbers?

A. 177   **B.** 165   **C.** 185   **D.** 160

Q.78 If $A = \{1,2,3\}, B = \{3,4\} and C = \{4,5,6\}$, Then $A \cup (B \cap C)$ is

A. { 3}   **B.** { 1,2,3,4}

C. { 1,2,5,6}   **D.** { 1,2,3,4,5,6}

Q.79 What will be the percentage profit after selling an article at a certain price if there occur a loss of 35% on selling the article $\frac{3}{5}$ of the selling price?

A. 8.33%   **B.** 6.67%   **C.** 12.25%   **D.** 6.33%

Ques (80-81):Direction: Study the following bar chart carefully and answer the questions given beside.

The following graph gives information about the number of students enrolled in three different disciplines in five different colleges.

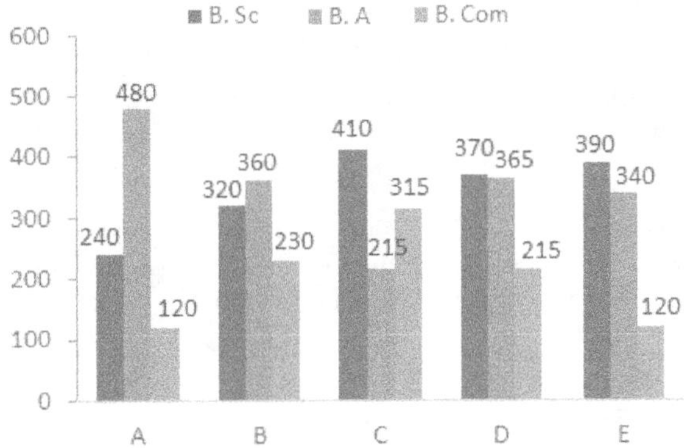

Q.80 What is the total number of students studying B.A. in all the colleges together?

A. 1750   **B.** 1780   **C.** 17090   **D.** 1760

Q.81 The total number of students studying B.Sc. in the colleges C and D together is approximately how much percent more than the total number of students studying B.Com. in the college's A and B together?

A. 44.87%   **B.** 122.86%

C. 120.20%   **D.** 220.86%

Q.82 The number $6n^2 + 6n$ for natural n is always divisible by

A. 6 only   **B.** 18   **C.** 12 only   **D.** 6 and 12

Q.83 In the given figure, if $\frac{QR}{XY} = \frac{14}{9}$ and $PY = 18\ cm$, what is the value (in cm) of PQ?

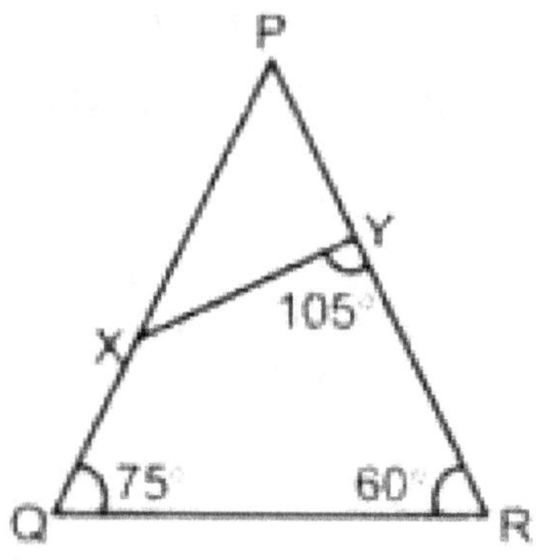

A. 28   **B.** 18   **C.** 21   **D.** 24

Q.84 In town males and females are in the ratio $3:2$. Out of males 25% are children and the rest are adults. If the adult male population of the town is 8100, find the total population of the town.

A. 22000   **B.** 24000   **C.** 20000   **D.** 18000

Q.85 The vertex angle of an isosceles triangle measures four times the sum of base angles. Find the measure of base angle.

A. 144°   **B.** 18°   **C.** 36°   **D.** 43°

Q.86 Five girls, Sneha, Leela, Alka, Neha, and Roji are standing in a circle facing the centre. Sneha is between Leela and Alka. Neha is to the immediate right of Leela. Who is to the left of Alka?

A. Roji

B. Neha

C. Sneha

D. Cannot be determined

Q.87 Directions: On the basis of the given figure, answer the question given below.

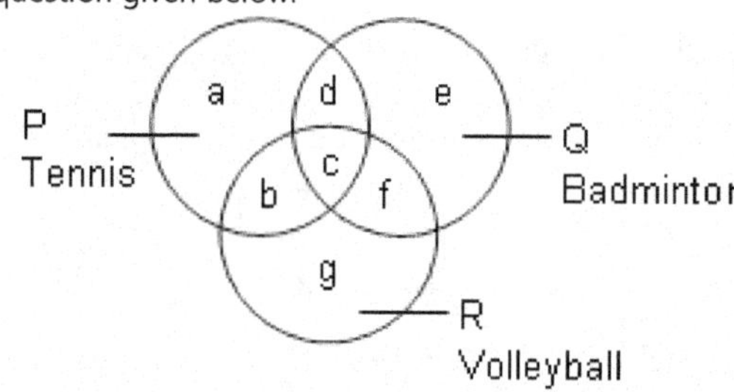

Which letter represents the set of persons who play all the three games?

A. b   **B.** c   **C.** f   **D.** g

Q.88 How many straight lines are needed to divide a regular hexagon into six identical triangles?

A. 1   **B.** 2   **C.** 3   **D.** 4

Q.89

For the figure given below, find the angle OAB (in degrees).

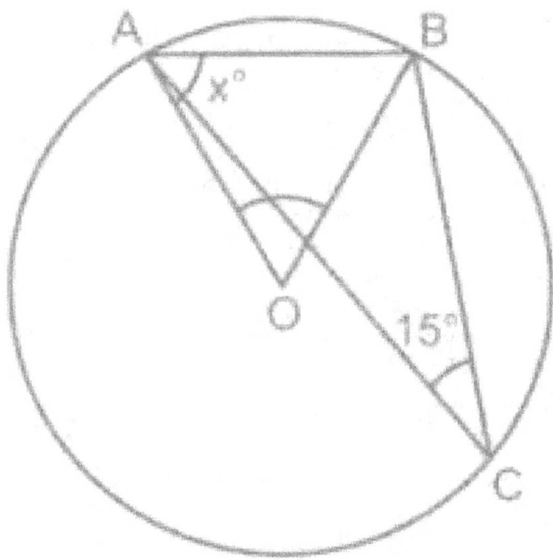

A. 25°   **B.** 50°   **C.** 75°   **D.** 90°

Q.90

What value should come in the place of the question mark(?) in the given number series?

24, 37, 54, 75, 100, 129, ?

A. 157509   **B.** 158   **C.** 161   **D.** 162

Q.91

A series is given with one term missing. Select the correct alternative from the given ones
that will complete the series.

111, 100, 87, ?, 55, 36

A. 1533 : 1615   **B.** 75   **C.** 81   **D.** 70

Q.92 Direction: Read the following questions carefully and choose the right answer.

If A varies directly as B and inversely as C and $A = 6$, when $B = 2$ and $C = 3$, what is the value of A when $B = 8$ and $C = 6$?

A. 12   **B.** 6   **C.** 18   **D.** 24

Q.93 Directions: Complete the series.

$12, 25, 53, 111, 229, 467, ?$

A. 578   **B.** 345   **C.** 945   **D.** 478

Q.94 What is the value of $2^x \times 1^x \times 3^x =?$. If x has the same value:

A. 16   **B.** 25   **C.** 36   **D.** 49

Q.95 Find the odd one out of the choices given therein.

A. Mango   **B.** Apple

C. Patato   **D.** Blackberry

Q.96 X's father's wife's father's granddaughter's uncle will be related to X as

A. Son   **B.** Nephew

C. Uncle   **D.** Grandfather

Q.97 <u>Directions:</u> Read the following information to answer the question,

Consider a group consisting of 4 students - Reena, Beena, Meena and Neena, who stand in a row. Reena and Beena stand respectively at the sixth and seventh positions from left. Meena and Neena stand respectively at the fourth and fifth positions from right. When Beena and Meena exchange their positions, Beena is fifteenth from left.

After the exchange of positions between Beena and Meena, what is Meena's position from right?

A. 5   **B.** 10

C. 12   **D.** None of these

Q.98 Direction: Study the following questions carefully and choose the right answer.

The sum of the squares is three consecutive odd numbers are 2531. find the numbers?

A. 21,23 and 25   **B.** 15,17 and 20

C. 27,29 and 31   **D.** 29,31 and 33

Ques (99-100):Direction: Study the following table chart carefully and answer the questions given beside.

The following table represents the number of employees in five different organizations in $2012, 2013, 2014$, and 2015.

Organization	2012	2013	2014	2015
P	5000	8800	3600	6200
Q	4800	10200	12100	8300
R	5500	6500	8800	4250
S	8000	4800	9000	5650
T	7600	7200	8400	3880

Q.99 Find the Total number of employees in all the organisations in 2013.

A. 35450   **B.** 32200   **C.** 37500   **D.** 36560

Q.100 Number of employees in organization P in 2013 and 2014 together is what percent of number of employees in organization R in 2014 and 2015 together?

A. 80.01%   **B.** 95.01%   **C.** 91.01%   **D.** 88.52%

// Smart Answer Sheet //

Correct — Indicates percentage of students who answered questions correctly.

Skipped — Indicates percentage of students who skipped questions.

Q.	Ans.	Correct / Skipped	Q.	Ans.	Correct / Skipped	Q.	Ans.	Correct / Skipped	Q.	Ans.	Correct / Skipped	Q.	Ans.	Correct / Skipped
1	A	13.1 % / 4.86 %	17	A	24.1 % / 4.3 %	33	B	89.09 % / 0.0 %	49	D	59.07 % / 1.24 %	65	B	85.92 % / 0.0 %
2	B	42.69 % / 1.09 %	18	D	23.67 % / 4.53 %	34	A	31.49 % / 3.66 %	50	C	84.37 % / 0.0 %	66	C	31.18 % / 3.47 %
3	B	20.59 % / 3.95 %	19	C	84.98 % / 0.0 %	35	A	86.71 % / 0.0 %	51	B	25.14 % / 4.78 %	67	B	13.48 % / 3.82 %
4	D	85.48 % / 0.0 %	20	C	27.9 % / 4.39 %	36	C	53.33 % / 1.03 %	52	D	47.72 % / 1.6 %	68	A	18.61 % / 3.46 %
5	A	19.05 % / 4.54 %	21	A	62.92 % / 1.98 %	37	A	88.63 % / 0.0 %	53	B	58.15 % / 1.61 %	69	D	26.34 % / 3.8 %
6	B	68.57 % / 1.21 %	22	A	22.15 % / 3.18 %	38	C	82.13 % / 0.0 %	54	C	45.49 % / 1.33 %	70	B	21.16 % / 3.03 %
7	A	64.59 % / 1.07 %	23	B	19.23 % / 3.5 %	39	A	64.14 % / 1.69 %	55	B	41.18 % / 1.2 %	71	D	52.87 % / 1.46 %
8	D	85.26 % / 0.0 %	24	A	11.21 % / 3.85 %	40	C	40.25 % / 1.15 %	56	C	60.34 % / 1.57 %	72	B	20.14 % / 3.81 %
9	A	22.31 % / 3.13 %	25	A	23.77 % / 3.02 %	41	C	79.39 % / 0.0 %	57	D	62.88 % / 1.55 %	73	C	78.12 % / 0.0 %
10	A	29.24 % / 3.2 %	26	A	86.31 % / 0.0 %	42	C	81.9 % / 0.0 %	58	A	11.68 % / 4.86 %	74	A	76.49 % / 0.0 %
11	D	42.0 % / 1.81 %	27	A	41.06 % / 1.76 %	43	D	65.62 % / 1.97 %	59	B	16.97 % / 4.3 %	75	A	55.92 % / 1.01 %
12	B	80.8 % / 0.0 %	28	A	23.26 % / 3.19 %	44	C	44.12 % / 1.02 %	60	A	51.15 % / 1.97 %	76	C	28.85 % / 4.1 %
13	A	16.68 % / 4.4 %	29	A	26.75 % / 3.86 %	45	D	62.45 % / 1.28 %	61	B	19.18 % / 3.82 %	77	A	80.27 % / 0.0 %
14	B	65.19 % / 1.92 %	30	C	25.17 % / 3.03 %	46	C	26.75 % / 4.92 %	62	C	49.32 % / 1.47 %	78	B	81.29 % / 0.0 %
15	D	89.46 % / 0.0 %	31	A	83.9 % / 0.0 %	47	B	81.69 % / 0.0 %	63	A	87.9 % / 0.0 %	79	A	50.75 % / 1.93 %
16	A	79.06 % / 0.0 %	32	D	88.6 % / 0.0 %	48	D	89.06 % / 0.0 %	64	B	65.49 % / 1.88 %	80	D	88.41 % / 0.0 %

Q.	Ans.	Correct / Skipped		Q.	Ans.	Correct / Skipped		Q.	Ans.	Correct / Skipped		Q.	Ans.	Correct / Skipped		Q.	Ans.	Correct / Skipped
81	B	40.14 % / 1.8 %		85	B	86.64 % / 0.0 %		89	C	58.71 % / 1.97 %		93	C	85.59 % / 0.0 %		97	C	15.58 % / 4.86 %
82	D	87.04 % / 0.0 %		86	A	69.25 % / 1.1 %		90	D	58.1 % / 1.94 %		94	C	78.68 % / 0.0 %		98	C	21.45 % / 3.14 %
83	A	42.68 % / 1.25 %		87	B	89.69 % / 0.0 %		91	A	59.77 % / 1.29 %		95	C	80.92 % / 0.0 %		99	C	21.98 % / 3.26 %
84	D	18.56 % / 4.45 %		88	C	84.79 % / 0.0 %		92	A	51.79 % / 1.4 %		96	C	40.48 % / 1.72 %		100	B	14.41 % / 3.74 %

Performance Analysis

Avg. Score (%)	33.0%
Toppers Score (%)	59.0%
Your Score	

General Awareness

Q.1 Which state launched the Sishu Suraksha Mobile App on the occasion of Children's Day?

A. Maharashtra 　　　　**B.** Rajasthan
C. Assam 　　　　　　**D.** West Bengal

Q.2 Which of the following became the second city in India after Ahmedabad to be inscribed on the World Heritage List?

A. Jaipur 　　　　　　**B.** Mumbai
C. Shimla 　　　　　　**D.** Bhubaneswar

Q.3 Which of the following is India's highest peacetime gallantry award?

A. Maha Vir Chakra 　　**B.** Ashok Chakra
C. Vir Chakra 　　　　**D.** Param Vir Chakra

Q.4 Which of the following is the driest place in the world?

A. Sahara Desert 　　　**B.** Danakil Depression
C. Djibouti 　　　　　**D.** Atacama Desert

Q.5 In which of the following years did the Kyoto Protocol come into force?

A. 1995 　　**B.** 1997 　　**C.** 2002 　　**D.** 2005

Q.6 Swachh Bharat (Clean India) campaign was launched on _______ birth anniversary of Mahatma Gandhi.

A. 140th 　　**B.** 142nd 　　**C.** 150th 　　**D.** 147th

Q.7 David Dixon Award is associated with

A. Commonwealth Games
B. FIFA World Cup
C. World Boxing Federation
D. Chess Olympiad

Q.8 When International Day for the Eradication of Poverty is observed?

A. 16 October 　　　　**B.** 17 October
C. 18 October 　　　　**D.** 19 October

Q.9 Which of the following articles of the Indian Constitution deals with the protection and improvement of the environment?

A. Article 48(A) 　　　**B.** Article 51(B)
C. Article 52(A) 　　　**D.** Article 55(C)

Q.10 Who were the first Europeans to trade with Indians?

A. French 　　　　　　**B.** Dutch
C. English 　　　　　**D.** Portuguese

Q.11 Famously known as Jhaveri Sisters, they have been making ceaseless efforts to preserve, perpetuate and propagate the art of this Indian classical dance style, of which they themselves are the talented exponents. Which Indian classical dance style are they exponents of?

A. Kuchipudi 　　　　**B.** Manipuri
C. Bharatanatyam 　　**D.** Odissi

Q.12 United Nations has declared 2011-2020 the

A. United Nations Decade on Wildlife.
B. United Nations Decade on Biodiversity.
C. United Nations Decade on Genetic Resources.
D. United Nations Decade on Habitat Protection.

Q.13 One of the characteristics of the Parliamentary System of Government in India is that the Council of Ministers is

A. responsible to the Parliament as well as the President.
B. collectively responsible to both the Houses of Parliament.
C. collectively responsible to the Lok Sabha.
D. responsible to the Head of the State.

Q.14 Which of the following articles of the Constitution of India states that no tax shall be levied or collected except by the authority of law?

A. Article 186 　　　　**B.** Article 265
C. Article 206 　　　　**D.** Article 346

Q.15 When was the National Literacy Mission launched?

A. May 5, 1988 　　　　**B.** September 5, 1988
C. December 5, 1988 　　**D.** March 5, 1988

Q.16 Direction: Match the following.

List - I	List - II
1. Elephants	A. Swampy mangrove forests
2. Wild asses	B. Moist and thick forests
3. One-horned rhinoceroses	C. Rann of Kutch
4. Tigers	D. Swampy and marshy lands of Assam

A. 1 - B, 2 - C, 3 - D, 4 - A
B. 1 - A, 2 - C, 3 - D, 4 - B
C. 1 - A, 2 - D, 3 - C, 4 - B
D. 1 - B, 2 - D, 3 - C, 4 - A

Q.17 Which of the following has launched 'Mission Satyanishtha' aimed at sensitizing its employees about the need to adhere to good ethics and to maintain high standards of integrity at work?

A. India Post 　　　　**B.** Railways
C. ONGC 　　　　　　**D.** NHAI

Q.18 World Health Day is observed on

A. April 7 　　　　　　**B.** July 7
C. October 16 　　　　**D.** December 16

Q.19 The headquarters of the International Cricket Council (ICC) is in

A. London 　　**B.** Dubai 　　**C.** Sydney 　　**D.** Brussels

Q.20 Which is the longest act passed by the British Parliament and was later split into two parts?

A. India Councils Act of 1904
B. Government of India Act of 1919
C. Government of India Act of 1935
D. Industrial Disputes Act of 1947

Q.21 Which of the following pairs of sports and trophies/awards is not matched correctly?
A. Sudirman Cup - Badminton
B. NatWest Trophy - Cricket
C. Davis Cup - Tennis
D. Sultan Azlan Shah Cup - Soccer

Q.22 Which of the following industries is the consumer of maximum water in India?
A. Engineering
B. Paper and pulp
C. Thermal power plant
D. Textiles

Q.23 The Minimum Wages Act, 1948 is applicable to
A. the whole of India.
B. the whole of India except Jammu and Kashmir state.
C. the whole of India except the states of Jammu and Kashmir, Goa, and Delhi.
D. the whole of India except the states of Punjab and Haryana.

Q.24 Naresh Harishchandra Patil has, was sworn-in as the new Chief Justice of
A. Calcutta High Court
B. Allahabad High Court
C. Karnataka High Court
D. Bombay High Court

Q.25 "Economics relates quite closely to philosophical disciplines; for example, the social choice theory makes intense use of mathematical logic and also draws on moral philosophy, so does the study of inequality and deprivation". Which Nobel Laureate said this?
A. Venkatraman Ramakrishnan
B. Kailash Satyarthi
C. Sir V. S. Naipaul
D. Amartya Kumar Sen

Q.26 Otten Thullal and Chakyar Koothu are folk dances of the Indian state of
A. Karnataka
B. Tamil Nadu
C. Kerala
D. Assam

Q.27 Who was the first foreigner to win the Bharat Ratna Award?
A. Khan Abdul Ghaffar Khan
B. Winston Churchill
C. Benazir Bhutto
D. None of them

Q.28 Why did the Government of India introduce the Wildlife (Protection) Act, 1972?
A. To regulate trade in wild plants and animals.
B. To identify and protect rare species of flora and fauna in India.
C. To protect and preserve species within natural boundaries.
D. To establish rules against poaching.

Q.29 EPFO would be crediting how much interest for the year 2018-19 in 6 crore accounts?
A. 8.65% **B.** 8.57% **C.** 8.60% **D.** 8.63%

Q.30 Several days are observed, and events are specially organized especially to highlight environmental problems to create general awareness. Likewise, Earth Day is celebrated annually on
A. October 11 **B.** May 17
C. April 22 **D.** January 10

Q.31 Which of the following countries is NOT a permanent member of the United Nations Security Council?
A. Russia **B.** France
C. China **D.** Germany

Q.32 The Home Ministry ordered that all personnel working in the Central Armed Police Forces will now retire at a uniform age of _______ years.
A. 56 **B.** 58 **C.** 60 **D.** 62

Q.33 The by-polls to two Rajya Sabha seats in Uttar Pradesh & Karnataka will be held on which date?
A. 22 November **B.** 28 November
C. 8 December **D.** 12 December

Q.34 In which of the following is the Foreign Direct Investment in India not allowed?
1. Real estate business
2. Atomic energy
3. Manufacturing of cigarette
4. Business of chit fund
5. Nidhi company
A. Only 2 **B.** 2, 4 and 5
C. Only 5 **D.** 1, 2, 3, 4 and 5

Q.35 Specify the number of women astronauts who did a spacewalk without the help of any male astronaut?
A. Two **B.** Three **C.** Four **D.** Five

Q.36 Kristalina Georgieva has been selected as the new Chief of which organization?
A. EU **B.** IMF **C.** ADB **D.** ECB

Q.37 Identify the correct chronological order of the following historic events - Dandi March, Foundation of Indian National Congress, Quit India Movement, and Khilafat Movement.
A. Foundation of Indian National Congress, Dandi March, Khilafat Movement, Quit India Movement
B. Dandi March, Foundation of Indian National Congress, Khilafat Movement, Quit India Movement
C. Foundation of Indian National Congress, Khilafat Movement, Dandi March, Quit India movement
D. Dandi March, Foundation of Indian National Congress, Quit India Movement, Khilafat Movement

Q.38 Where was the 3rd edition of the ScooNews Global Educators Fest (SGEF) held?
A. Lucknow
B. Udaipur
C. Pune
D. Mumbai

Q.39 Which of the following is a user interface that uses only a keyboard for input?
A. Graphical User Interface
B. Command Line Interface
C. Menu Driven Interface
D. All of the above

Q.40 In case no party enjoys an absolute majority in the Legislative Assembly of a state, the governor will go by
A. the advice of the former Chief Minister
B. the advice of the Prime Minister
C. the advice of the President
D. his own discretion

English Proficiency

Q.41 Direction: Complete the analogy.

Paranoia is to **Persecution** as **Alienation** is to
A. Ego
B. Estrangement
C. Scout
D. Barbaric

Q.42 Direction: Choose the option that best expresses the meaning of the idiom which is underlined.

I never want to rest on my laurels.
A. Be dissatisfied
B. Be eager
C. Be complacent
D. Be good

Q.43 Choose the word which can be substituted for the given phrase/sentence:

A photograph on transparent paper
A. Red print
B. Blueprint
C. Negative
D. Transparency

Q.44 Direction: Select the correct word or phrase to complete a grammatical and idiomatic sentence.

The match had ended in a draw, the first prize was shared ______.
A. Between Usha and I
B. By Usha and I
C. By Usha and me
D. Among me and Usha

Q.45 Direction: Choose the option that best expresses the meaning of the idiom which is underlined.

Don't tease him about his failure as it's like a red rag to a bull.
A. Provoke a violent action
B. Provoke an argument
C. Invite an angry bull
D. Commit a cowardly action

Q.46 Direction: Select the word that is antonymous to the given word.

PLIABLE

A. Plastic
B. Yielding
C. Rigid
D. Static

Q.47 Direction: Complete the analogy.

Abduction is to **Kidnapping** as **Larceny** is to
A. Rudder
B. Theft
C. Elegant
D. Dawdle

Q.48 Direction: Pick the odd one out.
A. Simmering
B. Seething
C. Boiling
D. Cooling

Q.49 Direction: Pick the odd one out.
A. Dwarf
B. Gnome
C. Pygmy
D. Huge

Q.50 Direction: Pick the odd one out.
A. Debutante
B. Novice
C. Seasoned
D. Fresher

Q.51 Choose the word which can be substituted for the given phrase/sentence:

A written declaration made on oath in the presence of a magistrate
A. Voucher
B. Dossier
C. Affidavit
D. Document

Q.52 Direction: Select the correct word or phrase to complete a grammatical and idiomatic sentence.

He has won the election because some of the votes ______ to have been miscounted.
A. Seem
B. Are seeming
C. Seems
D. Are

Q.53 Direction: Choose one word that substitutes the given phrase.

An offensively boastful person.
A. Atheist
B. Bloody
C. Ascetic
D. Braggart

Q.54 Direction: Choose the option that best expresses the meaning of the idiom which is underlined.

We decided to go Dutch for the party.
A. Share expenses
B. Visit a costly place
C. Indulge in drinking
D. Go wild

Q.55 Hydrophobia is to **Water** as **Photophobia** is to
A. Light
B. Camera
C. Photo
D. Stranger

Q.56 Direction: Choose the option that best expresses the meaning of the idiom which is underlined.

Zenus is in a pickle. His spouse and his girlfriend turned out to be best friends.
A. In a difficult situation
B. In a fit
C. Having fun
D. Shameful

Q.57 Direction: Read the sentence to find out whether there is any grammatical or idiomatic error in it. The error, if any, will be in one part of the sentence. The number of that part is the answer. If there is no error, the answer is (d). (Ignore the errors of punctuation, if any)

It is not an uncommon (a) misconception that rich (b) have nothing to worry about. (c) No error (d)

A. (a) **B.** (b) **C.** (c) **D.** (d)

Q.58 Directions: Read the sentence to find out whether there is any grammatical or idiomatic error in it. The error, if any, will be in one part of the sentence. The number of that part is the answer. If there is no error, the answer is (d). (Ignore the errors of punctuation, if any)

The solutions to the questions in the book (a) can be easily found in the guide (b) authored by the same person who is writing the book. (c) No error (d)

A. (a) **B.** (b) **C.** (c) **D.** (d)

Q.59 Direction: Read the sentence to find out whether there is any grammatical or idiomatic error in it. The error, if any, will be in one part of the sentence. The number of that part is the answer. If there is no error, the answer is (d). (Ignore the errors of punctuation, if any.)

If you have (a) informed him (b) he would have been happy. (c) No error (d)

A. (a) **B.** (b) **C.** (c) **D.** (d)

Q.60 Direction: Choose one word that substitutes the given phrase.

To change hostility into peace.

A. Gratify **B.** Slacken **C.** Placate **D.** Bewitch

Q.61 Direction: Choose the option that best expresses the meaning of the idiom which is underlined.

We failed to <u>read between the lines.</u>

A. Get the meaning
B. Understand implications
C. Read only the main points
D. Achieve the result

Q.62 Direction: Fill in the blank with the correct option.

We are hoping that the community will _____ in the waterfront clean-up efforts.

A. Connect **B.** Associate
C. Participate **D.** Concern

Q.63 Direction: Select the word that is antonymous to the given word.

GROUP

A. Disperse **B.** Assemble
C. Strengthen **D.** Accumulate

Q.64 Fill in the blank with a suitable noun:

What you heard was not _____.

A. Completely true **B.** The complete truth
C. True **D.** Only true

Q.65 Direction: Complete the analogy.

Slumber is to **Sleep** as **Stride** is to

A. Strength **B.** Walk **C.** Jump **D.** Sit

Ques (66-70):Direction: Read the following passage and answer the given question.

An earthquake comes like a thief in the night, without warning. It was necessary therefore to invent instruments that neither slumbered nor slept. Some devices were quite simple. One, for instance, consisted of rods of various lengths and thicknesses which would stand up on end like ninepins. When a shock came, it shook the rigid table upon which these stood. If it were gentle, only the more unstable rods fell. If it were severe, they all fell. Thus, the rods by falling and by the direction in which they fell, recorded for the slumbering scientist, the strength of a shock that was too weak to waken him and know the direction from which it came.

But instruments far more delicate than that were needed if any really serious advance was to be made. The ideal to be aimed at was to devise an instrument that could record with a pen on paper the movements of the ground or of the table as the quake passed by. While I write, my pen moves but the paper keeps still. With practice, no doubt, I could, in time, learn to write by holding the pen still while the paper moved. That sounds a silly suggestion, but that was precisely the idea adopted in some of the early instruments (seismometers) for recording earthquake waves. But when the table, pen holder, and paper are all moving, how is it possible to write legibly? The key to a solution to that problem lay in everyday observation. Why does a person standing on a bus or train tend to fall when a sudden start is made? It is because his feet move on, but his head stays still.

Q.66 The passage states that early instruments for measuring earthquakes were

A. Faulty in design
B. Expensive
C. Not sturdy
D. Not sensitive enough

Q.67 Why was it necessary to invent instruments to observe an earthquake?

A. Because an earthquake comes in the night.
B. To make people alert about earthquakes during their conscious as well as unconscious hours.
C. To prove that we are technically advanced.
D. To experiment with the control of man over nature.

Q.68 A simple device, which consisted of rods that stood up on end like ninepins, was replaced by a more sophisticated one because it failed

A. To measure a gentle earthquake
B. To measure a severe earthquake
C. To record the direction of the earthquake
D. To record the facts with a pen on paper

Q.69 The 'everyday observation' referred to in the passage relates to

A. A moving bus or train
B. The sudden start of a bus
C. The tendency of a standing person to fall when a bus or train moves suddenly
D. People standing on a bus or train

Q.70 The early seismometers adopted the idea that in order to record the earthquake, it is

A. The pen that should move just as it moves when we write on paper

B. The pen that should stay still and the paper should move

C. Both the pen and the paper that should move

D. Neither the pen nor the paper that should move

Maths and Logical Reasoning

Q.71 If $\dfrac{2x+3y}{2x-3y} = \dfrac{5}{2}$, what is the value of $y:x$?

A. $3:7$ **B.** $2:7$ **C.** $7:1$ **D.** $7:3$

Q.72 Directions: Study the following information carefully and answer the question given below.

There are seven students - A, B, C, D, E, F and G - in a class. Each of them has a different favourite subject - English, Mathematics, Physics, Chemistry, Biology, Sociology and Philosophy. All of them secure different marks in the examination. C secures second highest marks, and neither English nor Mathematics is his favourite subject. E secures the least marks, and neither Sociology nor Mathematics is his favourite subject. The favourite subject of D is Physics, and he secures more marks than B and G, but less than A. The favourite subject of B is Biology and his marks are more than the marks of E, but less than the marks of G. The favourite subject of A is Philosophy. The student, whose favourite subject is Chemistry, scores the highest marks.

Chemistry is the favourite subject of?

A. A **B.** C **C.** F **D.** G

Q.73 Directions: In the table below, the numbers of students studying in different standards of six different schools are given. Study the table carefully to answer the question that follows.

Standard → Schools ↓	I	II	III	IV	V	VI
A	42	54	48	58	50	38
B	50	60	58	45	45	46
C	40	48	58	56	42	54
D	45	55	46	40	52	50
E	48	55	44	55	52	48
F	52	52	54	42	60	54

The number of students studying in standard IV from school E is what percent of that from school D?

A. 128% **B.** 132.5% **C.** 124% **D.** 137.5%

Q.74 In the game of a one-day cricket match (50 overs), the run rate was 2.8 for the initial 15 overs. To reach the target of 252 runs, what should be the run rate for the remaining overs?

A. 6 **B.** 6.5 **C.** 7 **D.** 7.5

Q.75 Directions: Read the following passage carefully and answer the question given below.

An investor invested a certain amount of money into shares on January $1, 2004$. At the end of January, he sold all his shares and earned a profit of 25%. On February $1, 2004$, he reinvested his entire amount into the shares which he sold at the end of January and experienced a loss of 20%, when sold at the end of February. On March $1, 2004$, he again invested his entire amount in a company and at the end of the month, he earned a profit of 20% by selling it. On April $1, 2004$, he again invested his entire money into shares. At the end of the month, he sold his shares and earned Rs. $1,08,000$, incurring a loss of 10%.

What amount has the investor lost in the month of April?

A. Rs. $10,000$ **B.** Rs. $12,000$

C. Rs. $14,500$ **D.** Rs. $15,200$

Q.76

Directions: Study the given information carefully and answer the question that follows.

Question distribution among different sections of MBA entrance exams conducted by Rajput University from $2001 - 2005$:

Year/Sect ion	Verbal ability	Quantita tive ability	Logical reasoni ng	General knowle dge	Domain knowle dge
2001	48	50	46	46	60
2002	36	56	15	38	55
2003	45	68	12	45	30
2004	32	72	63	39	44
2005	15	39	38	15	43

(Assume there was no other section in MBA entrance exams apart from the given sections.)

The number of Logical Reasoning questions asked in the 2004 exam was what percent more than those asked in the 2001 exam?

A. 31.23% **B.** 32.58% **C.** 33.98% **D.** 36.96%

Q.77

Directions: Read the following information carefully to answer the question that follows.

Amount spent by five friends on electronic items.

Names\Articles	Refrigerat or	Air Conditi oner	Lapt op	Tot al
Manpre et	Rs. 26000		Rs. 21000	
Madhav	Rs. 35000	Rs. 35000	Rs. 24000	Rs. 94000
Rahul	Rs. 22000		Rs. 32000	
Amit	Rs. 21000	Rs. 36000		
Girish		Rs. 35000		Rs. 93000

If the shopkeeper sold an air conditioner after offering a 37% discount to Amit and still earned a 32% profit, what was the difference between the price at which the shopkeeper bought the air conditioner and the marked price of the air conditioner on which Amit was offered the discount?

A. Rs. 24560   **B.** Rs. 29870
C. Rs. 31000   **D.** Rs. 35691

Q.78

Directions: Answer the given question based on the following data.

FEDERAL SPENDING ON SECONDARY AND TERTIARY EDUCATION IN COUNTRY X, 1992-1998

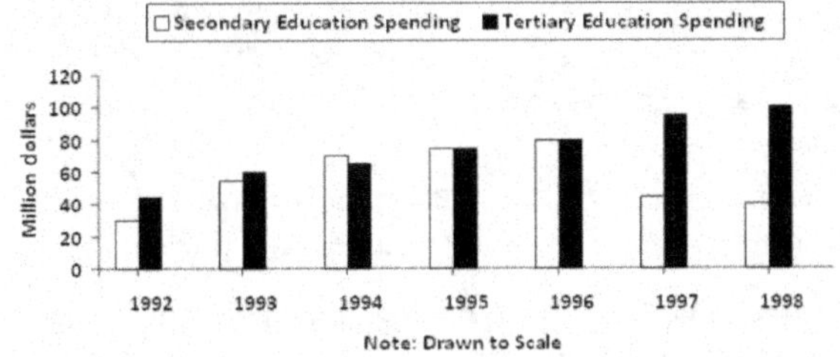

What is the median amount spent on secondary education by country X in the years shown?

A. $40 million   **B.** $45 million
C. $50 million   **D.** $55 million

Q.79 A survey of 100 people revealed that 72 of them had eaten at restaurant P and that 52 of them had eaten at restaurant Q . Which of the following could be the number of persons in the surveyed group who had eaten at both P and Q if each of the surveyed persons had eaten at least one restaurant?

A. 20   **B.** 24   **C.** 30   **D.** 50

Q.80 If 16th May 2017 was Tuesday, what was the day of the week on 13th May 2015?

A. Saturday   **B.** Friday
C. Thursday   **D.** Wednesday

Q.81 The given bar graph represents the number of different flowers grown in Sharon's garden.

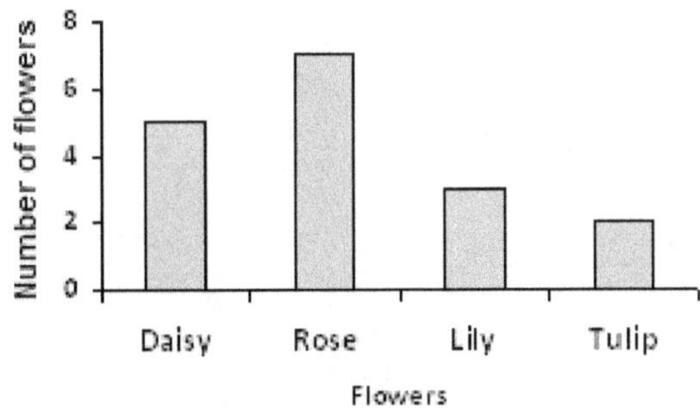

How many more Rose(s) than Lilies did she grow?

A. 1   **B.** 2   **C.** 3   **D.** 4

Q.82 The average marks of 8 students in a group are 65 . Three of them scored $75, 65$ and 50 marks. What are the average marks of the remaining 5 students?

A. 330   **B.** 50   **C.** 66   **D.** 1000

Q.83 How many triangles are there in the following figure?

A. 21   **B.** 25   **C.** 23   **D.** 27

Q.84 A mobile seller found that by selling 90 smartphones, he can earn the amount that is equal to the cost price of 120 smartphones, then what is the gain percent?

A. $32\frac{1}{4}\%$ **B.** $33\frac{1}{3}\%$ **C.** $33\frac{2}{3}\%$ **D.** 33%

Q.85 Which of the following option is correct about the value $\sqrt{3}$?

A. A rational number
B. An infinitely long non–repeating decimal
C. Equal to 1.732
D. None of these

Q.86 Direction: Read the given information carefully and answer the question that follows.

1. Seven students P, Q, R, S, T, U, and V take a series of tests.
2. No two students score the same marks.
3. V always scores more than P.
4. P always scores more than Q.
5. Each time, either R scores the highest and T scores the least or S scores the highest, and U or Q scores the least.

If S is ranked sixth and Q is ranked fifth, then which of the following statements can be true?

A. V is ranked either first or fourth
B. R is ranked either second or third
C. P is ranked either second or fifth
D. U is ranked either third or fourth

Q.87 In triangle ABC , BC is parallel to PQ . Find the value of x .

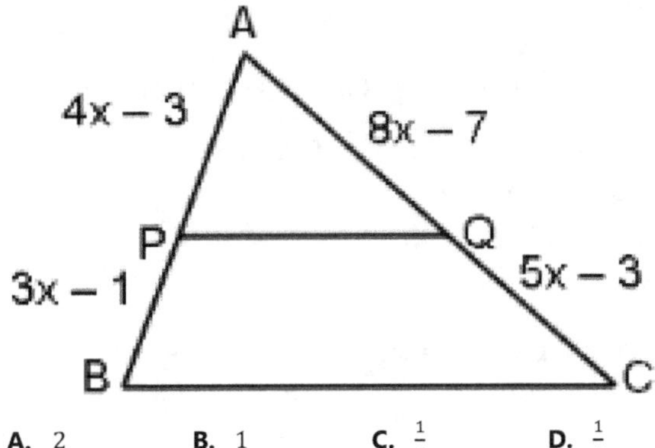

A. 2   **B.** 1   **C.** $\frac{1}{2}$ **D.** $\frac{1}{4}$

Q.88

Directions: Read the information carefully to answer the following question.

Number of income tax defaulters (in thousand)

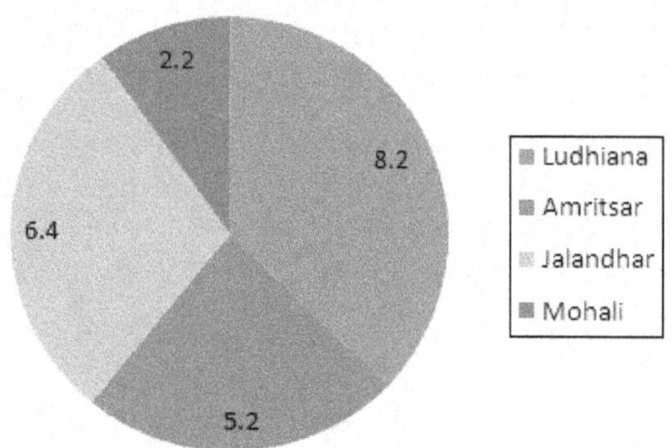

Fine imposed per person for the given cities

City	Fine imposed per person
Ludhiana	Rs. 700
Amritsar	Rs. 800
Jalandhar	Rs. 750
Mohali	Rs. 650

The total fine imposed on income tax defaulters from Jalandhar was what percent of that of those from Mohali?

A. 298.36%
B. 335.66%
C. 350.35%
D. 368.92%

Q.89 A total of nine athletes finish a race of 400 meters in a definite order. The athletes are Aaron, Benjamin, Charles, Denise, Ed, Frank, Gibbs, Hercules, and Ivan. They all complete at different times and their order of completion is as follows:

I. Frank completes before Aaron.

II. Denise completes before Benjamin and Ed.

III. Ivan comes first while Charles last.

IV. Gibbs, Hercules, Benjamin, and Ed complete after Aaron.

Which of the below positions can Aaron complete the race?

A. Second
B. Fifth
C. Fourth
D. Sixth

Q.90 Which of the following options will replace the question mark (?) in the given series?

FRP, HPQ, JNS, LLV,?

A. PKZ
B. NJZ
C. OJZ
D. MKZ

Q.91 Find the values of x and y if $x + 2y = 4$ and $2x - 3y = 5$.

A. $x = \frac{22}{7}, y = \frac{5}{7}$
B. $x = \frac{22}{7}, y = \frac{3}{7}$
C. $x = \frac{21}{7}, y = \frac{4}{7}$
D. $x = \frac{22}{5}, y = \frac{3}{7}$

Q.92 If A and B are finite sets and $A \subset B$, then

A. $n(A \cup B) = n(A)$
B. $n(A \cap B) = n(B)$
C. $n(A \cup B) = n(B)$
D. None of these

Q.93 In a group of persons, 70% of the persons are male and 30% of the persons are married. If two-seventh of the males are married, what fraction of the total females are unmarried?

A. $\frac{3}{5}$
B. $\frac{2}{3}$
C. $\frac{3}{2}$
D. $\frac{4}{3}$

Q.94 Directions: Study the following information carefully and answer the given question.

A, B, C, D, E, F, and G are sitting in a row facing North. F is to the immediate right of E. E is fourth to the right of G. C is the immediate neighbor of B and D. The person who is third to the left of D is at one of the ends.

What is the position of A?

A. Between E and C
B. At the extreme left
C. In the middle
D. At the extreme right

Q.95 Directions: Read the following information carefully and then answer the given question.

Ten persons are sitting in two rows. E, F, G, H and I are five boys sitting in one row facing south, while M, N, O, P and Q are five girls sitting in the other row parallel to the first row and are facing north. Every person is facing one of the persons sitting in the other row.

F, who is just next to the left of H, is facing Q. G and N are at extreme ends sitting diagonally opposite to each other. I is opposite to O, who is just next to the right of M. P is just next to the left of Q. M is at one of the ends of the row.

Who is sitting third to the right of O?

A. N
B. M
C. P
D. Q

Q.96 Directions: In the following question, a number series is given with one term missing. Choose the correct alternative that will continue the same pattern and replace the question mark (?) in the given series.

120, 99, 80, 63, 48, ?

A. 35
B. 38
C. 42
D. 46

Q.97 In the figure given below, if $AB \mid\mid CD$, then find the measure of $\angle BGF$.

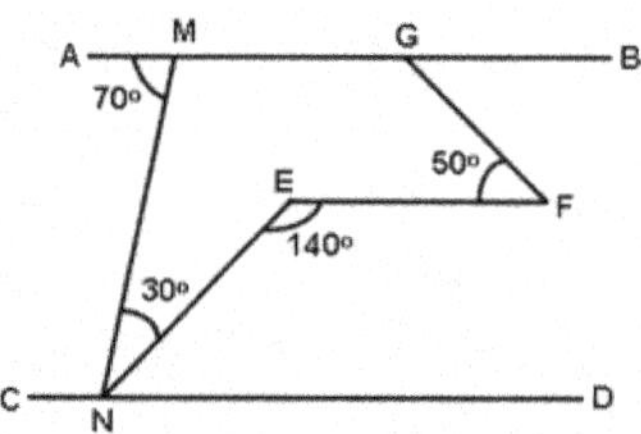

A. 60°
B. 50°
C. 70°
D. Data insufficient

Q.98 Directions: In making a decision about an important question, it is desirable to be able to distinguish between strong and weak arguments in so far as they are related to the question. Weak arguments may not be directly related to the question, maybe of minor importance, or maybe related to some insignificant aspect of the question.

The question given below is followed by two arguments numbered I and II. Decide which of the arguments is strong/weak. Mark your answer according to the codes given below:

(A) if only I is strong

(B) if only II is strong

(C) if either I or II is strong

(D) if neither I nor II is strong

Statement: Should the Indian cricket team be given more rest in-between the series?

Arguments:

I. Yes, because playing more cricket is affecting their performance.

II. No, more cricket means more money and people want to watch more cricket.

A. (A)   **B.** (B)   **C.** (C)   **D.** (D)

Q.99 Directions: Study the following information carefully and answer the question that follows.

In a school, there is total of 60 employees, out of which 25 are women. Also:

- 28 employees are married.
- 26 employees are postgraduate.
- 20 married employees are postgraduates.
- 15 males are postgraduates.
- 15 males are married.
- 11 married females are postgraduates.

How many unmarried females are postgraduates?

A. 0   **B.** 11   **C.** 9   **D.** 2

Q.100 Direction: The following figures show the same die in different orientations.

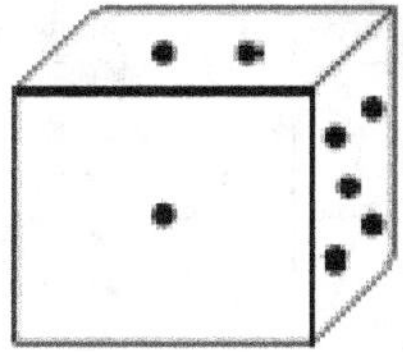 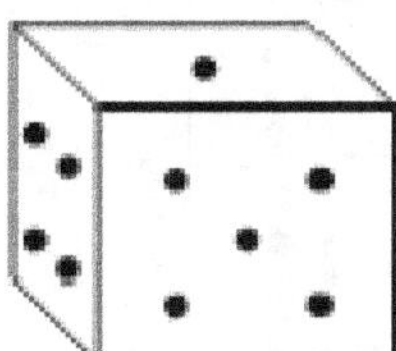

How many dots are there on the face opposite to the face having four dots?

A. 3   **B.** 2   **C.** 5   **D.** 6

// Smart Answer Sheet //

| Correct | Indicates percentage of students who answered questions correctly. |

| Skipped | Indicates percentage of students who skipped questions. |

Q.	Ans.	Correct / Skipped	Q.	Ans.	Correct / Skipped	Q.	Ans.	Correct / Skipped	Q.	Ans.	Correct / Skipped	Q.	Ans.	Correct / Skipped
1	C	21.82 % / 2.88 %	17	B	36.93 % / 27.58 %	33	D	11.51 % / 29.98 %	49	D	52.76 % / 34.77 %	65	B	45.08 % / 35.26 %
2	A	53.48 % / 22.78 %	18	A	35.73 % / 27.34 %	34	D	19.18 % / 28.78 %	50	C	51.32 % / 35.25 %	66	D	35.73 % / 36.69 %
3	B	39.09 % / 23.26 %	19	B	42.45 % / 27.33 %	35	A	34.05 % / 29.26 %	51	C	51.56 % / 35.49 %	67	B	55.4 % / 37.89 %
4	D	34.53 % / 23.98 %	20	C	29.26 % / 27.57 %	36	B	44.6 % / 29.26 %	52	A	38.37 % / 35.01 %	68	D	18.23 % / 38.12 %
5	D	16.07 % / 24.94 %	21	D	39.09 % / 28.06 %	37	C	41.49 % / 29.25 %	53	D	51.08 % / 35.25 %	69	C	56.35 % / 38.61 %
6	C	36.21 % / 24.22 %	22	C	39.33 % / 27.34 %	38	B	19.9 % / 30.22 %	54	A	33.09 % / 35.26 %	70	B	37.41 % / 38.85 %
7	A	19.18 % / 25.9 %	23	A	22.78 % / 28.06 %	39	B	27.1 % / 29.73 %	55	A	43.41 % / 35.01 %	71	B	48.2 % / 30.94 %
8	B	28.54 % / 26.62 %	24	D	27.82 % / 29.97 %	40	D	23.5 % / 28.78 %	56	A	57.55 % / 35.02 %	72	C	48.44 % / 35.97 %
9	A	29.26 % / 26.14 %	25	D	45.56 % / 28.78 %	41	B	47.72 % / 29.26 %	57	B	19.42 % / 35.26 %	73	D	50.84 % / 36.45 %
10	D	60.43 % / 25.66 %	26	C	30.22 % / 28.77 %	42	C	39.33 % / 33.09 %	58	C	40.77 % / 35.49 %	74	A	44.12 % / 37.65 %
11	B	26.62 % / 26.86 %	27	A	50.12 % / 28.06 %	43	D	22.06 % / 33.1 %	59	A	48.44 % / 35.01 %	75	B	32.85 % / 39.57 %
12	B	41.25 % / 26.62 %	28	C	30.22 % / 28.53 %	44	C	24.94 % / 33.57 %	60	C	34.77 % / 35.73 %	76	D	47.96 % / 37.41 %
13	C	24.94 % / 26.62 %	29	A	15.11 % / 30.21 %	45	A	46.52 % / 34.06 %	61	B	30.7 % / 35.01 %	77	B	23.26 % / 41.49 %
14	B	29.26 % / 28.29 %	30	C	48.44 % / 28.3 %	46	C	40.29 % / 35.25 %	62	C	57.79 % / 35.26 %	78	D	27.34 % / 39.09 %
15	A	18.94 % / 27.58 %	31	D	38.85 % / 28.3 %	47	B	53.0 % / 35.49 %	63	A	60.19 % / 35.25 %	79	B	49.88 % / 38.13 %
16	A	37.41 % / 27.34 %	32	C	33.09 % / 29.26 %	48	D	41.01 % / 34.53 %	64	B	43.41 % / 35.49 %	80	D	32.85 % / 38.85 %

Q.	Ans.	Correct / Skipped
81	D	53.96 %
		37.89 %
82	C	47.0 %
		37.65 %
83	D	6.0 %
		38.12 %
84	B	42.93 %
		39.8 %

Q.	Ans.	Correct / Skipped
85	C	24.46 %
		41.25 %
86	D	35.01 %
		38.85 %
87	B	38.37 %
		39.81 %
88	B	38.85 %
		40.53 %

Q.	Ans.	Correct / Skipped
89	C	39.57 %
		39.33 %
90	B	54.2 %
		39.56 %
91	B	49.64 %
		39.57 %
92	C	24.46 %
		42.21 %

Q.	Ans.	Correct / Skipped
93	B	37.65 %
		41.25 %
94	D	38.37 %
		39.81 %
95	A	34.77 %
		41.97 %
96	A	53.72 %
		39.09 %

Q.	Ans.	Correct / Skipped
97	B	40.77 %
		40.29 %
98	A	32.61 %
		40.77 %
99	A	23.5 %
		41.73 %
100	B	40.53 %
		41.24 %

Performance Analysis

Avg. Score (%)	40.0%
Toppers Score (%)	98.0%
Your Score	

Q.1 When did India compete in its First Fed Cup?
A. 1980 **B.** 1985 **C.** 1977 **D.** 1973

Q.2 Ishwar Chand Pandey is related to which of the following sports?
A. Hockey **B.** Football
C. Cricket **D.** Badminton

Q.3 Which country has won the maximum number of medals in the all time history of Commonwealth Games?
A. Australia **B.** England **C.** India **D.** Canada

Q.4 What are 'the camel', 'the mongoose', 'kaboom' and 'aluminum'?
A. Cricket bats **B.** Military codes
C. Squadrons **D.** Chess moves

Q.5 The National Income estimation in India is the responsibility of which of the following?

[RSMSSB Computor, 2018]

A. NSSO
B. CSO
C. Finance Ministry
D. National Income Committee

Q.6 When was NABARD established?
A. 1975 **B.** 1980 **C.** 1982 **D.** 1990

Q.7 Which country has the lowest corporate tax rate?
A. Germany **B.** China
C. Russia **D.** Switzerland

Q.8 Which five-year plan of India was based on the Harrod-Domar model?
A. First Five Year Plan
B. Second Five Year Plan
C. Third Five Year Plan
D. Fourth Five Year Plan

Q.9 Crescograph was invented by:
A. S.N. Bose **B.** P.C. Roy
C. J.C. Bose **D.** P.C. Mahalanobis

Q.10 Chandrayan - 1, India's first mission to Moon was launched successfully on _______ from, Sriharikota.
A. 22 October, 2008 **B.** 13 December, 2009
C. 30 March, 2010 **D.** 7 July, 2011

Q.11 India's first COVID-19 vaccine to get approval for children above 12 Years was _______.
A. Covaxin **B.** Sputnik
C. ZyCoV-D **D.** Covishield

Q.12 In December 2021, SpaceX has launched 52 Starlink internet satellites into orbit from California base. Which rocket has been used to launch these sattellites?
A. Voyger Cassini **B.** Falcon-9
C. Falcon-7 **D.** Rover-4

Q.13 Under the Constitution of India, which one of the following is not a Fundamental Duty?
A. To vote in Public Elections
B. To develop the scientific temper
C. To safeguard public property
D. To abide by the Constitution and respect its ideals

Q.14 Which one of the following is not a collective privilege of the members of Parliament?
A. Freedom of debates and proceedings.
B. The Right to regulate the internal matters of the Parliament.
C. Freedom from attendance as Witness.
D. The privilege of excluding strangers from the house.

Q.15 Which of the following actions of the government form(s) the part of the implementation of Directive Principles of State Policy (DPSP)?
1. Maternity Benefit Act
2. National Rural Employment Guarantee Act, 2005
3. Environment Protection Act, 1986
A. 1 only **B.** 2 and 3 only
C. 1 and 2 only **D.** 1, 2 and 3

Q.16 Which of the following Articles of Constitutional Bodies is/are correctly matched?

1. Article 324	a. Election Commission
2. Article 280	b. Finance Commission
3. Article 148	c. CAG (Comptroller and Auditor General of India)
4. Article 76	d. Attorney General of India

A. Only 1 and 2 **B.** Only 2 and 3
C. Only 1, 2 and 3 **D.** All are correct

Q.17 Consider the following statements regarding Karbi Anglong Autonomous Council (KAAC).
1. It is an autonomous district council, protected under the Sixth Schedule of the Indian Constitution.
2. The entire political discourse in this constituency comprising two districts of Karbi Anglong and West Karbi Anglong revolves around the demand for granting of "Autonomous State" status to the region.
Which of the statements given above is/are correct?
A. 1 only **B.** 2 only
C. Both 1 and 2 **D.** Neither 1 nor 2

Q.18 In which among the following cases, the Supreme Court of India propunded the theory of basic structure of the constitution?

A. Gopalan vs, State of Mdras

B. Golak Nath

C. Keshvanand Bharati

D. Minerva Mills

Q.19 With reference to the Constitution of India, prohibitions or limitations, or provisions contained in ordinary laws cannot act as prohibitions or limitations on the constitutional powers under Article 142. It could mean which one of the following?

[UPSC Prelims, 2019]

A. The decisions taken by the Election Commission of India while discharging its duties cannot be challenged in any court of law.

B. The Supreme Court of India is not constrained in the exercise of its powers by laws made by the Parliament.

C. In the event of grave financial crisis in the country, the President of India can declare Financial Emergency without the counsel from the Cabinet.

D. State Legislatures cannot make laws on certain matters without the concurrence of Union Legislature.

Q.20 Consider the following statements about Separation of Power

1. The doctrine of separation of power is a part of the basic structure of the Indian Constitution

2. Separation of Power is nowhere mentioned in the Indian Constitution

Which of the above statements is/are correct?

A. 1 only

B. 2 only

C. Both 1 and 2

D. Neither 1 nor 2

Q.21 Which of the following statements about Mahatma Gandhi's Satyagraha is/are correct?

1. It was during the course of his campaign against racialism in South Africa that Gandhiji first applied Satyagraha

2. The two vital ingredients of Satyagraha are 'truth' and 'non-violence'

3. The Satyagraha resists evil by inflicting suffering on himself and not by inflicting suffering in the opponent

4. In India, Satyagraha was first tried by Gandhiji in Champaran

A. 1 and 4 only

B. 2 only

C. 4 only

D. 1, 2, 3 and 4

Q.22 With reference to the changes made with the Indian army after the 1857 revolt, which of the following statement is NOT correct?

A. The East India Company's European forces were merged with the Crown troops.

B. The proportion of Europeans to Indians in the army was raised and fixed at one to two in the Bengal Army, Madras, and Bombay armies.

C. European troops were kept in key geographical and military positions.

D. The older policy of excluding Indians from the officer corps was strictly maintained.

Q.23 Examine the following statements:

A. A.O. Hume was responsible for the successful holding for the first session of the Indian National Congress (INC) in 1885.

B. It was decided to establish the Congress as a safety valve for the expression of people's discontent, sufferings and views.

Choose the correct answer:

A. Both A and B are correct.

B. Both A and B are incorrect.

C. Only A is correct

D. Only B is correct

Q.24 With reference to the Civil Administration in 1905, which of the statements is/are correct?

1. Lord Curzon decided to rearrange the provincial boundaries.

2. A new province was constituted, called East Bengal and Assam.

Select the correct answer using the codes given below:

A. 1 only

B. Both 1 and 2

C. 2 only

D. Neither 1 nor 2

Q.25 Consider the following statements regarding the 'Making Peace with Nature' report.

1. The report is released by Greenpeace in collaboration with World Wide Fund for Nature.

2. As per the report, climate change, biodiversity loss, and population add up to three self-inflicted planetary emergencies.

Which among the above statements is/are correct?

A. 1 only

B. 2 only

C. Both 1 and 2

D. Neither 1 nor 2

Q.26 The Environmental Performance Index is published by:

A. Yale University

B. World Wildlife Fund (WWF)

C. Oxford University

D. United Nations Environment Program (UNEP)

Q.27 Consider the following statements regarding the Governing Body of the International Labour Organization.

1. India has assumed the Chairmanship of the Governing Body of the International Labour Organization.

2. The Governing Body is the apex executive body of the ILO which decides policies and elects the Director-General.

Which among the above statements is/are correct?

A. 1 only

B. 2 only

C. Both 1 and 2

D. Neither 1 nor 2

Q.28 Which of the following statements with regards to Champaran Satyagraha is correct?

A. Gandhi used the technique of hunger strike for the first time in India.

B. Rajkumar Shukla requested Gandhi to look into the problems of farmers of Champaran area.

C. Both (A) and (B)

D. Neither (A) nor (B)

Q.29 With which of the following events of Indian National Struggle, did the Mappila Revolt merge with?

A. Civil Disobedience Movement

B. Quit India Movement
C. Deccan Riots
D. Khilafat Agitation

Q.30 Which of the following was/were one of the reason/reasons for the lack of economic developments in India in the 19th century?

1. Officially the British Government was committed to a policy of laissez-faire, but it was actually a policy of discriminatory intervention

2. European entrepreneurs had connections to banks and agency houses, while Indians had to rely on kin, family and caste men

3. When plantations were transferred to individual capitalist ownership, native investors were deliberately ignored.

Select the correct answer using the code below

A. 1 only
B. 2 and 3 only
C. 1 and 3 only
D. 1, 2 and 3

Q.31 The French East India Company was formed in 1664. Where and by whom was the first factory under French established in India?

A. Established by Colbert and at Surat
B. Established by Francis Caron and at Surat
C. Established by Colbert and at Masulipatnam
D. Established under Francis Caron and at Masulipatnam

Q.32 What is a biological community of interacting organisms and their physical surrourrdings' known as?

A. Biome
B. Ecosystem
C. Environment
D. Habitat

Q.33 Which of the following is not a Primary air pollutant?

A. Carbon Monoxide
B. Nitrogen Oxide
C. Ozone
D. Sulfur Oxide

Q.34 'Fly Ash' is the waste generated by:

A. Hydropower plant
B. Thermal power plant
C. Geothermal plant
D. Windmills

Q.35 Which one of the following gas is responsible for the Depletion of the ozone layer?

A. Nitrous Oxide
B. Methane
C. Chlorofluorocarbon
D. Carbon dioxide

Q.36 'Dandiya' is a popular dance of :

A. Punjab
B. Gujarat
C. Tamil Nadu
D. Maharashtra

Q.37 Who wrote 'Ramayana' grantha?

A. Surdaas
B. Kalidas
C. Ved Byas
D. Valmiki

Q.38 The Rath Yatra at Puri is celebrated in Honour of which Hindu deity?

A. Ram
B. Vishnu
C. Shiva
D. Jagannath

Q.39 The Hornbill Festival is one of the important festivals celebrated in ________.

A. Arunachal Pradesh
B. Nagaland
C. Mizoram
D. Meghalaya

Q.40 Which of the following committees' recommendation was recently accepted by the Government in relations to creating border infrastructure?

A. Shekatkar committee
B. Naresh Chandra Committee
C. Gadgil Committee
D. Santhanam committee

// Smart Answer Sheet //

Correct — Indicates percentage of students who answered questions correctly.

Skipped — Indicates percentage of students who skipped questions.

Q.	Ans.	Correct / Skipped
1	C	14.12 % / 4.88 %
2	C	85.05 % / 0.0 %
3	A	77.88 % / 0.0 %
4	A	45.89 % / 1.67 %
5	B	88.41 % / 0.0 %
6	C	84.54 % / 0.0 %
7	D	76.74 % / 0.0 %
8	A	87.21 % / 0.0 %
9	C	50.45 % / 1.9 %
10	A	56.53 % / 1.06 %
11	C	61.72 % / 1.46 %
12	B	53.3 % / 1.6 %
13	A	44.98 % / 1.85 %
14	C	76.25 % / 0.0 %
15	D	67.61 % / 1.84 %
16	D	56.14 % / 1.63 %
17	A	59.99 % / 1.6 %
18	C	22.88 % / 3.58 %
19	B	25.86 % / 3.57 %
20	C	78.48 % / 0.0 %
21	D	14.23 % / 4.13 %
22	B	78.72 % / 0.0 %
23	C	55.91 % / 1.48 %
24	B	56.1 % / 1.54 %
25	B	42.34 % / 1.13 %
26	A	40.49 % / 1.65 %
27	C	43.79 % / 1.24 %
28	B	50.86 % / 1.48 %
29	D	65.04 % / 1.22 %
30	D	64.59 % / 1.88 %
31	B	53.54 % / 1.17 %
32	B	46.51 % / 1.57 %
33	C	53.3 % / 1.48 %
34	B	43.24 % / 1.45 %
35	C	42.02 % / 1.93 %
36	B	84.17 % / 0.0 %
37	D	87.44 % / 0.0 %
38	D	89.24 % / 0.0 %
39	B	89.84 % / 0.0 %
40	A	46.32 % / 1.59 %

Performance Analysis

Avg. Score (%)	37.5%
Toppers Score (%)	62.5%
Your Score	

Q.1 Who among the following cricketers has won the ESPNcricinfo 'Captain of the Year' awards 2022?

A. Kane Williamson   **B.** KL Rahul

C. Virat Kohli   **D.** Babar Azam

Q.2 D Vishwa, who passed away recently, was an ace player of which game?

A. Tennis   **B.** Squash

C. Table Tennis   **D.** Fencing

Q.3 The 83rd Senior National Table Tennis Championship began in _______ in April 2022.

A. Nagaland   **B.** Mizoram

C. Meghalaya   **D.** Tripura

Q.4 The second Khelo India University Games 2021 is to start at the Sree Kanteerava Indoor Stadium, _______ on 24 April 2022.

A. Bengaluru   **B.** Chennai

C. Hyderabad   **D.** Kolkata

Q.5 Which of the following statements are correct?

1. When marginal revenue is positive, total revenue increases with an increase in output.
2. When marginal revenue is zero, the total revenue is maximum.
3. When marginal revenue becomes negative, total revenue falls with an increase in output.

Select the correct answer using the code given below:

A. 1 and 2 only   **B.** 2 and 3 only

C. 1 and 3 only   **D.** 1, 2, and 3

Q.6 An internal debt of the Government of India includes:

1. Loans raised by the government in the open market through treasury bills and government securities
2. Special securities issued to the RBI
3. Oil bonds

Choose the correct answer using the codes below:

A. Only 1 and 2   **B.** Only 2 and 3

C. Only 1 and 3   **D.** All of these

Q.7 Which country has surpassed China to become India's biggest trading partner in 2021-22?

A. USA   **B.** Saudi Arabia

C. UAE   **D.** Russia

Q.8 Which union minister has launched the Indian Business Portal in New Delhi on May 27, 2022?

A. Anupriya Patel   **B.** Narayan Rane

C. Anurag Thakur   **D.** Rajnath Singh

Q.9 The "Braille System" was invented by _______ and he is from _______.

A. Marie Curie, France

B. Hellen Keller, USA

C. Nicolas Appert, France

D. Louis Braille, Paris

Q.10 The world's first railway steam engine was invented by _______.

A. Otto Hahn   **B.** James Watt

C. Henri Becquerel   **D.** Ernest Rutherford

Q.11 What is the name of India's first manned space flight?

A. Gaganyaan   **B.** Vayuyaan

C. Pushpakyaan   **D.** Gagan Viman

Q.12 In the context of India's space research, 'Vyommitra' is the name of:

A. India's first manned Mars mission

B. An Indian spacecraft

C. An Indian robot

D. A newly found asteroid

Q.13 Which of the following statements is/are not correct?

1. As per the provisions of the Constitution, the Council of Ministers is collectively responsible to the Lok Sabha.
2. A censure motion must state the reason for its adoption.
3. A no-confidence motion must set out the grounds on which it is based.
4. If a no-confidence motion is passed by the Lok Sabha, the Council of Ministers is bound to resign.

Select the correct answer using the code given below:

A. 1, 2 and 4 only   **B.** 2 only

C. 3 only   **D.** 2, 3 and 4 only

Q.14 Consider the following statements regarding the National Commission for Scheduled Castes.

1. The Commission consists of a chairperson, a vice-chairperson, and 10 other members.
2. The Constitution of India under Article 338 assigns certain functions to this Commission.

Which among the above statements is/are correct?

A. 1 only   **B.** 2 only

C. Both 1 and 2   **D.** Neither 1 nor 2

Q.15 When can the Parliament make laws on the subjects mentioned in the State List?

1. When Rajya Sabha passes a resolution by simple majority.
2. During National Emergency.
3. When the legislation of a state passes a resolution requesting the Parliament.
4. To implement international agreements.

A. 1, 2 and 4 only   **B.** 2, 3 and 4 only

C. 2 and 4 only   **D.** All of the above

Q.16 Consider the following statements regarding the effects of National Emergency-

1. Centre assumes the executive power of the state and can give executive directions on 'any' subject.

2. Legislative power of the state is suspended and Parliament is empowered to make laws on any subject.

3. President can modify the constitutional distribution of revenues and such orders are at the discretion of President during emergency.

Which of the above statements is/are correct?

A. 1 only   **B.** 2 only
C. 3 only   **D.** 1 and 3 only

Q.17 Which of the following statement/s is/are correct about the Non-Cooperation movement?

1. The Hill tribes in northern Andhra violated the forest laws.

2. Foreign cloth being collected to be burnt in bonfires.

3. It entailed denial, renunciation, and self-discipline.

A. 1 only   **B.** 1 and 2 only
C. 2 and 3 only   **D.** 1, 2 and 3

Q.18 Which of the following statement/s is correct about Round Table Conference?

1. In January 1931, in order to create a conducive atmosphere for talks, the government lifted the ban on the Congress Party and released its leaders from prison.

2. In January 1932, the Non-cooperation Movement was resumed.

A. 1 only   **B.** 2 only
C. Both 1 and 2   **D.** Neither 1 nor 2

Q.19 Consider the following statements regarding Quit India Movement.

1. Aruna Asaf Ali, Sucheta Kripalani, and Usha Mehta are female leaders of the Quit India Movement.

2. Aruna Asaf Ali hoisted the Indian flag at Gowalia Tank Maidan in Mumbai.

Which of the statements given above is/are correct?

A. 1 only   **B.** 2 only
C. Both 1 and 2   **D.** Neither 1 nor 2

Q.20 Which of the following is not a part of Quit India Resolution?

A. An immediate end to British rule over India.
B. Formation of a provisional government of India.
C. Sanctioning a civil disobedience movement against British rule.
D. None of the above

Q.21 Which of the following countries is NOT a part of OPEC+?

A. Russia   **B.** Kazakhstan
C. Mexico   **D.** Nigeria

Q.22 The Genome Valley Excellence Award will be bestowed upon whom for their contributions to life sciences?

A. Dr James P. Allison and Dr Vas Narasimhan
B. Dr Carl H June and Dr Vas Narasimhan
C. Dr Steven Rosenberg and Dr James P. Allison
D. Dr Carl H June and Dr James P. Allison

Q.23 What is a carbon footprint?

A. The measure of radioactivity from a fossil.
B. Environmental impact because of used cells and batteries.
C. Total sets of greenhouse gas emissions by organizations, individual etc.
D. Amount of carbon content in the organic compounds.

Q.24 Members of Parliament Local Area Development Scheme (MPLADS) scheme is suspended for two years to boost the funding available for the COVID-19 fight. Before this, MPLADS funds were utilized for which of the following?

1. Purchase of Ambulances for sick/injured animals in Wildlife Sanctuaries and National Parks.

2. Purchase of books for schools, colleges, and public libraries belonging to Central, States, UTs, and Local Self-Government.

3. Helping poor families with the marriage of their first daughter

A. 1 and 2 only   **B.** 2 and 3 only
C. 1 and 3 only   **D.** 1, 2 and 3

Q.25 Kyoto protocol is related with _____.

A. Population   **B.** Resources
C. Global Warming   **D.** Pollution

Q.26 Swachh Bharat Abhiyan the mission aimed to achieve an "open-defecation free" (ODF) India by 2 October 2019, the _____ anniversary of the birth of Mahatma Gandhi.

A. 100th   **B.** 120th   **C.** 125th   **D.** 150th

Q.27 The protocol which decided to completely phase out CFC is known as :

A. Cartagena Protocol   **B.** Montreal Protocol
C. Kyoto Protocol   **D.** None of the above

Q.28 Which of the following is/are the source(s) of soil pollution?

A. Solid waste
B. Pesticides and chemical fertilizers
C. Effluent and sewage
D. All of the above

Q.29 The famous Khajurao Group of Monuments was constructed by the _______.

A. Chaulukyas   **B.** Chandelas
C. Gahadavalas   **D.** Solankis

Q.30 Akhil Bharatiya Kalidas Samaroh is organized in -

A. Bihar   **B.** Uttar Pradesh
C. Madhya Pradesh   **D.** Gujrat

Q.31 Ustad Amjad Ali Khan is famous for playing the _____.

A. tabla   **B.** violin   **C.** veena   **D.** sarod

Q.32 Gitanjali is a collection of poems by _____.

A. Rabindranath Tagore
B. Taslima Nasrin
C. Sunil Gangopadhyay
D. Bankim Chandra Chatterjee

Q.33 On which river is the Bhakra Nangal Dam situated?

A. Sutlej   **B.** Ghaggar   **C.** Ravi   **D.** Chenab

Q.34 Among the following which star is closest to Earth?

A. Alpha Centauri System

B. Proxima Centauri

C. Sirius

D. Antares

Q.35 'Sagarmatha' is the Nepali name for:

[AFCAT, 2021]

A. Mount Everest   **B.** Makalu

C. Kanchenjungha   **D.** Lhotse

Q.36 Kaziranga is known for-

A. Rhinoceros   **B.** Monkey

C. Birds   **D.** Lion

Q.37 Re-enactment of historic Dandi March of Mahatma Gandhi flagged off by Prime Minister Narendra Modi from Sabarmati Ashram reached Dandi on which day?

A. 4 April   **B.** 5 April   **C.** 6 April   **D.** 7 April

Q.38 Which among the following is first indigenous anti-radiation missile developed by India?

A. RUDRAM 1   **B.** NIRBHAY

C. BrahMos   **D.** AGNI

Q.39 Which of the following two states government have signed an agreement with the Union Ministry of Jal Shakti to implement the Ken-Betwa river interlinking project?

A. Rajasthan and Haryana

B. Uttar Pradesh and Madhya Pradesh

C. Punjab and Gujarat

D. Rajasthan and Gujarat

Q.40 The India Air Force recently gifted a legacy 1971 war helicopter to which among the following nations?

A. Pakistan   **B.** Israel

C. Bangladesh   **D.** Russia

// Smart Answer Sheet //

Correct Indicates percentage of students who answered questions correctly.

Skipped Indicates percentage of students who skipped questions.

Q.	Ans.	Correct / Skipped
1	C	77.29 % / 0.0 %
2	C	63.84 % / 1.75 %
3	C	81.31 % / 0.0 %
4	A	67.34 % / 1.94 %
5	D	28.39 % / 3.33 %
6	D	29.84 % / 4.81 %
7	A	16.69 % / 4.12 %
8	A	14.28 % / 4.93 %

Q.	Ans.	Correct / Skipped
9	D	76.45 % / 0.0 %
10	B	89.3 % / 0.0 %
11	A	87.55 % / 0.0 %
12	C	78.11 % / 0.0 %
13	C	62.76 % / 1.66 %
14	B	46.46 % / 1.84 %
15	C	43.97 % / 1.75 %
16	A	50.95 % / 1.9 %

Q.	Ans.	Correct / Skipped
17	D	42.06 % / 1.31 %
18	A	63.26 % / 1.15 %
19	C	51.43 % / 1.18 %
20	D	47.4 % / 1.13 %
21	D	62.07 % / 1.76 %
22	B	59.69 % / 1.39 %
23	C	42.18 % / 1.52 %
24	A	58.7 % / 1.18 %

Q.	Ans.	Correct / Skipped
25	C	56.24 % / 1.47 %
26	D	46.52 % / 1.1 %
27	B	54.7 % / 1.1 %
28	D	43.44 % / 1.38 %
29	B	66.12 % / 1.95 %
30	C	59.87 % / 1.14 %
31	D	43.09 % / 1.98 %
32	A	52.27 % / 1.2 %

Q.	Ans.	Correct / Skipped
33	A	53.84 % / 1.23 %
34	B	60.75 % / 1.67 %
35	A	41.06 % / 1.04 %
36	A	62.38 % / 1.58 %
37	B	55.97 % / 1.21 %
38	A	67.2 % / 1.46 %
39	B	44.18 % / 1.84 %
40	C	59.25 % / 1.62 %

Performance Analysis

Avg. Score (%)	32.5%
Toppers Score (%)	65.0%
Your Score	

Q.1 Brisbane will host the 2032 Olympics, In which country it is located?

A. Australia **B.** Portugal
C. New Zealand **D.** Sweden

Q.2 Which country won the 2022 U19 Cricket World Cup title?

A. India **B.** England
C. West Indies **D.** Sri Lanka

Q.3 According to the latest Reserve Bank of India study on State finances, capital spending is maximum on:

[Indian Military Academy (IMA), 2018], [Officers Training Academy (OTA), 2018]

A. rural development

B. water supply and sanitation

C. urban development

D. education

Q.4 The natural rate of unemployment hypothesis was advocated by:

[Indian Military Academy (IMA), 2018], [Officers Training Academy (OTA), 2018]

A. Milton Friedman **B.** A. W. Phillips
C. J. M. Keynes **D.** R. G. Lipsey

Q.5 With regard to the cabinet decision in July 2018, the percentage increase in Minimum Support Price (MSP) is maximum in which one of the following crops?

[Indian Military Academy (IMA), 2018], [Officers Training Academy (OTA), 2018]

A. Jowar (Hybrid) **B.** Bajra
C. Maize **D.** Soya bean

Q.6 The Economic historian, who has used the data collected by Buchanan-Hamilton to support the thesis of deindustrialization in the 19th century India, is:

[Indian Military Academy (IMA), 2018], [Officers Training Academy (OTA), 2018]

A. Tirthankar Roy

B. Amiya Kumar Bagchi

C. Sabyasachi Bhattacharya

D. Irfan Habib

Q.7 _______ was invented by laser.

A. Ah-taylor **B.** TH-Mammon
C. Le de forest **D.** Thomas Edison

Q.8 Which technology company has introduced the health monitoring device 'Halo Band'?

A. Microsoft **B.** Apple
C. Google **D.** Amazon

Q.9 Bluetooth technology allows:

A. Wireless communication between equipments

B. Signal transmission on mobile phones only

C. Landline to mobile phone communication

D. Satellite television communication

Q.10 "Chunauti"- Next Generation Start-up Challenge Contest, recently in news is launched by which of the following ministry?

A. Ministry of Agriculture

B. Ministry of Trade and Commerce

C. Ministry of Electronics and Information Technology

D. NITI Aayog

Q.11 The Foreign Minister of which country is on a two-day visit to India from 5 April 2021?

A. Russia **B.** Mongolia
C. Turkey **D.** China

Q.12 The Aero India 2021 gathering, the premier aerospace and defense exhibition in the world, kicked off at _______.

A. Air Force Station Yelahanka, Bengaluru

B. Air Force Station Jodhpur, Rajasthan

C. Air Force Station Hasimara, West Bengal

D. Air Force Station Agartala, Tripura

Q.13 Who bagged Dadasaheb Phalke Awards for 'Best Actor' in February 2021?

A. Akshay Kumar **B.** Salman Khan
C. Hrithik Roshan **D.** Amitabh Bachchan

Q.14 The river Godavari originates in the state of _____.

A. Madhya Pradesh **B.** Chhatisgarh
C. Maharashtra **D.** Odisha

Q.15 Which of the following countries share the longest international border with India?

A. Bangladesh **B.** China
C. Pakistan **D.** Myanmar

Q.16 Which cities are connected by Golden Quadrilateral?

A. Srinagar-Tamilnadu- Silchar-Porbandar

B. Delhi-Amritsar

C. Delhi-Mumbai-Chennai-Kolkata

D. Delhi- Assam-Bangalore-Gujarat

Q.17 Which Indian state produces the largest quantity of Pulses?

A. Madhya Pradesh **B.** Uttar Pradesh
C. Rajasthan **D.** Bengal

Q.18 Agreement on Subsidies and Countervailing Measures (ASCM) is related to which of the following organizations?

A. United States Trade Representative (USTR)

B. World Trade Organization (WTO)

C. United Nations Office for Outer Space Affairs

D. United Nations Conference on Trade and Development (UNCTAD)

Q.19 NIRVIK Scheme, recently in news is related to -

A. National Programme for Public Distribution System

B. Pension scheme for retail traders and self-employed persons

C. Provide enhanced insurance cover and reduce premium for exporters.

D. Assistance to the North Eastern States to build well-endowed resources

Q.20 WHO's REPLACE campaign is related to

A. Replace all cooling systems in government buildings with energy efficient cooling system.

B. Replace all petrol and diesel vehicles to Electric Vehicles by 2030.

C. Eliminate industrially produced trans-fatty acids from the global food supply.

D. Provide protein rich food to children in the government schools.

Q.21 Eat Right Movement has been launched by which among the following?

A. Food Safety and Standards Authority of India (FSSAI)

B. World Health Organisation (WHO)

C. World Trade Organization (WTO)

D. Food and Agricultural Organization

Q.22 What is the meaning of "Incineration" in waste disposal method?

A. Burning of waste

B. Deposit the refused and compost it with the builder

C. Combustion in absence of oxygen

D. Spreading the waste on fields

Q.23 What does the pollution in simple terms means :

A. Uncontaminated environment

B. Contaminated environment

C. Uncontaminated and contaminated environment

D. Nice environment

Q.24 'Mohiniyattam', is a traditional dance which originated in the state of ______ in India.

A. Assam   **B.** West Bengal

C. Kerala   **D.** Andhra Pradesh

Q.25 Which of the following questions is/are correct regarding Preamble to the Indian Constitution?

1. The Congress party adopted a resolution to establish a socialist pattern of society in its Avadi session in 1955.

2. The word socialist is added by the 42nd amendment in 1976 in the Preamble of the Indian Constitution.

3. Preamble is a part of the Constitution and is justiciable.

A. 1 and 2 only   **B.** 2 and 3 only

C. 1 and 3 only   **D.** 1, 2 and 3

Q.26 Which of the following statements is/are correct about the Finance Commission of India?

1. The eligibility of members of the Finance Commission is determined by the President.

2. The First Finance Commission was constituted in 1951.

3. The President of India constitutes the Finance Commission every 5 years.

4. Chairman of Finance Commission submits his report to the Parliament of India.

A. 1 and 2 only   **B.** 2 and 3 only

C. 3 and 4 only   **D.** 1 and 4 only

Q.27 The expenditure charged upon the Consolidated Fund of India is not subjected to vote but the discussion can be held. which of the following forms a part of the expenditure charged upon the CFI?

1. Expenditure declared by the constitution or by Parliament by law to be so charged.

2. Debt charges for which the Government of India is liable.

3. Any sums required to satisfy any judgment, decree, or award of any Court.

4. Salary, allowances, and pension payable to or in respect of the Comptroller and Auditor General of India and the Judges of the Supreme Court.

A. 1, 2 and 3 only   **B.** 2, 3 and 4 only

C. 1, 3 and 4 only   **D.** 1, 2, 3 and 4

Q.28 The constitution of India describes India as-

A. A Union of States

B. Quasi-federal

C. A federation of state and union territories

D. A Unitary State

Q.29 Which of the following statements is not correct with respect to Pitts India Act of 1784?

A. It distinguished between the commercial and political functions of the Company.

B. It provided for the establishment of a Supreme Court at Calcutta.

C. It created a new body called Board of Control.

D. The territories in India were for the first time called the 'British possessions in India'.

Q.30 Consider the following statements with reference to Indian Councils Act, 1861

1. Legislative councils had no control over budget.

2. Legislative councils could discuss the executive action.

3. Secretary of state could disallow a legislation.

Which of the above statements are incorrect?

Select the correct answer using the code given below:

A. 1 and 2 only   **B.** 1 and 3

C. 2 only   **D.** 1, 2 and 3 only

Q.31 Mahatma Gandhi worked as an editor in which of the following newspapers?

A. Indian Opinion

B. The Leader

C. Independent

A. A and B   **B.** Only B   **C.** B and C   **D.** Only A

Q.32 Free trade with Britain led to de-industrialization in (up to 1880s) India due to which of the following reasons?

1. Free trade was only one-sided as Indian goods were still charged with heavy levies.

2. Indian handmade goods were at disadvantage competing with machine-based British goods.

3. Indian goods were never popular in the western market and Indian weavers had thrived only on the Indian market.

A. 1 only   **B.** 2 and 3

C. 1 and 2   **D.** 1, 2 and 3

Q.33 Bharat Mahila Parishad was founded by who among the following women reformers?

A. Sarla Devi Chaudhurani

B. Ramabai Ranade

C. Pandita Ramabai Saraswati

D. Mehribai Tata

Q.34 Lord Curzon formed Police commission under the leadership of ______.

A. Sir John Shore   **B.** Sir Andrew Fraser

C. Sir William Hunter   **D.** None of the Above

Q.35 Which of the following routes was selected by C. Rajaji for the Salt Satyagraha March?

A. Tiruchirappalli to Vedaranyam

B. Erode to Salem

C. Tiruchirappali to Erode

D. Erode to Vedaranyam

Q.36 Which of the following publications was started by Khan Abdul Gaffar Khan in 1928?

A. Khudai Khitamatgar

B. Pakhtoon

C. Young India

D. India Awakens

Q.37 The Constituent Assembly (elected for an undivided India) met for the first time on ______.

A. 14th August 1947

B. 9th December 1946

C. 3rd June 1947

D. 15th November 1939

Q.38 Who among the following was the first permanent President of the Constituent Assembly of India?

[Super TET Paper - I, 2019]

A. Dr. Sachchidananda Singh

B. Dr. Rajendra Prasad

C. Dr. B. R. Ambedkar

D. Prof. H. C. Mookerjee

Q.39 ____ Schedule of the Constitution of India deals with the names of the states and their territorial jurisdiction.

A. First   **B.** Second   **C.** Third   **D.** Fourth

Q.40 Which of the following Union Territories has a Chief Minister?

A. Dadra and Nagar Haveli

B. Andaman and Nicobar Islands

C. Puducherry

D. Chandigarh

// Smart Answer Sheet //

Correct Indicates percentage of students who answered questions correctly.

Skipped Indicates percentage of students who skipped questions.

Q.	Ans.	Correct / Skipped
1	A	55.1 % / 1.44 %
2	A	54.03 % / 1.28 %
3	A	67.87 % / 1.76 %
4	A	41.64 % / 1.96 %
5	B	64.85 % / 1.74 %
6	B	44.76 % / 1.29 %
7	B	61.02 % / 1.05 %
8	D	62.03 % / 1.47 %

Q.	Ans.	Correct / Skipped
9	A	45.03 % / 1.95 %
10	C	50.37 % / 1.06 %
11	A	56.83 % / 1.07 %
12	A	54.98 % / 1.84 %
13	A	65.73 % / 1.88 %
14	C	44.41 % / 1.38 %
15	A	42.15 % / 1.37 %
16	C	66.06 % / 1.21 %

Q.	Ans.	Correct / Skipped
17	A	59.03 % / 1.62 %
18	B	27.3 % / 3.55 %
19	C	30.33 % / 3.0 %
20	C	17.65 % / 4.31 %
21	A	20.61 % / 4.64 %
22	A	63.46 % / 1.37 %
23	B	59.28 % / 1.85 %
24	C	63.16 % / 1.62 %

Q.	Ans.	Correct / Skipped
25	A	15.84 % / 4.92 %
26	B	48.57 % / 1.45 %
27	D	48.51 % / 1.72 %
28	A	69.71 % / 1.52 %
29	B	60.52 % / 1.21 %
30	C	65.88 % / 1.5 %
31	D	43.62 % / 1.3 %
32	C	57.84 % / 1.29 %

Q.	Ans.	Correct / Skipped
33	B	55.31 % / 1.42 %
34	B	57.39 % / 1.21 %
35	A	43.59 % / 1.68 %
36	B	43.05 % / 1.59 %
37	B	43.17 % / 1.82 %
38	B	62.64 % / 1.4 %
39	A	41.53 % / 1.41 %
40	C	67.99 % / 1.41 %

Performance Analysis	
Avg. Score (%)	55.0%
Toppers Score (%)	55.0%
Your Score	

Q.1 Three persons walking together in the morning. The distance of their one footstep is 80 cm, 85 cm, and 90 cm respectively. How much minimum distance they cover so that distance can be measured with the complete number (integer number) of their footsteps completely?

A. 122.40 m   **B.** 123.45 m
C. 244. 80 m   **D.** 122.50 m

Q.2 A student obtained 87 average marks in 8 subjects. If the students highest gaining subject is 2 marks more than the second-ranked subject. If these two subjects are eliminated then the average of the remaining subjects will become 85. The highest marked subject is:

A. 91   **B.** 89   **C.** 94   **D.** 96

Q.3 A shopkeeper sells rice on 10% profit and also uses 20% less weight, his total percent of profit is:

A. 25%   **B.** 20%
C. 10%   **D.** None of these

Q.4 What is the value of $\left(\cot 60° + \dfrac{1}{\sqrt{3}}\right)$?

A. $\dfrac{4}{\sqrt{3}}$ **B.** $\dfrac{(2\sqrt{2}+\sqrt{3})}{2}$
C. $\dfrac{2}{\sqrt{3}}$ **D.** $\dfrac{2\sqrt{2}+1}{\sqrt{2}}$

Q.5 Direction: What will come in place of the question mark (?) in the following number series?

$$8, \; 24, \; 12, \; 36, \; 18, \; 54, \; ?$$

A. 27   **B.** 108   **C.** 68   **D.** 72

Q.6 If $\dfrac{(2\sin\theta - \cos\theta)}{(\cos\theta + \sin\theta)} = 1$ then the value of $\cot\theta$ is:

A. $\dfrac{1}{2}$ **B.** $\dfrac{1}{3}$ **C.** 3   **D.** 2

Ques (7-10):Direction: Study the data carefully and answer the questions given below:

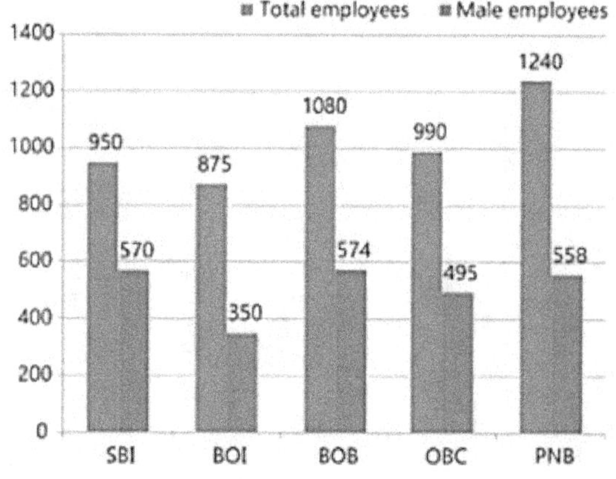

Q.7 The number of female employees working in OBC and PNB together is approximately how much percentage less than the total number of employees working in PNB?

A. 10%   **B.** 8%   **C.** 5%   **D.** 12%

Q.8 What is the average number of female employees working in all the banks?

A. 503.6   **B.** 523.6
C. 533.6   **D.** None of these

Q.9 What is the ratio of number of male employees who are working in SBI and BOI together to the number of female employees who are working in same bank?

A. 190 : 193   **B.** 83 : 90
C. 184 : 181   **D.** 101 : 104

Q.10 The total number of employees who are working in BOI is 80% of the total number of employees who are working in BOB. Find the percentage of female employees who are working in BOI if the number of male employees is 648.

A. 75%   **B.** 60%   **C.** 80%   **D.** 25%

Q.11 If $\sqrt{1 + \dfrac{y}{16}} = \dfrac{7}{4}$, then find the value of 5y – 15.

A. 110   **B.** 130   **C.** 150   **D.** 160

Q.12 If $\tan^4\theta + \tan^2\theta = 1$, then the value of $\cos^4\theta + \cos^2\theta$ is:

A. 8   **B.** 10   **C.** 1   **D.** 2

Q.13 The ratio of the three numbers is $2 : 3 : 4$. If the sum of its squares is 1856, then the number are:

A. 8, 12, 16   **B.** 16,24, 32
C. 12, 18, 24   **D.** None of these

Q.14 Calculate the distance (in cm) of the chord from the centre of the circle, if the chord of length 48 cm is drawn in the circle of radius 25 cm.

A. 7   **B.** 14   **C.** 49   **D.** 56

Q.15 The value of sin (45° + θ) – cos (45° – θ) is:

A. 1   **B.** 0   **C.** 2 cos θ   **D.** 2 sin θ

Q.16 In ΔABC, ∠ABC = 70°, ∠BCA = 40°. O is the point of intersection of the perpendicular bisectors of the sides, then the angle ∠BOC is

A. 100°   **B.** 120°   **C.** 130°   **D.** 140°

Q.17 Select the option that is related to the third term in the same way as the second term is related to the first term.

Pitch : Cricket :: Arena : ?

A. Baseball   **B.** Football
C. Wrestling   **D.** Skating

Q.18 In the following question, select the odd letter/letters from the given alternatives.

A. DHM **B.** GKO **C.** IMQ **D.** LPT

Q.19 In the following question, select the missing number from the given series.

1, 2, 6, 42, ?

A. 1696 **B.** 1036 **C.** 1806 **D.** 984

Q.20 Direction: In a certain code language, '×' represents '+', '÷' represents '×', '-' represents '÷' and '+' represents '-'. Find out the answer to the following question.

42 + 36 − 6 ÷ 15 × 8 ÷ 20 + 20 − 5 = ?

A. 100 **B.** 108 **C.** 105 **D.** 101

Q.21 Direction: In the question below there are three statements followed by three conclusions I, II and III. You have to take the three given statements to be true even if they seem to be at variance from commonly known facts and then decide which of the given conclusions logically follows from the given statements disregarding commonly known facts.

Statements:

I. Some cats are dogs.

II. All dogs are monkeys.

III. All monkeys are pigs.

Conclusions:

I. Some cats are monkeys.

II. No pig is cat.

III. All dogs are pigs.

A. Only conclusion I and III follow

B. Only conclusion II follows

C. Only conclusion II and III follow

D. None of the above

Q.22 Four pairs of number have been given, out of which three are alike in some manner, while one is different. Choose out the odd one.

A. 23 - 18 **B.** 30 - 20 **C.** 62 - 8 **D.** 21 - 9

Q.23 Pointing to a child, a lady named Sheela said, "He is the son of my maternal grandmother's only daughter". How is the child's father related to Sheela?

A. Father **B.** Son

C. Son-in-law **D.** Uncle

Q.24 A series is given with one term missing. Select the correct alternative from the given ones that will complete the series.

EJK, DIJ, BGH, ?

A. YDE **B.** XED **C.** YED **D.** XCE

Q.25 Six friends are sitting around a circular table facing towards the center. A and B sitting opposite to each other. C sits exactly in the middle of B and D. D sits second to the right of F. D and E are sitting opposite to each other. Who among the following is sitting immediate left of A?

A. D **B.** F **C.** C **D.** B

Q.26 Direction: In the following question, four words are given, out of which three are alike in a certain manner and the fourth one is different. Choose the odd one.

A. Rhombus **B.** Trapezium

C. Parallelogram **D.** Pentagon

Q.27 In the following question, four words are given, out of which three are alike in a certain manner and the fourth one is different. Choose the different one.

A. Cattail **B.** Cactus

C. Lotus **D.** Water Lilly

Q.28 Find the wrong term in following series.

256, 289, 324, 351, 400, 441.

A. 351 **B.** 400 **C.** 289 **D.** 441

Q.29 Ankit walks 7 km from school, turns right, and walks 5 km, then he turns left and walks 11 km. Again turns right and walks for 5 km. In the end, he notices that he is facing towards the east. In which direction was the school from the present place?

A. North - East **B.** South – West

C. South **D.** South - East

Q.30 What should come in the place of question mark (?) in the following number series?

27, 40.5, 60.75, 91.125, ?,

A. 135.6875 **B.** 136.6875

C. 137.6875 **D.** 138.6875

// Smart Answer Sheet //

| Correct | Indicates percentage of students who answered questions correctly. |

| Skipped | Indicates percentage of students who skipped questions. |

Q.	Ans.	Correct / Skipped		Q.	Ans.	Correct / Skipped		Q.	Ans.	Correct / Skipped		Q.	Ans.	Correct / Skipped		Q.	Ans.	Correct / Skipped
1	A	25.95 % / 10.95 %		7	C	31.55 % / 25.19 %		13	B	49.11 % / 20.61 %		19	C	19.08 % / 23.41 %		25	B	48.09 % / 28.75 %
2	C	50.89 % / 11.2 %		8	D	21.37 % / 35.37 %		14	A	43.0 % / 18.32 %		20	B	71.5 % / 11.2 %		26	D	45.55 % / 32.57 %
3	D	31.81 % / 18.06 %		9	C	41.98 % / 26.98 %		15	B	24.43 % / 24.42 %		21	A	63.1 % / 17.05 %		27	B	41.73 % / 31.04 %
4	C	55.47 % / 15.78 %		10	D	18.83 % / 35.11 %		16	D	40.71 % / 17.31 %		22	A	53.69 % / 15.01 %		28	A	51.65 % / 23.16 %
5	A	55.47 % / 22.65 %		11	C	38.42 % / 21.12 %		17	C	53.69 % / 16.03 %		23	A	40.71 % / 24.18 %		29	B	35.37 % / 39.95 %
6	A	24.17 % / 30.79 %		12	C	28.5 % / 18.57 %		18	A	42.24 % / 34.35 %		24	A	40.46 % / 16.79 %		30	B	45.29 % / 23.16 %

Performance Analysis

Avg. Score (%)	43.33%
Toppers Score (%)	100.0%
Your Score	

Q.1 What will come at the place of question mark ?

1, 9, 25, 49, ?, 121

A. 100   **B.** 91   **C.** 64   **D.** 81

Q.2 What will come at the place of question mark?

4, 7, 12, 19, 28, ?

A. 49   **B.** 36   **C.** 30   **D.** 39

Q.3 The numerical value of $\dfrac{5}{\sec^2\theta} + \dfrac{2}{1+\cot^2\theta} + 3\sin^2\theta$ is?

A. 5   **B.** 2   **C.** 3   **D.** 4

Q.4 A bag contains 5 green, 7 yellow, and 4 red balls. Three balls are drawn at random, find the probability that all the balls are of the same color.

A. $\dfrac{5}{46}$ **B.** $\dfrac{9}{70}$ **C.** $\dfrac{7}{78}$ **D.** $\dfrac{7}{80}$

Q.5 P can do a piece of work in 15 days and Q in 20 days. With help of R, they finish the work in 5 days. In how many days R alone can do the same work?

A. 10   **B.** 12   **C.** 15   **D.** 18

Q.6 A cricketer scored some runs in his continuous 9 innings. He scored 100 runs in his 10th innings and increases his average by 8 runs. What was the average of his runs at the end of 10th innings?

A. 20   **B.** 24   **C.** 28   **D.** 32

Ques (7-10):Directions: Study the following information to answer the given question.

Total number of passengers travelling from Patna Junction to different districts = 12000

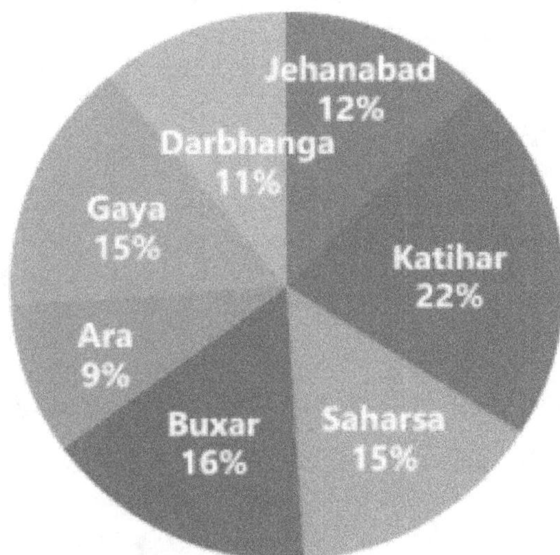

Q.7 The number of passengers travelling from Patna to Buxar is what per cent more than the number of passengers travelling to Jehanabad?

A. 20%   **B.** 25%   **C.** $33\frac{1}{3}\%$ **D.** $66\frac{2}{3}\%$

Q.8 The number of passengers travelling from Patna to Gaya is what per cent of the total number of passengers travelling from Patna to Darbhanga and Ara together?

A. $133\frac{1}{3}\%$ **B.** 75%   **C.** $66\frac{2}{3}\%$ **D.** 33%

Q.9 What is the average number of passengers travelling from Patna to Saharsa, Katihar and Buxar together?

A. 2140   **B.** 2220   **C.** 2020   **D.** 2120

Q.10 Among the passengers who are travelling from Patna to Katihar, 42% are female adults and 38% are male adults. What is the number of children? (Transgenders are not to be considered.)

A. 268   **B.** 278

C. 288   **D.** None of these

Q.11 Direction: What will come in place of the question mark (?) in the following number series?

$17, 18, 57, 290, ?$

A. 1455   **B.** 1746   **C.** 2037   **D.** 2228

Q.12 Find the minimum number of straight lines required to make the given figure.

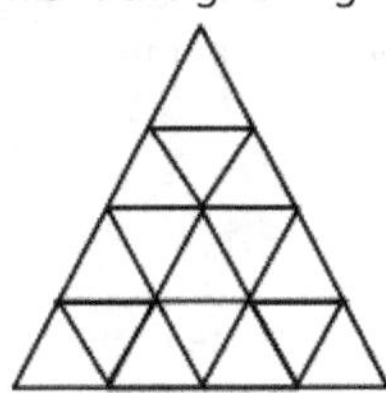

A. 11   **B.** 12

C. 13   **D.** None of these

Q.13 The greatest five digit number which is exactly divisible by the number $12, 18, 21,$ and 28 is:

A. 98,286   **B.** 92,888   **C.** 99,284   **D.** 99,792

Q.14 A train of length 350 meters can cross a pole and platform of a certain length in 21 seconds and 36 seconds respectively, then what is the length of the platform?

A. 200 meters   **B.** 250 meters

C. 350 meters   **D.** 300 meters

Q.15 Find the simple interest on Rs. 3000 at $\dfrac{25}{4}\%$ per annum for the period from 4th Feb, 2005 to 18th April, 2005.

A. Rs. 45.70   **B.** Rs. 34.65

C. Rs. 38.50   **D.** Rs. 37.50

Q.16 In the following question, find out the alternative which will replace the question mark.

Pediatricians : Children :: Podiatrists : ?

A. Ankle   **B.** Intestine   **C.** Uterus   **D.** Liver

Q.17 A person buys several fruits at the rate of 16 for Rs 24 and sells them at the rate of 8 for Rs 18. What is his gain percent?

A. 50%   **B.** 60%   **C.** 40%   **D.** 25%

Q.18 Find the odd word from the given following alternatives?

A. Tuticorin   **B.** Paradip   **C.** Haldia   **D.** Delhi

Q.19 Direction: In following alphabet series, one term missing as shown by question mark. Choose missing term from options.
SGU, VJX, ?, BPD, ESG

A. ZMA   **B.** YMA   **C.** YNA   **D.** YMB

Q.20 Direction: Find the next term of the given series :
124, 62, 60, 30, 28, ?

A. 26   **B.** 20   **C.** 15   **D.** 14

Q.21 Select the correct option that will fill in the blank and complete the series.
2, 3, 11, 38, __, 227, 443

A. 98   **B.** 100   **C.** 102   **D.** 104

Q.22 A man is facing north-west. He turns 45° in the clockwise direction, then 90° in the anticlockwise direction and then another 180° in the same direction. Finally he turns 45° in clockwise direction. Which direction is he facing now?

A. North - west   **B.** South - east
C. North - east   **D.** South - west

Q.23 Direction: In these series, you will be looking at both the letter pattern and the number pattern. Fill the blank in the middle of the series or end of the series.

CMM, EOO, GQQ, _____, KUU

A. GRR   **B.** GSS   **C.** ISS   **D.** ITT

Q.24 In the following question choose the appropriate option from the given alternatives.

Pigeon : Peace : : White flag : ?

A. Friendship   **B.** Victory
C. Surrender   **D.** War

Q.25 Find the odd word from the given alternatives.

A. Teacher   **B.** Lawyer   **C.** Doctor   **D.** Manager

Q.26 Direction: Study the following information and answer the question given below.

M, N, P, R, T, W, F, and H are sitting around a circle facing the centre. P is third to the left of M and second to the right of T. N is second to the right of P. R is second to the right of W, who is second to the right of M. F is not an immediate neighbour of P. Who is to the immediate right of P?

A. H   **B.** F   **C.** R   **D.** M

Q.27 The average age of three girls is 16 years. If their ages are in the ratio $4:5:7$, then the age of the youngest girl is

A. 21 years   **B.** 15 years   **C.** 12 years   **D.** 16 years

Q.28 Direction: In the question below are given two statements followed by two conclusions numbered I and II. You have to take the given statements to be true even if they seem

to be at variance with commonly known facts. Read all the conclusions and then decide which of the given conclusions logically follows from the given statements disregarding commonly known facts.

Statements:

Some pens are bags.

Some gates are bags.

Conclusions:

I. All pens are gates.

II. Some pens are gates.

A.   Only I follows
B.   Only II follows
C.   Either I or II follows
D.   Neither I nor II follows

Q.29 The following equation is incorrect. Which two signs should be interchanged to correct the equation?

18 ÷ 2 - 25 × 9 + 6 = 38

A. + and ×   **B.** + and ÷   **C.** - and +   **D.** ÷ and ×

Q.30 In the following question, select the related letters from the given alternatives.

ADVICE : WZREVX :: MATURE : ?

A. ZNGZVI   **B.** FNZGVI
C. ZNFGVI   **D.** ZNFGIV

// Smart Answer Sheet //

Correct Indicates percentage of students who answered questions correctly.

Skipped Indicates percentage of students who skipped questions.

Q.	Ans.	Correct / Skipped
1	D	54.23 % / 7.46 %
2	D	53.23 % / 12.94 %
3	A	42.29 % / 19.4 %
4	D	24.38 % / 16.42 %
5	B	35.82 % / 29.35 %
6	C	32.34 % / 32.83 %

Q.	Ans.	Correct / Skipped
7	C	63.18 % / 14.43 %
8	B	44.28 % / 27.86 %
9	D	44.28 % / 16.91 %
10	D	34.33 % / 29.85 %
11	C	25.37 % / 28.86 %
12	B	41.29 % / 29.85 %

Q.	Ans.	Correct / Skipped
13	D	38.31 % / 20.89 %
14	B	45.77 % / 22.39 %
15	D	21.89 % / 27.36 %
16	A	32.84 % / 28.85 %
17	A	41.29 % / 18.41 %
18	D	38.81 % / 33.33 %

Q.	Ans.	Correct / Skipped
19	B	32.34 % / 31.84 %
20	D	78.11 % / 6.96 %
21	C	39.8 % / 17.91 %
22	B	44.78 % / 12.93 %
23	C	63.18 % / 23.39 %
24	C	38.31 % / 27.36 %

Q.	Ans.	Correct / Skipped
25	D	30.85 % / 36.31 %
26	A	36.82 % / 27.36 %
27	C	62.69 % / 22.88 %
28	D	50.25 % / 10.45 %
29	A	22.39 % / 42.78 %
30	C	57.71 % / 9.95 %

Performance Analysis

Performance Analysis	
Avg. Score (%)	43.33%
Toppers Score (%)	100.0%
Your Score	

Ques (1-4):Direction: Answer the following question based on the information given below.

The table below shows the number of cases of various crimes reported at police stations in different states in 2015-16.

State	Domestic Violance	Dowry	Rape	Molestation	Trafficking
UP	354	496	263	132	342
MP	376	225	216	125	117
HP	87	125	53	56	57
Kerala	535	352	226	364	126
Gujarat	455	225	252	175	144
Bihar	475	576	675	764	852
Punjab	245	256	259	261	263
Assam	278	274	276	252	363

Q.1 The Domestic violance and Dowry cases reported in Bihar are what percent more/less than the Rape and Trafficking cases reported in Punjab?

A. 98.7% less   **B.** 101.3% more

C. 101.3% less   **D.** 98.7% more

Q.2 Based on the average number of Rape and Molestation cases reported per state, Molestation is approximately how many times as prevalent as Rape?

A. 1.04   **B.** 0.96   **C.** 0.92   **D.** 0.86

Q.3 The total number of Dowry and Molestation cases reported in UP is approximate what percent of the total cases reported in that state, across all crimes?

A. 40   **B.** 45   **C.** 37   **D.** 47

Q.4 In which state are the least number of cases reported?

A. UP   **B.** Punjab   **C.** MP   **D.** HP

Q.5 In triangle ABC, right-angled at B, if $\tan A = \dfrac{1}{\sqrt{3}}$, find the value of:

$$\sin A \cos C + \cos A \sin C$$

A. 1   **B.** 2   **C.** 3   **D.** 4

Q.6 Evaluate the following:

$$\frac{\sin 30° + \tan 45° - cosec\, 60°}{\sec 30° + \cos 60° + \cot 45°}$$

A. $\dfrac{44-24\sqrt{3}}{11}$ **B.** $\dfrac{43-24\sqrt{3}}{11}$ **C.** $\dfrac{45-24\sqrt{3}}{11}$ **D.** $\dfrac{46-24\sqrt{3}}{11}$

Q.7 Evaluate:

$$\frac{\sin^2 63° + \sin^2 27°}{\cos^2 17° + \cos^2 73°}$$

A. 1   **B.** 2   **C.** 3   **D.** 4

Q.8 A man sells an article on Rs. 280 and gets 40% profit. Then find the cost price of the article.

[AFCAT, 2021]

A. Rs. 180   **B.** Rs. 200   **C.** Rs. 240   **D.** Rs. 220

Q.9 Two numbers are respectively 20% and 50% of a third number. What percent is the first number of the second?

A. 10%   **B.** 20%   **C.** 30%   **D.** 40%

Q.10 In $\triangle ABC, O$ is the incentre and $\angle BOC = 135°$. The measure of $\angle BAC$ is:

A. 80°   **B.** 45°   **C.** 90°   **D.** 55°

Q.11 Find the surface area of a sphere of radius 14 cm.

A. 616 cm²   **B.** 2584 cm²

C. 2464 cm²   **D.** 1232 cm²

Q.12 The product of two numbers is $\dfrac{y}{x}$ If one of the numbers is $\dfrac{x}{y^2}$ then the other number is:

A. $\dfrac{y^3}{x^2}$ **B.** y **C.** $\dfrac{x^3}{y^3}$ **D.** $\dfrac{y^3}{x}$

Q.13 A train 220 m long is running at a speed of 36 km/hr. What time will it take to cross a 110 m long tunnel?

A. 21 sec   **B.** 27 sec   **C.** 30 sec   **D.** 33 sec

Q.14 A car travels a certain distance at 70 km/h and comes back at 30 km/h. Find the average speed for total journey.

A. 42 km/hr   **B.** 50 km/hr   **C.** 34 km/hr   **D.** 58 km/hr

Q.15 The score of 9 Students are : $7, 5, 4, 3, 9, 8,\ 2, 6, 5$. Then find the median of the score is?

A. 6   **B.** 3   **C.** 4   **D.** 5

Q.16 A and B together can do a piece of work in 12 days while A alone can do the same work in 30 days. B alone can do it in

A. 18 days   **B.** 20 days   **C.** 15 days   **D.** 22 days

Q.17 The LCM of two numbers is 90 times their HCF. The sum of LCM and HCF is 1456 . If one of the number is 160 , then what is the other number?

[Territorial Army Officer, 2019]

A. 120   **B.** 136   **C.** 144   **D.** 184

Q.18 At what rate of interest will a sum of Rs. 4,500 amount to Rs. 6,525 at simple interest for 5 years?

A. 8%   **B.** 9%   **C.** 10%   **D.** 12%

Q.19 Select the missing number from the given series?

3, 11, 38, 102, ?

A. 201   **B.** 103   **C.** 227   **D.** 305

Q.20 Four number-pairs have been given, out of which three are alike in some manner and one is different. Choose out the odd one.

A. 9 : 738 **B.** 6 : 210 **C.** 8 : 504 **D.** 7 : 336

Q.21 Six People A, B, C, D, E and F, are sitting in two rows with three people in each row. E is not sitting at any end of any row. D is sitting on the left of F and is at second place. C is sitting next to E and diagonally opposite to D. B is sitting next to F. On the basis of given information who is sitting opposite to B?

A. D **B.** F **C.** A **D.** E

Q.22 In the following questions, a series is given with one term missing. Choose the correct alternative from the given options.

7, 20, 59, 176, ___ , 1580

A. 527 **B.** 526 **C.** 524 **D.** 555

Q.23 City P is to the East of city Q and city R is to the south of city P. If city S is to the west of city R, then in which direction is city S located in respect of city P?

A. South **B.** North East
C. South West **D.** West

Q.24 Choose the odd numerical pair/group in the following options.

A. 55 - 62 **B.** 34 - 43 **C.** 62 - 71 **D.** 83 - 92

Q.25 Direction: In the following question below are given some statements followed by some conclusions. Taking the given statements to be true even if they seem to be at variance from commonly known facts, read all the conclusions and then decide which of the given conclusions logically follows the given statements.

Statements:

I. All doors are room.

II. No room is a window.

Conclusions:

I. No door is a window.

II. No window is a room.

A. Only conclusion (I) follows

B. Only conclusion (II) follows

C. Both conclusion follow

D. Neither conclusion (I) nor conclusion (II) follows

Q.26 Four letter clusters have been given, out of which three are alike in some manner, while one is different. Select the odd letter cluster.

A. EGKQ **B.** ACGM **C.** GIMT **D.** KMQW

Q.27 11 $ 11 = 99, 45 $ 15 = 615, 44 $ 12 = 472, then find the value of 32 $ 11 = ?

A. 115 **B.** 272 **C.** 600 **D.** 309

Q.28 In the given matrix which option will replace the question mark.

11	7	16
27	19	64
39	22	?

A. 441 **B.** 625 **C.** 289 **D.** 169

Q.29 Identify the odd one from the given groups of letters.

A. IR **B.** OL **C.** EV **D.** CX

Q.30 In the following question, select the related letters from the given alternatives.

OPEN : PRHR : : CLOSE : ?

A. DNRWJ **B.** PRJQD **C.** DMPRF **D.** BKNQD

// Smart Answer Sheet //

Correct Indicates percentage of students who answered questions correctly.

Skipped Indicates percentage of students who skipped questions.

Q.	Ans.	Correct / Skipped
1	B	28.46 % / 26.92 %
2	B	18.46 % / 28.46 %
3	A	20.0 % / 37.69 %
4	D	39.23 % / 25.39 %
5	A	20.0 % / 46.92 %
6	B	20.77 % / 40.0 %

Q.	Ans.	Correct / Skipped
7	A	34.62 % / 37.69 %
8	B	26.92 % / 45.39 %
9	D	33.85 % / 40.77 %
10	C	18.46 % / 45.39 %
11	C	40.0 % / 32.31 %
12	A	37.69 % / 29.23 %

Q.	Ans.	Correct / Skipped
13	D	33.85 % / 34.61 %
14	A	43.08 % / 25.38 %
15	D	41.54 % / 36.15 %
16	B	47.69 % / 26.16 %
17	C	36.92 % / 30.77 %
18	B	35.38 % / 44.62 %

Q.	Ans.	Correct / Skipped
19	C	36.92 % / 34.62 %
20	A	25.38 % / 32.31 %
21	D	33.85 % / 18.46 %
22	A	46.92 % / 16.93 %
23	C	36.92 % / 26.93 %
24	A	42.31 % / 27.69 %

Q.	Ans.	Correct / Skipped
25	C	36.15 % / 36.93 %
26	C	33.08 % / 24.61 %
27	D	16.15 % / 45.39 %
28	C	18.46 % / 44.62 %
29	D	23.85 % / 36.92 %
30	A	24.62 % / 28.46 %

Performance Analysis

Avg. Score (%)	**30.0%**
Toppers Score (%)	**100.0%**
Your Score	

Ques (1-2):Direction: In the following question, choose the word opposite in meaning to the given word.

Q.1 Born in **squalid** surroundings of the slums she rose to stardom overnight.

A. Dirty
B. Clean
C. Disorderly
D. Mean

Q.2 Mrs. Nisha made a **fervent** appeal to the members of the club to maintain unity.

A. Active
B. Impassive
C. Cold
D. Passionate

Ques (3-7):Direction: Read the following passage carefully and answer the question given below it.

True, it is the function of the army to maintain law and order in abnormal times. But in normal times there is another force that compels citizens to obey the laws and to act with due regard to the rights of others. The force also protects the lives and the properties of law-abiding men. Laws are made to secure the personal safety of its subjects and to prevent murder and crimes of violence. They are made to secure the property of the citizens against theft and damage to protect the rights of communities and castes to carry out their customs and ceremonies, so long as they do not conflict with the rights of others. Now the good citizen, of his own free will obey these laws and he takes care that everything he does is done with due regard to the rights and well-being of others.

But the bad citizen is only restrained from breaking these laws by fear of the consequence of his actions. And the necessary steps to compel the bad citizen to act as a good citizen are taken by this force. The supreme control of law and order in a State is in the hands of a Minister who is responsible to the State Assembly and acts through the Inspector General of Police.

Q.3 The expression 'customs and ceremonies' means:

A. fairs and festivals
B. habits and traditions
C. usual practices and religious rites
D. superstitions and formalities

Q.4 A suitable title for the passage would be:

A. the function of the army
B. laws and the people's rights
C. the fear of the law and citizen's security
D. the functions of the police

Q.5 Which of the following is not implied in the passage?

A. Law protects those who respect it.
B. Law ensures peoples' religious and social rights absolutely and unconditionally.
C. A Criminal is deterred from committing crimes only for fear of the law.
D. The forces of law help to transform irresponsible citizens into responsible ones.

Q.6 According to the writer, which one of the following is not the responsibility of the police?

A. To protect the privileges of all citizens.
B. To check violent activities of citizens.
C. To ensure peace among citizens by safeguarding individual rights.
D. To maintain peace during extraordinary circumstances.

Q.7 Which of the following reflects the main thrust of the passage?

A. If deals with the importance of the army in maintaining law and order.
B. It highlights the role of the police as superior to that of the army.
C. It discusses the roles of the army and the police in different circumstances.
D. It points to the responsibility of the Minister and the Inspector General of Police.

Ques (8-10):Direction: In the following question a part of the sentence is bold. Below are given alternatives to the bold part at (A), (B), and (C) which may improve the sentence. Choose the correct alternative. In the case of no improvement, your answer is (D).

Q.8 The **car's doors are loose**.

A. car-doors are loose
B. doors of the car are loose
C. the doors to the car are loose
D. No improvement

Q.9 When a man has to give evidence he must **have a clean breast** of the whole matter.

A. make a clean breast
B. obtain a clean breast
C. possess a clean breast
D. No improvement

Q.10 I did not accept an award for **assisting him with help.**

A. Helping him
B. I had helped him
C. I did help him
D. No improvement

Ques (11-12):Direction: Choose the best option to fill in the blank.

Q.11 My mother upset the kettle of boiling water and .... her right hand badly.

A. wounded **B.** sizzled **C.** scorched **D.** scalded

Q.12 Please do not .... an offer made by the Chairman.

A. refrain **B.** refute **C.** refuge **D.** refuse

Ques (13-15):Direction: In the following question, a part of a sentence is given in bold, it is then followed by alternatives that try to explain the meaning of the idiom/phrase given in bold. Choose the alternative which explains the meaning of the

phrase correctly without altering the meaning of the sentence given a question.

Q.13 Being an introvert, he will only **eat his heart out.**

A. eat too much   **B.** keep brooding
C. invite trouble   **D.** suffer silently

Q.14 He is **not worth his salt** if he fails at his juncture.

A. quite worthless
B. very proud of himself
C. quite strange
D. very strange

Q.15 She exhibited remarkable **sangfroid** during the crisis.

A. temper   **B.** irritation
C. composure   **D.** anger

Ques (16-17):Direction: In the following question, groups of four words are given. In each group, one word is correctly spelt. Find the correctly spelt word.

Q.16 (A) Duration   (B) Dustur
(C) Electrisity   (D) Economicel

A. (A)   **B.** (B)   **C.** (C)   **D.** (D)

Q.17 (A) Poresistance (B) Thesaurus
(C) Conspicous (D) Renaisance

A. (A)   **B.** (B)   **C.** (C)   **D.** (D)

Ques (18-19):Direction: In the following question out of the four alternatives, choose the one which is best expresses the meaning of the given word

Q.18 Ramifications

A. Uses   **B.** Developments
C. Consequences   **D.** Conclusions

Q.19 Gimcrack

A. Expensive   **B.** Worthless
C. Rare   **D.** Smuggled

Ques (20-24):Direction: Select the most appropriate word from the options against each number:

Temperatures ___(1)___ than 30 degrees Celsius can be bad for your smartphone in the long run. Indeed, if left out in the sun for too long, a smartphone's touch-screen will stop working ___(2)___, warns German telecommunications portal Teltarif.de. Batteries can also give ___(3)___ their charge faster in the heat, meaning it's best if mobile devices are carried in bags during warm weather. If you accidentally let your phone overheat, put it in the shade to cool ___(4)___. Don't go ___(5)___ and try to cool it off quickly in the refrigerator or freezer. Too rapid a change in temperature will let condensation build up in the housing, which could ___(6)___ to a short circuit.

Q.20 Which of the following is the most appropriate option for blank ___(1)___?

A. Basic   **B.** Lower   **C.** Higher   **D.** Lesser

Q.21 Which of the following is the most appropriate option for blank ___(2)___?

A. Befittingly   **B.** Properly

C. Truly   **D.** Healthy

Q.22 Which of the following is the most appropriate option for blank ___(3)___?

A. Up   **B.** Over   **C.** Under   **D.** In

Q.23 Which of the following is the most appropriate option for blank ___(4)___?

A. Of   **B.** Off   **C.** Than   **D.** At

Q.24 Which of the following is the most appropriate option for blank ___(5)___?

A. Overcome   **B.** Overhear
C. Overdo   **D.** Overboard

Ques (25-27):Direction: Select the correct direct form of the given sentence.

Q.25 I told my brother not to mess up the things in the cupboard.

A. I said to my brother, "You will not mess up the things in the cupboard."

B. I said to my brother, "Didn't mess up the things in the cupboard."

C. I said to my brother, "Not mess up the things in the cupboard."

D. I said to my brother, "Don't mess up the things in the cupboard."

Q.26 She asked me how much I had paid for the mangoes.

A. She said to me, "How much did you pay for the mangoes?"

B. She said to me, "How much I paid for the mangoes?"

C. She said to me, "How I paid for the mangoes?"

D. She said to me, "How much did I pay for the mangoes?"

Q.27 The shopkeeper requested the lady to hurry up as it was time to close the shop.

A. The shopkeeper said to the lady, "Please hurry up, it will be time for the shop to be closed."

B. The shopkeeper said to the lady, "Please hurry up, it is time for the shop to be closed."

C. The shopkeeper said to the lady, "Please hurry up, it is time to closed the shop."

D. The shopkeeper said to the lady, "Please hurry up, it was time for the shop to be closed."

Q.28 Direction: Select the option that is the passive form of the sentence.

This man has stolen the clothes from the wardrobe.

A. The clothes from the wardrobe have been stolen by this man.

B. The clothes from the wardrobe has been stolen by this man.

C. The clothes from the wardrobe have being stolen by this man.

D. The clothes from the wardrobe were stolen by this man.

Q.29 Direction: Select the correct passive form of the given sentence.

The frog made the nightingale practise day in and day out.

A. The nightingale is made to practice day in and day out by the frog.

B. The nightingale did made to practise day in and day out by the frog.

C. The nightingale was made to practise day in and day out by the frog.

D. nightingale was made to practise by the frog day in and day out.

Q.30 Direction: In the following question, some part of the sentence is underlined. Which of the options given below the sentence should replace the part underlined to make the sentence grammatically correct? If the sentence is correct as it is given then choose option (D) 'No Correction required' as the answer.

He did not like <u>me to smoking</u> in the presence of our teacher yesterday.

A. that I smoke

B. my smoking

C. me smoking

D. No correction required

// Smart Answer Sheet //

Correct — Indicates percentage of students who answered questions correctly.

Skipped — Indicates percentage of students who skipped questions.

Q.	Ans.	Correct / Skipped
1	B	50.0 % / 2.62 %
2	B	30.95 % / 3.1 %
3	C	59.52 % / 6.43 %
4	D	20.24 % / 5.0 %
5	B	31.43 % / 6.9 %
6	D	41.19 % / 7.62 %

Q.	Ans.	Correct / Skipped
7	C	48.57 % / 6.67 %
8	B	65.71 % / 5.24 %
9	A	34.05 % / 5.24 %
10	A	86.43 % / 6.19 %
11	D	24.52 % / 4.77 %
12	D	79.29 % / 4.76 %

Q.	Ans.	Correct / Skipped
13	D	80.0 % / 4.52 %
14	A	80.71 % / 4.29 %
15	C	74.29 % / 5.71 %
16	A	89.05 % / 4.76 %
17	B	50.24 % / 2.38 %
18	C	57.62 % / 3.81 %

Q.	Ans.	Correct / Skipped
19	B	54.52 % / 4.53 %
20	C	30.0 % / 66.19 %
21	B	30.0 % / 66.19 %
22	A	28.1 % / 66.19 %
23	B	30.24 % / 66.19 %
24	D	25.95 % / 66.19 %

Q.	Ans.	Correct / Skipped
25	D	26.9 % / 66.2 %
26	A	21.43 % / 66.19 %
27	B	24.05 % / 66.19 %
28	A	17.86 % / 66.19 %
29	C	26.9 % / 66.2 %
30	B	10.0 % / 66.19 %

Performance Analysis

Avg. Score (%)	56.67%
Toppers Score (%)	100.0%
Your Score	

Q.1 Direction: Choose the best option to fill in the blank.

If only I _____ his address, I would most certainly have told you.

A. know

B. knew

C. had known

D. would have known

Q.2 Direction: Choose the option that best expresses the meaning of the idiom which is underlined.

Diana took to swimming <u>like a duck to water</u> even before she was 3 years old.

A. Like an expert

B. Having natural ability

C. Swim the way a duck does

D. Showing passion for

Q.3 Direction: Select the word that is antonymous to the given word.

Gloat

A. Exult

B. Relish

C. Sympathise

D. Jubilate

Q.4 Direction: Choose the best option to fill in the blank.

Clothes ___ jeans and t-shirts are my favourite casual wears.

A. unlike

B. like

C. alike

D. likely

Q.5 Direction: Choose the alternative that explains the given idiomatic expression.

To shed crocodile tears

A. To weep bitterly and long

B. To pretend to feel sadness

C. To behave like a clever person

D. To deceive by telling tales of misfortune

Q.6 Direction: Choose the alternative that explains the given idiomatic expression.

To tempt providence

A. To invite punishment

B. To achieve a fortune

C. To take reckless risks

D. To have god's favour

Ques (7-9):Direction: Read each sentence to find out whether there is any grammatical error in the bracketed part. If there is no error, the answer is (D).

Q.7 (We discussed about the) problem so thoroughly on the eve of the examination that I found it very easy to work it out.

A. We are discussed about the

B. We are discussing about the

C. We discussed the

D. No error

Q.8 An Indian ship laden with merchandise (got drowned in the Pacific Ocean).

A. got drown in the Pacific Ocean

B. get sink in the Pacific Ocean

C. got sank in the Pacific Ocean

D. No error

Q.9 (I could not put up in a hotel) because the boarding and lodging charges were exorbitant.

A. I could not put up at a hotel

B. I could not put up on a hotel

C. I could not puting up at a hotel

D. No error

Ques (10-11):Direction: In the following sentence, there are two blank spaces. Find out which pair of words can be used to fill in the blanks in the same sequence to make the sentence meaningfully complete.

Q.10 A more _____ strategy to _____ away from its reliance on diamonds is to attract more tourists.

A. practical, distract

B. viable, get

C. realistic, diversify

D. cogent, conduct

Q.11 In her interviews and emails, she is prickly and cautious, as though _____ incursions into the worlds she has _____ her readers.

A. defending, abstained

B. fending off, bequeathed

C. soliciting, summoned

D. avoiding, celebrated

Ques (12-16):Direction: Read the following passage carefully and answer the question given below it.

India embarked on a gradual shift towards capital account convertibility with the launch of the reforms in the early 1990s. Although foreign natural persons except NRIs are prohibited from investing in financial assets, such investments were permitted through Foreign Institutional Investor (FIIs) and Overseas Corporate Bodies (OCBs) with suitable restrictions. Ever since September 14, 1992, when FIIs were first allowed to invest in all the securities traded on the primary and secondary markets, including shares, debentures and warrants issued by companies which were listed or were to be listed on the Stock Exchanges in India and in the schemes floated by domestic mutual funds, the holding of a single FII and of all FIIs, Non-resident Indians (NRIs) and OCBs in any company were subject to the upper limit of 5 per cent and 24 per cent of the company's total issued capital, respectively. Furthermore, funds invested by FIIs had to have at least 50 participants with no one holding more than 5 per cent to ensure a broad base and preventing such investment acting as a camouflage for individual investment in the nature of Foreign Direct Investment (FDI) and requiring Government approval.

Initially the idea of allowing FIIs was that they were broad-based, diversified funds, leaving out individual foreign investors and foreign companies. The only exceptions were the NRI and OCB portfolio investments through the secondary market, which were subject to individual ceilings of 5 per cent to prevent a possible "take over." OCB investments through the portfolio route have been banned since November, 2001.

In February 2000, the FII regulations were amended to permit foreign corporate and high net worth individuals to also invest as sub-accounts of Securities and Exchange Board of India (SEBI)-registered FIIs. Foreign corporate and high net worth individuals fall outside the category of diversified investors. FIIs were also permitted to seek SEBI registration in respect of sub-accounts for their clients under the regulations. A Working Group for Streamlining of the Procedures relating to FIIs constituted in April, 2003 by the Government, inter alia, recommended streamlining of SEBI registration procedure, and suggested that dual approval process of SEBI and RBI be changed to a single approval process of SEBI. This recommendation has been implemented.

Like in other countries, the restrictions on FII investment have been progressively liberalized. From November 1996, any registered FII willing to make 100 per cent investment in debt securities were permitted to do so subject to specific approval from SEBI as a separate category of FIIs or sub-accounts as 100 per cent debt funds. Moreover, investments were allowed only in debt securities of companies listed or to be listed in stock exchanges. Investments were free from maturity limitations.

Q.12 Which of the following best introduces the above passage?

A. Evolution of FII investment policy

B. Significance of foreign investment

C. The emergence of different types of foreign funds

D. Impact of FII on Indian reforms

Q.13 How was a foreign natural person, except NRI, allowed to enter in Indian equity market?

A. Converting himself into Overseas Corporate Body or FII

B. Acquiring at least 5% capital of an Indian company

C. Selecting the primary market route to enter into Indian market

D. Contributing up to 5% in the funds of a Foreign Institutional Investor

Q.14 Which of the following, according to the passage, shows the feasibility to invest in Indian companies?

A. FII and OCB taking up a combined 20% of the issued capital of an Indian company

B. Any person outside India investing in Indian companies after taking government approval

C. A Foreign Institutional Investor applying for more than 5% of the capital of Indian company

D. Thirty persons coming up to form an FII and investing 5% of the total issued capital

Q.15 What can serve as the possible reason for limiting the individual investments to only 5% of the issued capital of Indian companies?

A. Providing the upper edge to the Non-Indian Residents

B. Preventing hostile bids for acquiring control over Indian Companies

C. Serving the equal opportunity to the foreign investors to invest into the Indian market

D. Restraining the black money coming into the Indian economy

Q.16 How, according to the passage, did the foreign companies manage to invest directly into the Indian share market?

A. By passing out special resolution and forming itself as an Overseas Corporate Body

B. By proposing to bring in Foreign Direct Investment to help Indian companies

C. By becoming sub-accounts of existing registered Foreign Institutional Investors

D. By assuring to invest firstly into debt securities issued by Indian companies

Ques (17-21):Direction: Each of the following passages in this section has some blank spaces with four words or groups of word given. Select whichever word or group of words you consider most appropriate for the blank space.

Researchers in Singapore have ______(1) smart clothing which they say can boost signals and save battery life on wireless devices ______(2) headphones and smartwatches. The invention ______(3) "metamaterial" allows radio waves like Bluetooth and Wi-Fi to glide across clothing between wearable devices ______(4) of radiating outwards in all directions. This means sensors and wearable ______(5) such as Apple Watches and AirPods can establish ______(6) connections faster and save energy, the scientists at the National University of Singapore said. "This T-shirt ______(7) the wireless connectivity of devices around my body ______(8) 1,000 times," said assistant professor John Ho, donning a sports shirt laced with comb-shaped strips of the metamaterial textile. Mr. Ho, who oversaw a 10-member team that ______(9) the technology over a year, said it ______(10) used for measuring the vital signs of athletes or hospital patients.

Q.17 Which of the following is the most appropriate option for blank 1?

A. Discarded	**B.** Relinquished
C. Invented	**D.** Repudiated

Q.18 Which of the following is the most appropriate option for blank 3?

A. Dismissed	**B.** Called
C. Ousted	**D.** Rescinded

Q.19 Which of the following is the most appropriate option for blank 4?

A. Regardless	**B.** Instead
C. Although	**D.** Through

Q.20 Which of the following is the most appropriate option for blank 5?

A. Tradition	**B.** Norm
C. Rule	**D.** Technology

Q.21 Which of the following is the most appropriate option for blank 6?

A. Stronger	**B.** Bleaker
C. Puny	**D.** Diminutive

Q.22 Direction: A sentence has been given in Active/Passive Voice. Out of the four alternatives suggested, select the one which best expresses the same sentence in Passive/Active voice.

Ads on Facebook increase the sale of any commodity.

A. The sale of any commodity is being increased by the ads on Facebook.

B. The sale of any commodity are increased by the ads on Facebook.

C. The sale of any commodity are being increased by the ads on Facebook.

D. The sale of any commodity is increased by the ads on Facebook.

Q.23 A sentence has been given in Active Voice. Choose the option which best expresses the given sentence in Passive Voice.

Some boys were helping the wounded man.

[Army Public School (PRT), 2019]

A. The wounded man was being helped by some boys.

B. The wounded man was helped by some boys.

C. The wounded man has been helped by some boys.

D. The wounded man was been helped by some boys.

Q.24 Direction: Choose the most appropriate form of Indirect speech for the given sentence.

The teacher said to Hari, "Why did you not do your homework yesterday?"

A. The teacher asked Hari why had he not done his homework the previous day?

B. The teacher asked Hari why he had not done his homework the previous day.

C. The teacher said to Hari why had he not done their homework the previous day?

D. The teacher said Hari that he had not done his homework the previous day.

Ques (25-26):Direction: In the following question, a sentence is given in Direct/Indirect speech. Out of the four alternatives choose the one which best expresses the sentence in Indirect/Direct Speech.

Q.25 The teacher said to the students, "Do not create a nuisance in the class."

A. The teacher requested the students to not create a nuisance in the class.

B. The teacher forbade the students to not create a nuisance in the class.

C. The teacher advised the students to not create a nuisance in the class.

D. The teacher forbade the students to create a nuisance in the class.

Q.26 The person said to me, "How many places have you visited today?"

A. The person asked me how many places you had visited today.

B. The person asked me how many places had I visited that day.

C. The person asked me how many places I had visited today.

D. The person asked me how many places I had visited that day.

Ques (27-28):Direction: Each item in this section consists of a sentence with an underlined word followed by four options. Select the option that is nearest in meaning to the underlined word.

Q.27 His language is political and <u>vitriolic</u>.

A. Imaginative   B. Sprightly

C. Vivacious   D. Abusive

Q.28 The Industrial Revolution saw a <u>massive</u> rise in the population of Europe.

A. Enormous   B. Erroneous

C. Hazardous   D. Perilous

Ques (29-30):Direction: Choose the word which best expresses the opposite meaning of the underlined word in the sentences given below.

Q.29 He looked <u>elated</u> on hearing the news

A. Depressed   B. Exasperated

C. Anxious   D. Jubilant

Q.30 He stood gazing at the <u>serene</u> expanse of the sea.

A. Ruffled   B. Clear   C. Scenic   D. Tranquil

// Smart Answer Sheet //

Correct — Indicates percentage of students who answered questions correctly.

Skipped — Indicates percentage of students who skipped questions.

Q.	Ans.	Correct / Skipped
1	C	44.8 % / 4.07 %
2	B	61.99 % / 4.53 %
3	C	39.82 % / 8.14 %
4	B	85.07 % / 5.88 %
5	B	74.21 % / 4.98 %
6	C	47.51 % / 5.88 %

Q.	Ans.	Correct / Skipped
7	C	48.87 % / 5.43 %
8	C	49.77 % / 6.79 %
9	A	63.35 % / 6.79 %
10	B	61.99 % / 6.34 %
11	B	37.1 % / 4.98 %
12	A	49.77 % / 8.15 %

Q.	Ans.	Correct / Skipped
13	D	23.08 % / 8.59 %
14	A	18.1 % / 7.24 %
15	B	44.8 % / 9.95 %
16	C	32.13 % / 6.78 %
17	C	34.39 % / 60.63 %
18	B	31.22 % / 61.09 %

Q.	Ans.	Correct / Skipped
19	B	29.41 % / 60.64 %
20	D	35.75 % / 60.63 %
21	A	31.67 % / 60.64 %
22	D	25.34 % / 58.82 %
23	A	28.51 % / 61.08 %
24	B	23.53 % / 60.18 %

Q.	Ans.	Correct / Skipped
25	D	14.93 % / 59.73 %
26	D	16.29 % / 59.73 %
27	D	10.86 % / 61.09 %
28	A	36.2 % / 61.09 %
29	A	21.72 % / 61.09 %
30	A	24.43 % / 61.09 %

Performance Analysis

Avg. Score (%)	56.67%
Toppers Score (%)	96.67%
Your Score	

Ques (1-2):Direction: In the following question, some parts of the sentences have errors and some have none. Find out which part of the sentence has an error. If there is no error, the answer would be (D).

Q.1 (A) I find
(B) cinema preferable
(C) than dramatics
(D) No Error

A. (A) **B.** (B) **C.** (C) **D.** (D)

Q.2 (A) They'd go
(B) with us.
(C) Wouldn't they?
(D) No Error

A. (A) **B.** (B) **C.** (C) **D.** (D)

Ques (3-4):Direction: In the following question, sentences are given with blanks to be filled in with an appropriate word(s) Some alternatives are suggested for each question. Choose the correct alternative out of the given alternatives as your answer.

Q.3 _______ seen my brother, I came home.
A. After **B.** Having
C. After having **D.** Not

Q.4 Though he is rich, ___ he is not happy.
A. yet **B.** but **C.** still **D.** and

Q.5 Direction: In the following question, out of the four alternatives, choose the one which is best expresses the meaning of the given word.

Expulsion
A. Breakage **B.** Debarment
C. Spate **D.** Influx

Ques (6-8):Direction: In the following question, choose the word opposite in meaning to the given word.

Q.6 Credence
A. Crucial **B.** Review
C. Disbelief **D.** Conspiracy

Q.7 Obscure
A. Discernible **B.** Roasted
C. Refresh **D.** Relieve

Q.8 Augment
A. Casual **B.** Decrease
C. Regenerate **D.** Avoid

Q.9 Find the correctly spelled word:
A. Motely **B.** Deceitful
C. Conglomarate **D.** Nebulous

Q.10 Find the correctly spelled word:

A. Redundant **B.** Redundunt
C. Redundent **D.** Redendant

Ques (11-12):Direction: In the following question, four alternatives are given for the meaning of the given idiom/Phrase. Choose the alternative which best expresses the meaning of the Idiom/Phrase.

Q.11 Root and branch
A. Complementary **B.** Completely
C. Strictly **D.** Constantly

Q.12 To show a clean pair of heels
A. Escape **B.** Forget
C. Hide **D.** Remember

Q.13 Direction: In the following question, a sentence has been given in Active Voice/ Passive Voice. Out of the four alternatives suggested, select the one which best expresses the same sentence in Passive/Active Voice.
The teacher was respectfully addressed by Abhinav.
A. Abhinav respectfully addressed the teacher.
B. Respectfully Abhinav addressed the teacher.
C. Abhinav addressed the teacher respectfully.
D. The teacher was respectfully addressed.

Ques (14-15):Direction: In the following question, a part of the sentence is bold. Below are given alternatives to the bold part at (A), (B), and (C) which may improve the sentence. Choose the correct alternative. In the case of no improvement, your answer is (D).

Q.14 All parents desire that their offspring are fit and healthy.
A. Every parent want
B. Each parent want
C. Each of parent desire
D. No improvement

Q.15 The boat lay **below** several feet of water.
A. Under **B.** Beneath
C. Within **D.** No improvement

Q.16 Direction: In the following question, a sentence has been given in Direct/Indirect. Out of the four alternatives suggested, select the one which best expresses the same sentence in Indirect/ Direct.
The girl said that she had to go to Delhi the next day.
A. The girl said, "I have to go to Delhi the next day".
B. The girl said, "I am going to Delhi the next day".
C. The girl said, "she has to go to Delhi tomorrow".
D. The girl said, "I have to go to Delhi tomorrow".

Ques (17-21):Direction: Read the passage given below and answer the questions by selecting the -correct/most appropriate options:

The make-up room had the look of a hair-cutting salon with lights at all angles around half a dozen large mirrors. They were all incandescent lights, so you can imagine the fiery misery of those subjected to make-up. The make-up department was first headed by a Bengali who became too big for a studio and left. He was succeeded by a Maharashtrian who was assisted by a Dharwar Kannadiga, an Andhra, a Madras Indian Christian, an Anglo-Burmese and the usual local Tamils. All this shows that there was a great deal of national integration long before A.I.R. and Doordarshan began broadcasting programmes on national integration. This gang of nationally integrated make-up men could turn any decent-looking person into a hideous crimson-hued monster with the help of truck-loads of pancake and a number of other locally made potions and lotions. Those were the days of mainly indoor shooting, and only five percent of the film was shot outdoors. I suppose the sets and studio lights needed the girls and boys to be made to look ugly in order to look presentable in the movie.

A strict hierarchy was maintained in the make-up department. The chief make-up man-made the chief actors and actresses ugly, his senior assistant the 'second' hero and heroine, the junior assistant the main comedian, and so forth. The players who played the crowd were the responsibility of the office boy. (Even the make-up department of the Gemini Studio had an 'office boy'!) On the days when there was a crowd shooting, you could see him mixing his paint in a giant vessel and slapping it on the crowd players. The idea was to close every pore on the surface of the face in the process of applying make-up. He wasn't exactly a 'boy'; he was in his early forties, having entered the studios years ago in the hope of becoming a star actor or a top screenwriter, director or lyrics writer. He was a bit of a poet.

Q.17 Why were the actors loaded with extensive makeup?

A. The makeup artists, then, were not learned enough.

B. The makeup artist of the studio was an amateur who had been hired on personal grounds.

C. The script called for looks that portrayed heavy makeup.

D. The lights of the studio were such that only extensively painted faces looked presentable on the screen.

Q.18 The word 'incandescent' means:

A. Colorful

B. Gloomy

C. Luminous

D. Dull

Q.19 The word 'hideous' means:

A. Disguised

B. Delightful

C. Disgusting

D. Divine

Q.20 Identify the part of the following sentence which has an error in it.

Those were the days of mainly (a)/ indoor shooting, and only five (b)/ percent of the film (c)/ was shoot outdoors. (d)

A. (a)

B. (b)

C. (c)

D. (d)

Q.21 Why did the office boy join the Gemini Studios?

A. To hone his makeup skills

B. To hone his talent in team management

C. To become a star actor/ write/ director

D. To earn a living since his family could barely make the ends meet

Ques (22-26):Direction: Each of the following sentences in this section has a blank space with four words or group of words given. Select whichever word or group of words you consider most appropriate for the blank space.

Today India's teachers are being trained in hordes, like industrial workers. The assumption is that the B.Ed.-certified teacher will (1) the quality of teaching, and this in turn will improve children's education. Unfortunately, the assumptions don't (2). Being trained keeps one away from much-needed contact with the ground and (3) the anxiety to get a certificate, and then a job. The certificate (4) more important than what you do, and thus what you do matters (5). Orwellian workers, going through the motions, cannot (6) a living, fear-free, celebrative system. They can only go through the motions and (7) the energy of the young, while somehow staying out of their superior's bad books. Unfortunate, (8) movement in the name of education, that preys on the future. But there are individuals who are willing to try something that has not been tried. This hopeful group is shut (9) by the board, 'qualified teachers only'. The certificate matters more than the human being who is willing to learn on the job. No one knows where to take this ship, and the B.Ed. certificate (10) the status quo.

Q.22 Which of the following is the most appropriate option for blank 1?

A. Tackle

B. Raise

C. Refer

D. Enunciate

Q.23 Which of the following is the most appropriate option for blank 2?

A. Dodge

B. Permit

C. Contempt

D. Add up

Q.24 Which of the following is the most appropriate option for blank 3?

A. Accords

B. Causes

C. Accentuates

D. Mollify

Q.25 Which of the following is the most appropriate option for blank 4?

A. Becomes

B. Deems

C. Portray

D. Seem

Q.26 Which of the following is the most appropriate option for blank 5?

A. More

B. Often

C. Much

D. Little

Q.27 Direction: Changed the sentence from direct speech to indirect speech.

Sneha's mother said to her, "What were you doing at eight o'clock last night?"

A. Sneha's mother said to her what she had been doing at eight o'clock last night.

B. Sneha's mother said to her what she was doing at eight o'clock last night.

C. Sneha's mother asked her what she had been doing at eight o'clock the night before.

D. Sneha's mother told her what she had been doing at eight o'clock last night.

Q.28 Direction: Select the most appropriate indirect form of the given sentence.

Amit said to me, "Your parents are waiting for you."

[SSC CGL, 2020]

A. Amit told me that his parents were waiting for me.
B. Amit told me that your parents are waiting for you.
C. Amit asked me if my parents were waiting for me.
D. Amit told me that my parents were waiting for me.

Q.29 Select the correct passive form of the sentence.

We should never neglect the time which is meant for us.

A. The time which is meant for us never should be neglected.
B. The time which is meant for us should never be neglected.
C. The time which is meant for us should never have been neglected.
D. The time never neglected by us which is meant for us.

Q.30 Select the correct active form of the given sentence.

The migrant was bidden to leave the country by the authority.

A. The authority bid the migrant to leave the country.
B. The authority bade the migrant leave the country.
C. Let the migrant bade to leave the country.
D. The authority bade the migrant to leave the country.

// Smart Answer Sheet //

Correct Indicates percentage of students who answered questions correctly.

Skipped Indicates percentage of students who skipped questions.

Q.	Ans.	Correct / Skipped
1	C	38.3 % / 1.59 %
2	D	43.62 % / 3.19 %
3	B	35.11 % / 5.32 %
4	A	42.02 % / 5.32 %
5	B	47.87 % / 5.32 %
6	C	58.51 % / 6.38 %

Q.	Ans.	Correct / Skipped
7	A	39.36 % / 5.32 %
8	B	46.28 % / 5.85 %
9	D	73.4 % / 5.86 %
10	A	67.55 % / 5.32 %
11	B	51.6 % / 5.31 %
12	A	51.06 % / 5.85 %

Q.	Ans.	Correct / Skipped
13	C	64.89 % / 5.32 %
14	D	42.55 % / 5.32 %
15	A	40.43 % / 5.31 %
16	D	68.09 % / 5.85 %
17	D	27.13 % / 64.89 %
18	C	24.47 % / 64.89 %

Q.	Ans.	Correct / Skipped
19	C	25.0 % / 64.89 %
20	D	25.53 % / 64.9 %
21	C	28.19 % / 64.9 %
22	B	27.66 % / 64.89 %
23	D	21.28 % / 64.36 %
24	C	15.43 % / 64.89 %

Q.	Ans.	Correct / Skipped
25	A	23.4 % / 64.9 %
26	D	23.94 % / 64.89 %
27	C	31.91 % / 64.9 %
28	D	30.85 % / 64.89 %
29	B	34.04 % / 64.9 %
30	C	1.6 % / 64.89 %

Performance Analysis

Avg. Score (%)	53.33%
Toppers Score (%)	100.0%
Your Score	

General Awareness

Q.1 Which one of the following objectives is NOT embodied in the Preamble to the Constitution of India?

A.   Liberty of thought
B.   Liberty of movement
C.   Liberty of belief
D.   Liberty of expression

Q.2 The Radcliffe Committee was appointed to _________.

A.   draw the boundaries between India and Pakistan
B.   give effect to the Independence Bill
C.   solve the problems of minorities in India
D.   enquire into the riots in East Bengal

Q.3 Who, in India, has the power to summon or prorogue either House of the Parliament?

A. President
B. Home Minister
C. Prime Minister
D. Vice President

Q.4 The Indian Supreme Court's judgement on triple talaq refers to which of its forms?

A. Talaq-e-Ahsan
B. Talaq-e-Hasan
C. Talaq-e-Biddat
D. All of the above

Q.5 The number $'1729'$ is considered as an interesting number as it is the smallest natural number that can be written as the sum of cubes in two ways - sum of the cubes of 12 and 1 and the sum of the cubes of 10 and 9. What is this number $'1729'$ popularly known as?

A.   Landau-Ramanujan Constant
B.   Hardy-Ramanujan Number
C.   Ramanujan-Soldner Number
D.   None of the above

Q.6 The key document that legally entitles registered households to apply for work under MGNREGA is _________.

A. Aadhar Card
B. Ration Card
C. PAN Card
D. Job card

Q.7 "Halfway to Heaven" is the slogan adopted to promote tourism by which Indian state?

A.   Meghalaya
B.   Jammu and Kashmir
C.   Sikkim
D.   Uttarakhand

Q.8 'Adam's Apple' is the common name for which organ in the human body?

A. Esophagus
B. Thyroid cartilage
C. Thoracic cavity
D. Phalange

Q.9 Which tribal community in Madhya Pradesh celebrates the Bhagoria festival?

A. Bhil
B. Gond
C. Mariya
D. Bhariya

Q.10 In February 2017, ISRO launched PSLV-C37 which carried 104 satellites belonging to seven countries, including India. How many of these were Indian satellites?

A. 96
B. 3
C. 1
D. 4

Q.11 Who has authored the book 'The Remembered Village'?

A. M.N. Srinivas
B. Iravati Karve
C. T.N. Madan
D. G.S. Ghurye

Q.12 The recipient of the Nobel Prize for Economics in the year 2017 contributed to which field of research?

A.   Macroeconomic theory
B.   Development Economics
C.   Behavioural Economics
D.   All of the above

Q.13 The first Census of independent India was conducted in the year_________.

A. 1950
B. 1951
C. 1949
D. 1948

Q.14 Which indicator(s) is/are used by the International Food Policy Research Institute to compute the 'Global Hunger Index Report'?

A. Undernourishment
B. Child stunting
C. Child mortality
D. All of the above

Q.15 For which of the following parameters does the Census of India NOT collect data?

A.   Household size
B.   Household ownership status
C.   Income
D.   Occupation

Q.16 Which men's single title did badminton player Kidambi Srikanth win in 2017?

A.   Badminton World Championship
B.   All England Open Badminton Championship
C.   French Open Superseries Badminton
D.   Dubai World Superseries

Q.17 The control of a significant share of the supply or production of a particular good or service by a firm is called __________.

A. crony capitalism
B. monopsony
C. monopoly
D. None of the above

Q.18 Tenali Raman was to _____________ as Birbal was to Akbar.

A.   Raghunatha Nayak
B.   Krishna Deva Raya
C.   Krishnaraj Wodiyaar
D.   Mahendra Varman

Q.19 Consider the following three statements and indicate which of these is/are CORRECT

i) Sex is a biological concept; Gender is a social construct

ii) Sex is a natural or biological feature; Gender is a cultural or learned feature

iii) Both terms mean the same and can be used interchangeably

A. (i) and (ii)   **B.** Only (ii)

C. (i) and (iii)   **D.** Only (iii)

Q.20 Vishaka Guidelines are a set of procedural guidelines that apply to which type of criminal cases?

A. Paedophilia

B. Dowry deaths

C. Human Trafficking

D. Sexual harassment of women at workplace

Q.21 Pradhan Mantri Jan Dhan Yojana has been launched for

__________.

A. providing housing loan to poor people at cheaper interest rates

B. providing financial help to small enterprises in rural areas

C. promoting financial inclusion in the country

D. promoting women's self help groups in backward areas

Q.22 In which Indian city is the world's first solar powered airport located?

A. Delhi   **B.** Udaipur   **C.** Jaipur   **D.** Kochi

Q.23 Which of the following sports involves animals?

A. Jallikattu   **B.** Mallakhamb

C. Lagori   **D.** Vallamkali

Q.24 The 'Apu Trilogy' was directed by __________.

A. Bimal Roy   **B.** Ritwik Ghatak

C. Satyajit Ray   **D.** Mrinal Sen

Q.25 The Padmapani and Vajrapani paintings are found in which caves in India?

A. Elephanta Caves, Maharashtra

B. Udayagiri Caves, Odissa

C. Badami Caves, Karnataka

D. Ajanta Caves, Maharashtra

Q.26 The word 'Zeta' refers to:

A. a letter in the Greek alphabet

B. a national currency

C. a mathematical symbol

D. the name of a galaxy

Q.27 'Rashtriya Garima Abhiyaan' is a national campaign to

__________.

A. rehabilitate the homeless and destitute persons and provide them with shelter and livelihood opportunities

B. free bonded labourers of their bondage and rehabilitate them

C. rehabilitate sex workers through alternative sources of livelihood

D. eradicate the practice of manual scavenging and rehabilitate manual scavengers

Q.28 The United States of America declared its withdrawal from the Paris Agreement in 2017. What was the stated reason for their withdrawal?

A. Unfair benefits to India and China due to the Agreement

B. Loss of it's status within the United Nations to India and China

C. Non-inclusion of India and China in the Agreement

D. Lack of penalties for India and China in the Agreement

Q.29 Find the odd one out.

A. Punam Raut   **B.** Harmanpreet Kaur

C. Mitali Raj   **D.** Anjum Chopra

Q.30 Considering the chronological order, identify the social media site that is the NEWEST among those given here.

A. Instagram   **B.** Twitter

C. Facebook   **D.** Snapchat

Q.31 'Pledge for 9' is the slogan for which national programme?

A. Janani Suraksha Yojana

B. Beti Bachao, Beti Padhao Yojana

C. Pradhan Mantri Surakshit Matritva Abhiyan

D. Janani Shishu Suraksha Karyakram

Q.32 According to the 2011 Population Census, which of the following groups of states occupies the THREE top places with respect to literacy?

A. Kerala, Lakshadweep, Mizoram

B. Kerala, Chandigarh, Goa

C. Kerala, Mizoram,Tripura

D. Kerala, Goa, West Bengal

Q.33 Who was awarded the Jnanpith award in 2017?

A. Shankha Ghosh

B. Bhalchandra Nemade

C. Amarkant

D. Krishna Sobti

Q.34 Who first deciphered the edicts or inscriptions of Emperor Ashoka?

A. Georg Bilhler   **B.** William Jones

C. Max Mueller   **D.** James Prinsep

Q.35 According to the WHO 2017 Report maximum number of Indians suffer from __________.

A. depressive disorders   **B.** drug use disorders

C. schizophrenia   **D.** anxiety disorders

Q.36 Match List I (Book) and List II (Author) and select the correct answers using the codes given below:

List I(Books)	List II (Authors)
a. In Custody	(i) Amartya Sen
b. Sea of Poppies	(ii)Jhumpa Lahiri
c.The Argumentative Indian	(iii)Anita Desai
d. Unaccustomed Earth	(iv)Amitav Ghosh

A. a-iii, b-iv, c-i, d-ii   **B.** a-iv, b-i, c-ii, d-iii

C. a-i, b-iii, c-iv, d-ii   **D.** a-iv, b-iii, c-ii, d-i

Q.37 Which of the following represents billion bytes?

A. Gigabytes   **B.** Megabytes
C. Kilobytes   **D.** Terabytes

Q.38 A low sex ratio in a particular place can indicate
___________.

A. practice of significant sex selective foeticide
B. high male in-migration
C. Both of the above
D. None of the above

Q.39 Which international body benchmarks countries on the 'Global Gender Gap Index'?
A. World Economic Forum
B. UN Women
C. The World Bank
D. World Health Organisation

Q.40 One of the ways in which the National Food Security Act empowers women is by ____________.

A. allocation of 10 kg extra food grain for women headed households
B. issue of ration card in the name of the eldest woman in eligible households
C. issuing separate ration cards for all women in eligible households with dependent children
D. None of the above

English Proficiency

Q.41 Direction: Complete the sentence with the correct option.

The teacher added the stipulation that all projects had to be _______; no student could carry out research on an area that had already been explored by someone else.
A. original   **B.** constructive
C. extensive   **D.** convincing

Q.42 "Had you been at the disaster site, you would have understood the magnitude of the destruction. Of the given options, which one does NOT mean 'magnitude' as used in the above sentence?
A. enormity   **B.** scale
C. significance   **D.** quantum

Q.43 Which option does NOT mean ' handed' in the sentence ' She handed the documents to the revenue officer'?
A. delivered   **B.** gave
C. handled   **D.** passed

Q.44 Direction: Choose the option that would make the sentence grammatically most correct.

The group of nurses are complaining about the lack of safety precautions in the hospital.
A. No change. The sentence is correct as is.
B. is complaining
C. were complained
D. did complaining

Q.45 Direction: Read the given statement and answer the question that follows:

Whenever I eat an icecream, I get a cold.

Which of the following statements is/are definitely true:
I. If I never eat an icecream, I will never get a cold.
II. Eating an icecream is one of the reasons for me to get a cold.
III. If I have a cold, I must have eaten an icecream.
A. II only   **B.** I, II and III
C. Both I and III   **D.** III only

Q.46 Direction: Complete the sentence with the correct option.
We were so delayed that the football match ___ by the time we ___.
A. already finished, arrived
B. had already finished, arrive
C. already finish, arrived
D. had already finished, arrived

Q.47 Direction: Choose the option that would make the sentence grammatically most correct.
Who's life is it anyway?
A. No change. The sentence is correct as is.
B. Whose life is it anyway?
C. Who life is it anyway?
D. Whose's life is it anyway?

Q.48 Direction: Complete the sentence with the correct option.
My wife and ___ will attend the function.
A. me   **B.** him   **C.** myself   **D.** I

Q.49 Direction: Choose the option that would make the sentence grammatically most correct.
The house as well as the garden were to be treated for a termite infestation.
A. No change, the sentence is correct as is.
B. The house as well as the garden is to be treated for a termite infestation.
C. The house as well as the garden are going to be treated for a termite infestation.
D. The house as well as the garden need to be treated for a termite infestation.

Q.50 Direction: Complete the sentence with the correct option
Nearly _______ by disease and the destruction of their habitat, Koalas are now found only in isolated parts of eucalyptus forests.
A. damaged   **B.** destroyed
C. decimated   **D.** dispersed

Q.51 Which of the following is the closest in meaning to the word 'retribution'?
A. return   **B.** reinstatement
C. reiteration   **D.** revenge

Ques (52-53):Direction: Identify the error in the sentence, if any:

Q.52 Modern cinematography/(1) techniques are far superior to/(2) that employed in the past./(3) No Error/(4)
A. Modern cinematography
B. are far superior to
C. that employed in the past

D. No Error

Q.53 He wondered whether he could make it/(1) through the storm as there was no safe haven in sight/(2) and it was pouring cats and dogs, with the roads full of gushing water./(3) Error./(4).

A. he could make it

B. no safe haven in sight

C. full with gushing water

D. No Error

Ques (54-56):Direction: Complete the sentence with the correct option.

Q.54 It's a wonder that _______ still such a popular band even after twenty years of being on the music charts!

A. they're   **B.** their's   **C.** there   **D.** their

Q.55 None of the students prepared for the examination. As far as answering the examination paper was concerned, they were all______________.

A. making their mark

B. sailing in the same boat

C. scoring a sitter

D. barking up the wrong tree

Q.56 The itinerary set by their travel agent included so many stops in a _______ amount of time that they received only the most _________ impressions of the places they visited.

A. sufficient, cursory   **B.** generous, abiding

C. brief, fleeting   **D.** limited, lasting

Q.57 Direction: Identify the error in the sentence, if any:

In this way nuclear fission/(1) or the splitting of the atoms/(2) have been achieved./(3) No Error./(4)

A. In this way nuclear fission

B. or the splitting of the atoms

C. have been achieved

D. No Error

Ques (58-59):Direction: Complete the sentence with the correct option:

Q.58 Ms. Kapoor recommended perseverance and _______ in dealing with the activists rather than the uncompromising approach the government had adopted.

A. patience   **B.** persistence

C. joviality   **D.** acrimony

Q.59 The land reforms were diluted, if not sabotaged, in ______________ with politicians and highly placed legal officials.

A. collusion   **B.** agreement

C. pandemonium   **D.** cooperation

Q.60 Direction: Identify the error in the sentence, if any:

Neither the Bank manager nor the other/(1) staff members was able/(2) to calm the distressed client./(3) No Error/(4)

A. nor the other   **B.** was able

C. the distressed client   **D.** No Error

Ques (61-65):Direction: Read the following passage and answer the question that follow.

To those who do listen, the desert speaks of things with an emphasis quite different from that of the shore, the mountain, the valley or the plains. Whereas these invite action and suggest limitless opportunity and exhaust less resources, the implications and the mood of the desert are something different. For one thing, the desert is conservative and not radical. It is more likely to provide awe than to invite conquest. The heroism which it encourages is the heroism of endurance, not that of conquest. It brings man up against this limitation, turns him upon himself and suggests values which more indulgent regions suppress. Sometimes it includes contemplation in men who have never contemplated before. And of all the answers to the question- what is a desert good for - 'contemplation' is perhaps the best.

Q.61 In order to receive the desert's message, the beholder needs to be

A. a good listener

B. courageous in his reaction

C. reflective by nature

D. conservative in his responses

Q.62 The phrase "it brings man up against this limitations" indicates that __________

A. man feels hopeless about his limitations.

B. man is made aware of his limitations..

C. man is persuaded to overcome his limitations.

D. man is compelled to fight against his limitations

Q.63 The desert is unique among landscapes in that it is relatively______.

A. constant   **B.** judgemental

C. adventurous   **D.** conventional

Q.64 The writer calls the desert "conservative rather than radical" because it provides an environment that ______.

A. inspires one to test one's endurance

B. makes one gloomy

C. inspires man to explore it

D. offers unlimited opportunity to conquer it

Q.65 If one responds with insight to the mood of the desert, it evokes:

A. intense conflict   **B.** deep thoughtfulness

C. heroic conquest   **D.** resourcefulness

Ques (66-70):Direction: Read the following passage and answer the question that follow.

Before the grass has thickened on the roadside verges and leaves have started growing on the trees is a perfect time to look around and see just how dirty Britain has become. The pavements are stained with chewing gum that has been spat out and the gutters are full of discarded fast food cartons. Years ago I remember travelling abroad and being saddened by the plastic bags, discarded bottles and soiled nappies at the edge of every road. Nowadays, Britain seems to look at least as bad. What has gone wrong?

The problem is that the rubbish created by our increasingly mobile lives lasts a lot longer than before. If it is not cleared up and properly thrown away, it stays in the undergrowth for years; a semi-permanent reminder of what a tatty little country we have now.

Firstly, it is estimated that 10 billion plastic bags have been given to shoppers. These will take anything from 100 to 1,000 years to rot. However, it is not as if there is no solution to this. A few years ago, the Irish government introduced a tax on non-recyclable carrier bags and in three months reduced their use by 90%. When he was a minister, Michael Meacher attempted to introduce a similar arrangement in Britain. The plastics industry protested, of course. However, they need not have bothered; the idea was killed before it could draw breath, leaving supermarkets free to give away plastic bags.

What is clearly necessary right now is some sort of combined initiative, both individual and collective, before it is too late. The alternative is to continue sliding downhill until we have a country that looks like a vast municipal rubbish tip. We may well be at the tipping point. Yet we know that people respond to their environment. If things around them are clean and tidy, people behave cleanly and tidily. If they are surrounded by squalor, they behave squalidly. Now, much of Britain looks pretty squalid. What will it look like in five years?

Q.66 It is general knowledge that

A. people behave according to what they see around them

B. people are like a vast municipal rubbish tip.

C. people are clean and tidy

D. people are squalid

Q.67 Michael Meacher

A. issued orders to follow the Irish example with a tax on plastic bags.

B. tried to follow the Irish example with a tax on plastic bags.

C. followed the Irish example with a tax on plastic bags.

D. questioned the plastics industry who weren't bothered about the tax

Q.68 According to the writer, years ago, things used to be

A. the same abroad as compared to Britain

B. better abroad as compared to Britain

C. worse abroad as compared to Britain

D. worse, but now things are better abroad

Q.69 For the writer, the problem is that:

A. rubbish lasts longer than it used to.

B. Britain is a tatty country.

C. rubbish is not cleared up.

D. our society is increasingly mobile

Q.70 The writer thinks

A. we need to work together to solve the problem.

B. we are at the tipping point.

C. it is too late to do anything.

D. there is no alternative.

Maths and Logical Reasoning

Q.71 Which of the following dates fall on the same day of the week in any given month?

A. 4 and 24

B. 6 and 30

C. 13 and 27

D. 11 and 22

Q.72 If 15 August 1905 was a Tuesday, which day was 15 August in 1895?

A. Friday

B. Wednesday

C. Thursday

D. Tuesday

Q.73 The following table gives the percentage distribution of population of five states, $P, Q, R, S,$ and T on the basis of poverty line and also on the basis of sex.

State	Percentage of population below the poverty line	Proportion of Males and Females	
Below Poverty Line		Above Poverty Line	
M:F		M:F	
P	35	5:6	6:7
Q	25	3:5	4:5
R	24	1:2	2:3
S	19	3:2	4:3
T	15	5:3	3:2

If the male population above poverty line for State R is 1.9 million, then the total population of State R is?

A. 6.25 million

B. 5.35 million

C. 4.5 million

D. 4.85 million

Q.74 The figures given here show three distributions. Based on these figures, which of the following statements is FALSE?

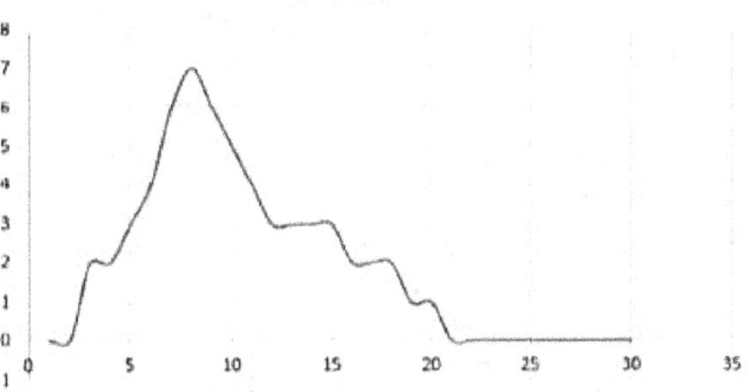

Distribution - 3

A. In Distribution- 1, Mean=Median
B. In Distribution- 3, Mean>Median
C. In Distribution- 2, Mean
D. Mean for Distribution- 2 < Mean for Distribution- 3

Q.75 How many times do the hands of a clock overlap in 24 hours?

A. 11　　**B.** 22　　**C.** 24　　**D.** 12

Q.76 If $\tan(A) = 0$ and $\sin(A) = 0$. what is the value of $\cos(A)$?

A. Inf
B. 1
C. 0
D. Undefined

Q.77 1 ml. salt is added to 19 ml. of distilled water. What is the percentage of salt in the dilution?

A. 10%　　**B.** 5%　　**C.** 4%　　**D.** 0.05%

Q.78 Which number should come next in the following series:

$4,12,28,52$______,

A. 92
B. 84
C. 108
D. None of the above

Q.79 Of the given FOUR sets of five numbers each, find the ODD ONE out.

A. 1,2,19,23,11
B. 841,169,9,361,4
C. 23,29,7,5,27
D. 1,121,169,289,25

Q.80 For a series of 5 numbers, the mean is 20, the median and mode are both 10, the highest number in the series is 50 and one of the numbers is 20. Find the number of times the modal value appears in the series.

A. 4　　**B.** 1　　**C.** 2　　**D.** 3

Q.81 From the data given in the table, which of the following two statements is TRUE:

1. Average annual temperatures for year 2011 are more than average annual temperatures for years 2013 .

2. Average annual temperatures for year 2010 are more than average annual temperatures for years 2012 .

Average Monthly Tempratures in Degree C				
	January	April	July	October
2010	14	32	24	28
2011	12	30	22	30
2012	16	32	24	32
2013	16	34	24	30

A. Both statements are true
B. Statement 1 is false but Statement 2 is true
C. Statement 1 is true but Statement 2 is false
D. Both statements are false

Q.82 Find the odd one out from the following list of numbers:

$161,203,104,112,91$

A. 91
B. 104
C. 112
D. None of the above

Q.83 Mohit was looking for his father. He went 90 meters to the East before turning to his right. He went 20 meters before turning to his right again to look for his father in his uncle's house 30 meters away from this point. His father was not there. From here he went 100 meters to the North before meeting his father in a street. How far away did the son meet his father from the starting point?

A. 140 meters
B. 260 meters
C. 100 meters
D. 80 meters

Q.84 Fill in the missing number in the series:

$7,13,21,$____$,43,57$

A. 35　　**B.** 30　　**C.** 31　　**D.** 34

Q.85 There are a 100 students in a graduating class. Of these, 80 students have passed (let us call this Set A), 20 have failed (let us call this Set B). 90 students from this class got a job (let us call this Set C). Given this information, which of the following statements is TRUE?

A. Set C intersects Set A but not Set B
B. Set B is a subset of Set C
C. Set A is a subset of Set C
D. Set C is a subset of the Union of Set A and Set B

Q.86 If all angles in a triangle are equal, which of the following statements is true?

A. All sides are equal
B. Opposite sides are equal
C. Adjacent sides are equal
D. No side is equal to another

Q.87 If the ratio of the number of men to the number of women on a committee of 30 is $7:8$, how many members are women?

A. 7　　**B.** 8　　**C.** 16　　**D.** 14

Q.88 Find the missing set of letters in the following series

$BAD, DAB, CAE, EAC,$____

A. DAE　　**B.** DAC　　**C.** CAD　　**D.** DAF

Q.89 If all apples are red, and some apples are juicy, which of the following statements is true?

i) All apples are juicy.

ii) Some juicy apples are red.

iii) Some red apples are juicy.

A. First statement
B. Second and Third Statement

C. Third Statement

D. None of the above

Q.90 Father's age and daughter's age add upto 55. Daughter's age is reverse of her father's and difference in their ages is more than 10. How old is the daughter?

A. 21 **B.** 14 **C.** 23 **D.** 32

Q.91 The canteen sells 4 types of chocolates - A, B, C, D. A costs Rs. 10, B costs Rs. 5, C costs Rs. 8 and D costs Rs. 11. I have Rs. 100 with me to spend. If I buy, 4 chocolates of type D and 5 chocolates of type C, then how many chocolates of type A and B can I buy so that I use the maximum of the Rs. 100 that I have.

A. 3 of Type B and 1 of Type A

B. 2 of Type B and 1 of Type A

C. 1 of Type B and 1 of Type A

D. None of the above

Q.92 If the sequence $2,4,2,4,2,4, \ldots$ continues as shown, then the sum of the first 19 terms is______?

A. 62 **B.** 56 **C.** 54 **D.** 60

Q.93 What percentage of 1425 is 68.04?

A. 4.30% **B.** 4.60% **C.** 4.80% **D.** 4.50%

Q.94 If Number A is $(0.99)^2 \times (0.99)^3$ and Number B is $(0.99)^6$, then which number is bigger?

A. Number A

B. Number B

C. Both numbers are equal

D. Cannot be determined

Q.95 Direction: The following two figures show the contribution of the agricultural, industrial and services sectors to the economies of India and China respectively in the time period between 1940 and 2015. Based on the data represented in these figures, which of the following statements is TRUE:

1) India and China have both experienced similar economic trends in the past 75 years

2) The Chinese economy is dominated by industry whereas the Indian economy is dominated by the services sector

3) The Chinese economy is stronger than the Indian economy

India

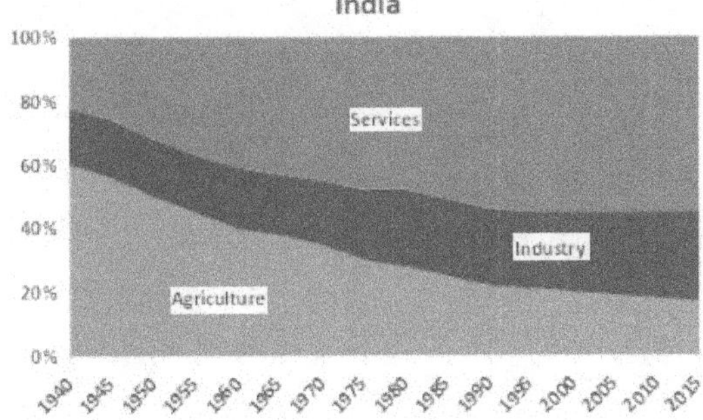

China

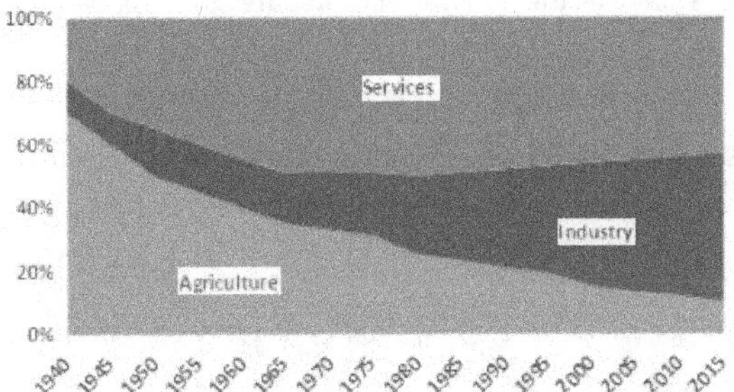

A. The first two statements are true and the third statement cannot be assessed based on the graph

B. The first statement is true and the other two cannot be assessed based on the graph

C. None of the statements can be assessed based on the graph

D. All of the statements are true

Q.96 If two numbers are in a ratio of $7:9$ and their sum is 112, then which is the larger number?

A. 49 **B.** 72 **C.** 56 **D.** 63

Ques (97-98):Direction: The given line graph shows the percentage of the number of candidates who qualified in an examination out of the total number of candidates who appeared for the examination over a period of seven years from 1994 to 2000. Answer the following two questions based on the graph

Percentage of Candidates Qualified to Appeared in an Examination over the Years.

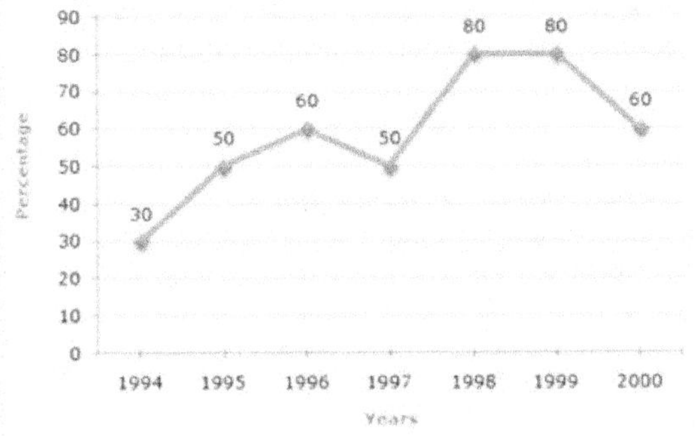

Q.97 The percentage of candidates who qualified in the examination increased between 1994 and 1997 as well as between 1995 and 2000. Of these two time periods, in which time period was the percentage increase in the qualification of candidates the maximum?

A. 1995 to 2000

B. The two time periods cannot be compared

C. Increase was the same in both time periods

D. 1994 to 1997

Q.98 If the number of candidates that qualified in 1998 was 21200, what was the number of candidates that appeared in 1998?

A. 28500   **B.** 25000   **C.** 26500   **D.** 32000

Ques (99-100):Direction: The following bar chart shows the education level of men in Village X. Please answer the following two questions based on the bar chart.

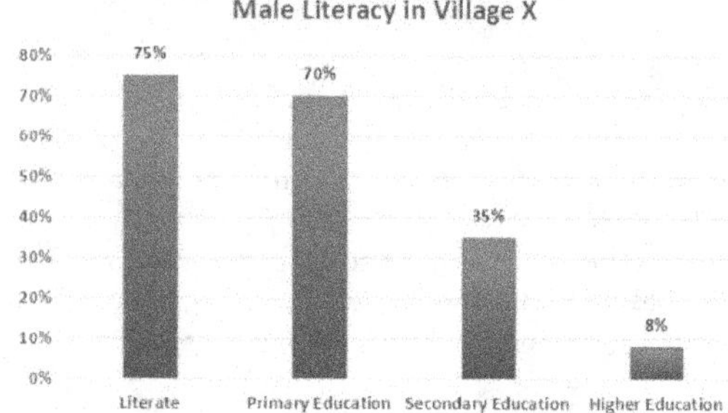

Q.99 If the number of literate men is 1200, what is the number of men who have attained secondary level education?

A. 560   **B.** 288   **C.** 392   **D.** 420

Q.100 If the population ratio (i.e., the proportion of men and women) in Village X is $10:8$, and female literacy is 60%, estimate the number of literate women in Village X

A. 960   **B.** 576   **C.** 768   **D.** 720

// Smart Answer Sheet //

Correct — Indicates percentage of students who answered questions correctly.

Skipped — Indicates percentage of students who skipped questions.

Q.	Ans.	Correct / Skipped
1	B	37.12 % / 27.02 %
2	A	41.92 % / 37.37 %
3	A	51.77 % / 34.85 %
4	C	28.54 % / 38.63 %
5	B	32.07 % / 39.65 %
6	D	17.17 % / 37.12 %
7	A	21.46 % / 38.14 %
8	B	38.89 % / 36.62 %
9	A	21.46 % / 39.4 %
10	B	19.44 % / 38.39 %
11	A	24.49 % / 38.89 %
12	C	17.42 % / 38.64 %
13	B	49.24 % / 34.09 %
14	D	44.19 % / 37.88 %
15	C	14.65 % / 37.37 %
16	C	17.17 % / 38.64 %

Q.	Ans.	Correct / Skipped
17	C	37.12 % / 39.4 %
18	B	43.69 % / 37.37 %
19	A	33.59 % / 17.17 %
20	D	44.7 % / 36.11 %
21	C	26.26 % / 34.85 %
22	D	34.34 % / 37.63 %
23	A	57.58 % / 32.07 %
24	C	41.16 % / 39.4 %
25	D	25.51 % / 39.14 %
26	A	33.33 % / 37.63 %
27	D	18.69 % / 35.86 %
28	A	30.56 % / 40.15 %
29	D	25.76 % / 36.36 %
30	D	47.98 % / 36.87 %
31	C	22.73 % / 38.89 %
32	A	25.25 % / 35.86 %

Q.	Ans.	Correct / Skipped
33	D	16.67 % / 36.61 %
34	D	18.94 % / 38.38 %
35	A	33.33 % / 37.12 %
36	A	28.28 % / 39.4 %
37	A	25.0 % / 39.14 %
38	C	39.14 % / 37.12 %
39	A	29.8 % / 38.89 %
40	B	23.99 % / 39.65 %
41	A	48.48 % / 32.83 %
42	C	31.31 % / 38.13 %
43	C	50.0 % / 38.38 %
44	B	30.05 % / 38.89 %
45	A	46.46 % / 38.64 %
46	D	49.49 % / 39.15 %
47	B	43.69 % / 39.39 %
48	D	50.0 % / 39.14 %

Q.	Ans.	Correct / Skipped
49	B	21.21 % / 39.4 %
50	C	32.58 % / 39.89 %
51	D	19.95 % / 39.9 %
52	C	24.49 % / 39.65 %
53	C	20.96 % / 39.9 %
54	A	52.78 % / 39.64 %
55	B	49.49 % / 39.65 %
56	C	33.08 % / 39.65 %
57	C	36.62 % / 40.15 %
58	A	41.41 % / 39.65 %
59	A	19.19 % / 39.9 %
60	B	43.94 % / 39.9 %
61	C	10.61 % / 39.9 %
62	B	10.86 % / 40.4 %
63	A	12.37 % / 41.17 %
64	A	39.14 % / 40.91 %

Q.	Ans.	Correct / Skipped
65	B	28.54 % / 41.41 %
66	A	45.45 % / 41.92 %
67	B	40.15 % / 42.68 %
68	C	27.53 % / 42.92 %
69	A	26.26 % / 43.18 %
70	A	37.37 % / 42.93 %
71	C	44.44 % / 35.86 %
72	C	15.91 % / 38.89 %
73	A	16.41 % / 44.7 %
74	D	13.89 % / 44.95 %
75	B	22.47 % / 37.63 %
76	D	15.91 % / 41.92 %
77	B	40.91 % / 38.64 %
78	B	37.12 % / 39.9 %
79	C	19.19 % / 40.15 %
80	D	28.54 % / 40.4 %

Q.	Ans.	Correct
		Skipped
81	D	24.49 %
		39.9 %
82	B	23.23 %
		38.64 %
83	C	25.51 %
		39.89 %
84	C	46.46 %
		38.14 %

Q.	Ans.	Correct
		Skipped
85	D	37.37 %
		38.14 %
86	A	36.62 %
		40.15 %
87	C	49.49 %
		39.15 %
88	D	48.48 %
		30.56 %

Q.	Ans.	Correct
		Skipped
89	C	18.18 %
		36.37 %
90	B	39.9 %
		37.37 %
91	C	40.66 %
		39.64 %
92	B	48.23 %
		36.11 %

Q.	Ans.	Correct
		Skipped
93	C	37.63 %
		40.91 %
94	A	17.42 %
		40.41 %
95	B	12.37 %
		41.42 %
96	D	46.21 %
		35.61 %

Q.	Ans.	Correct
		Skipped
97	D	16.41 %
		42.18 %
98	C	36.36 %
		42.93 %
99	A	30.05 %
		36.87 %
100	C	22.22 %
		39.65 %

Performance Analysis

Avg. Score (%)	34.0%
Toppers Score (%)	96.0%
Your Score	

General Awareness

Q.1 Which of the following is the salient feature of Indian Constitution?

A. Directive Principles **B.** CJI
C. President of India **D.** None of the above

Q.2 The term hegemony refers to which of the following?

A. A dominant ideology that legitimizes cultural power only
B. A dominant ideology that legitimizes economic, political and cultural power
C. A dominant ideology that legitimizes economic power only
D. None of the above

Q.3 What is meant by the term "Tragedy of Commons"?

A. Normal problems faced by common people
B. Tragedies caused by nature
C. Interest tension due to individual control over resources meant for the collective
D. None of the above

Q.4 Which Indian state has received president's assent for the "Good Samaritan and Medical professional bill, 2016"?

A. Kerala **B.** MP
C. Rajasthan **D.** Karnataka

Q.5 Which of the following is not a characteristic of totalitarian societies?

A. a complete lack of democracy
B. widespread personality cultism
C. absolute control over the economy,
D. Complete freedom of movement for citizens

Q.6 Who founded the satya shodhak samaj?

A. Swami Vivekanand
B. Swami Dayanand
C. Jyotirao Phule
D. Raja Ram Mohan Rai

Q.7 The renowned Hindustani musician Annapurna devi, who passed away in 2018 was a:

A. Surbahar **B.** Surshri
C. Surkokila **D.** None of the above

Q.8 Malthusian theory of population explored relationship between:

A. Supply and sales
B. Optimum growth and resources
C. Production and supply
D. None of the above

Q.9 What is zero hour in parliament?

A. When members can raise important questions
B. Lunch time
C. Time taken by the speaker
D. None of the above

Q.10 Name of the light combat aircraft developed by India indigenously?

A. Sukhoi **B.** Tejas
C. Chinook **D.** None of the above

Q.11 Who is the author of the book "Ants among elephants"?

A. Shashi Tharoor **B.** Karanveer Thapa
C. Sujatha Gidla **D.** None of the above

Q.12 Jangarh singh shayam, the acclaimed artist was associated with which form of painting?

A. Gond **B.** Rajasthani
C. Marathi **D.** None of the above

Q.13 According to B.R. Ambedkar, which one of the following was considered as the "Heart and Soul" of Indian constitution?

A. Right to constitutional remedies
B. Right to constitutional amendments
C. Right to freedom of speech
D. None of the above

Q.14 National Health Mission of Indian seeks to achieve

__________.

A. Universal access to toilet
B. Universal access to equitable, affordable & quality health care services
C. Universal access to food
D. None of the above

Q.15 Which of the following is not correct about "yellow vest" movement?

A. Protestors demanding favorable policy for the immigrants
B. Known as yellow jackets movement
C. began in France in October 2018
D. None of the above

Q.16 Which two teams reached the finals of Men's Hockey World Cup 2018 held in Odisha?

A. Belgium and Russia
B. Belgium and Brazil
C. Belgium and Netherlands
D. None of the above

Q.17 Which Indian River crosses Tropic of Cancer twice?

A. Ganga **B.** Mahi **C.** Yamuna **D.** Jhelum

Q.18 Which writ means "We command"?

A. Mandamus **B.** Habeas Corpus
C. Certiorari **D.** None of the above

Q.19 Which is the highest sport honour of India?

A. Arjuna Award
B. Padam Bhushan

C. Rajiv Gandhi Khel Ratna Award
D. None of the above

Q.20 Who led the Salt Satyagraha movement along with Mahatma Gandhi?
A. Ahilya Bai Holkar
B. Kamaladevi Chattopadhyay
C. Sarojini Naidu
D. None of the above

Q.21 Nobel Prize for Medicine in 2018 was awarded for which of the following?
A. Discovery of cancer therapy by inhibition of positive immune regulation
B. Discovery of AIDS therapy by inhibition of negative immune regulation
C. Discovery of cancer therapy by inhibition of negative immune regulation
D. None of the above

Q.22 Which gas is the most toxic greenhouse gas?
A. Nitrogen Oxide
B. Carbon dioxide
C. Carbon monoxide
D. None of the above

Q.23 An economy reached 'Take-off' stage when ________.
A. Rapid growth in limited group of sectors is achieved
B. When small businesses are established
C. Slow growth in the economy
D. None of the above

Q.24 With reference to computers and the world wide web, what is the function of cookies?
A. To debug the websites
B. To block the viruses
C. To maintain and save site and user information
D. None of the above

Q.25 Punjab is referred as "The land of five waters" Select the set of rivers/water bodies it refers to ________.
A. Yamuna, Chenab, Jhelum, Sutlej, and Beas
B. Jhelum, Chenab, Ravi, Sutlej, and Beas
C. Jhelum, Chenab, Ravi, Sutlej, and Kaveri
D. None of the above

Q.26 Salome Zurabishvili was elected as the first female president of which country?
A. Georgia
B. Ireland
C. Canada
D. None of the above

Q.27 Which Hindi movie is based on English classic "Macbeth" by William Shakespeare?
A. Ishq Jaan
B. Maqbool
C. Mashgool
D. None of the above

Q.28 Who were the first European settlers in India?
A. Portuguese
B. Britishers
C. Irish
D. None of the above

Q.29 Where will India's first indigenous film festival be held in February 2019?
A. Kerala
B. Andhra Pradesh
C. Odisha
D. Karnataka

Q.30 The UN sustainable development goals, launched in September 2015, have how many goals and targets?
A. 22, 172
B. 17, 169
C. 21, 85
D. 17, 144

Q.31 Global Environment outlook is ________.
A. Reports released on World Environment Day
B. A series of reports on the environment prepared by the UN
C. Reports submitted by NGO to UN
D. None of the above

Q.32 Which has not been decriminalized by the Indian Judiciary?
A. Active Euthanasia
B. Section 377
C. Both of the above
D. None of the above

Q.33 First non-Indian to receive Bharat Ratna?
A. Khan Abdul Gaffar
B. Mohammad Raja
C. Shah bin Mohammad
D. None of the above

Q.34 Treaty of Versailles marked the end of which war?
A. World War 1
B. World War 2
C. American Civil War
D. None of the above

Q.35 Which one of the following Indian states does not have a common international border with Bangladesh?
A. Manipur
B. West Bengal
C. Tripura
D. Assam

Q.36 In 2018, Mary Kom won her 6th gold medal in the 48 Kg category at World Boxing Championships. Whom did she defeat?
A. Kanna Okopa
B. Hanna Okhota
C. Shala Okhota
D. None of the above

Q.37 In 2018, "The future policy" Gold Award of the UN Food & Agricultural Organization was given to ________.
A. Kerala
B. Sikkim
C. Rajasthan
D. Karnataka

Q.38 In India, Right to Property is a ________.
A. Legal Right
B. Fundamental Right
C. Constitutional Right
D. None of the above

Q.39 Choose correct film and director combination that was India's entry in Best Foreign Film Category for 2018 Oscar Awards.
A. Village Rockstars-Rashi Das
B. Urban Rockstars-Rima Banerji
C. Village Rockstars-Rima Das
D. None of the above

Q.40 Which is not correct about Fundamental Duties under the Constitution of India?
A. Uphold and protect the sovereignty, unity and integrity of India
B. Defend the country and render national service when

called upon to do so
C.   Safeguard public property and to abjure violence
D.   To vote in public elections

English Proficiency

Q.41 Which of the underlined parts has an error.
<u>Tulika could</u> <u>easily deceive</u> her <u>credulous parents.</u>
    1   2   3
A. 1   **B.** 2   **C.** 3   **D.** No error

Q.42 The charges against the police made by the local residents are serious ranging from indifference to ______.
A. actuation   **B.** initiation
C. encouragement   **D.** instigation

Q.43 At this time of the year, it is noticeable that the ______ is getting ______ by the day.
A. weather; bad   **B.** weather; worse
C. weather; worst   **D.** None of the above

Q.44 Which of the following is the antonym of Soothe?
A. Inflame   **B.** Calm
C. Comfort   **D.** None of the above

Q.45 The idea that my homeland has an obesity problem is difficult for me to digest. India, after all, is ________ for its high malnutrition rates, higher than even sub-Saharan Africa. But lately, it's also a place where obesity has ________ into a national crisis.
A.   notorious; skyrocketed
B.   great, come
C.   notorious, come
D.   None of the above

Q.46 Find the odd one out.
A. Statute   **B.** Act
C. Ordinance   **D.** Lawyer

Q.47 Synonym of Pedestrian is:
A. Exciting   **B.** Inspired
C. Ordinary   **D.** None of the above

Q.48 Synonym of Uncanny.
A. Canny   **B.** Ordinary
C. Extraordinary   **D.** None of the above

Q.49 Jatin could not catch the bus because by the time he ______ the bus stand, the bus ______.
A. leave, had left   **B.** reached; had left
C. reach, left   **D.** None of the above

Q.50 Antonym of Frustrated:
A. Gratified   **B.** Unhappy
C. Ordinary   **D.** None of the above

Q.51 Oil prices continued to ______ in 2018, amid weaker global demand & increased output n the United States, so that supply exceeded consumer demand. This is the ______ price in 2018 so far.
A. plummet; highest   **B.** plummet; lower

C. plummet; lowest   **D.** None of the above

Q.52 Which part has the error?
How many (A) / cups of tea (B) / she drinks (C) / everyday (D)?
A. A   **B.** B   **C.** C   **D.** D

Q.53 A section of dual ________ forming part of the outer ring road was closed due to ______.
A.   carriageway; alterations
B.   contribution; alterations
C.   carriageway; altering
D.   None of the above

Q.54 Read each sentence to find out whether there is any grammatical error in it. The error, if any, will be in one part of the sentence. Mark the number of that part as your answer.
Raju have won a prize of (1)/ two million dollars which (2)/ has to be shared (3)/ with all his team members. (4)
A. 1   **B.** 2   **C.** 3   **D.** 4

Q.55 Read each sentence to find out whether there is any grammatical error in it. The error, if any, will be in one part of the sentence. Mark the number of that part as your answer.
I do not understand (1)/ about how the payment (2)/ was made without (3)/ the manager's permission. (4)
A. 1   **B.** 2   **C.** 3   **D.** 4

Q.56 The road ______ involving two vehicles was ______ by a stray dog.
A. accident; done   **B.** accident; cause
C. accident; caused   **D.** None of the above

Q.57 Find the incorrect part.
<u>People are</u> <u>venturing</u> into hydroponics to provide an option for the <u>urban populous</u>.
      1   2
        3
A. 1   **B.** 2
C. 3   **D.** None of the above

Q.58 Find the incorrect part.
<u>There are</u> one <u>Spoon</u> and one knife <u>in my hand.</u>
    1   2   3
A. 1   **B.** 2
C. 3   **D.** None of the above

Q.59 To become a successful teacher, one must understand the role of both, the curriculum and the pedagogy. The school curriculum is about ______ to teach the next generation the decision about curriculum occurs logically prior to how to teach it.
A. Which   **B.** What
C. that   **D.** None of the above

Ques (60-64):Direction: Read the following passage carefully and answer the questions given below it.

Planning in India has essentially been an effort to determine the overall direction of the economy by directing public investment accordingly. It was possible to conceive of outcomes on the basis of government spending between 1947 and 1985 when the public sector made up more than half the gross domestic product. Now that is neither possible nor desirable. The private sector accounts for three-fourths of the gross domestic product, reducing the role of public expenditure in meeting growth targets. Besides, decades of the government occupying the commanding heights of the economy merely resulted in low rates of growth and nearly two-fifth of the population living below the poverty line till 1991.

How can planning contribute to today's economy? It should be reconceived as a think tank that works at maximizing outcomes from investments in social and physical infrastructure by identifying problems of governance. Outcomes in health and education are crucial to realize the potential of our billion-plus population, while shortcomings in power and port handling facilities can hold up future growth. Where public-private partnerships involve a number of government agencies, the Commission can work as a nodal body that takes a larger view of projects and ensures their smooth implementation.

Planners should aim at meeting growth targets by ensuring that markets function efficiently. They can advise the government on market-specific policies that address lack of access to information. They can identify sunrise areas in the next decade and promote research and innovation through public-private partnership. Simultaneously, planners should explore markets for products made by unskilled workers.

The Eleventh Plan aims at 9 per cent 'inclusive' growth by raising investment in infrastructure from 5 per cent of GDP to 9 per cent. Of the $475 billion investment needed for infrastructure, $130–140 billion is expected to come from the private sector. Public sector enterprises are expected to raise resources internally, with the Plan proposing lower support for them. The Plan has got its priorities right by reducing support for PSEs and increasing social sector allocations. Education is a big-ticket item, with the Planning Commission earmarking Rs. 2,75,289 crore for it alone with a view to meeting the skills shortage. Sadly, health has not been given the same emphasis. But, generally speaking, we are on the right track.

Q.60 Which of the following was/were the outcome/s of the government controlling the economy?

(a) Public expenditure could easily meet growth targets.

(b) Rates of growth were marginal.

(c) About 40% people had to live below the poverty line.

A. only (a)   **B.** only (b)

C. only (c)   **D.** Both (b) and (c)

Q.61 What does the author expect the planners to do about the products manufactured by unskilled workers?

A. To explore the market for importing necessary raw material

B. To provide adequate finance to unskilled workers

C. To provide skill development training

D. None of these

Q.62 Which of the following is NOT appreciated by the author in the Eleventh Plan?

A. Education has been given undue favour

B. The area of health has been given a secondary treatment

C. Reduction in support for public sector enterprises

D. Increase in fund allocation to social sector

Q.63 According to the Eleventh Plan what percentage contribution is expected to come from private sector for investment in infrastructure (approximately)?

A. 35.40   **B.** 7.12   **C.** 5.9   **D.** 25.30

Q.64 Read each sentence to find out whether there is any grammatical error in it. The error, if any, will be in one part of the sentence. Mark the number of that part as your answer.

The noise was (1)/ so faintly that (2)/ one had to strain (3)/ one's ears to hear it. (4)

A. 1   **B.** 2   **C.** 3   **D.** 4

Q.65 Select the word or phrase that is nearest in meaning to the word in capital letters.

Exiguous

A. very urgent   **B.** very small

C. extravagant   **D.** very exciting

Ques (66-70):Direction: Read the following passage carefully and answer the questions given below it.

The core policies and institutions for creating more opportunities involve complementary actions to stimulate overall growth, make markets work for poor people, and build their assets including addressing deep-seated inequalities in the distribution of such endowments as education.

Investment and technological innovation are the main drivers of growth in jobs and labor incomes. Fostering private investment requires reducing risk for private investors-through stable fiscal and monetary policy, stable investment regimes, sound financial systems, and a clear and transparent business environment. But it also involves ensuring the rule of law and taking measures to fight corruption-tackling business environments based on kickbacks, subsidies for large investors, special deals, and favored monopolies. Special measures are frequently essential to ensure that microenterprises and small businesses, which are often particularly vulnerable to bureaucratic harassment and the buying of privilege by the well-connected, can participate effectively in markets. Such measures include ensuring access to credit by promoting financial deepening and reducing the sources of market failure; lowering the transactions costs of reaching export markets by expanding access to Internet technology, organizing export fairs, and providing training in modern business practices; and building feeder roads to reduce physical barriers. Creating a sound business environment for poor households and small firms may also involve deregulation and complementary institutional reform, for example, reducing restrictions on the informal sector, especially those affecting women, and tackling land tenure or registry inadequacies that discourage small investments. Private investment will have to be complemented by public investment to enhance competitiveness and create new market opportunities. Particularly important is complementary public investment in expanding infrastructure and communications and upgrading the skills of the labor force.

International markets offer a huge opportunity for job and income growth- in agriculture, industry, and services. All countries that have had major reductions in income poverty have made use of international trade. But opening to trade can create losers as well as winners, and it will yield substantial benefits only when countries have the infrastructure and institutions to underpin a strong supply response. Thus the opening needs to be well designed, with special attention to country specifics and to institutional and other bottlenecks. The sequencing of policies should encourage job creation and manage job destruction. A more pro-poor liberalization is not necessarily a slower one; moving fast can create more opportunities for the poor. And explicit policies should offset transitory costs for poor people, as the grants for small Mexican maize producers did in the wake of the North American Free Trade Agreement (NAFTA). The opening of the capital account has to be managed prudently-in step with domestic financial sector development-to reduce the risk of high volatility in capital flows. Long-term direct investment can bring positive externalities, such as knowledge transfer, but short-term flows can bring negative externalities, particularly volatility. Policies need to address them separately. Creating human, physical, natural, and financial assets that poor people own or can use requires actions on three fronts. First, increase the focus of public spending on poor people in particular, expanding the supply of basic social and economic services and relaxing constraints on the demand side (through, for example, scholarships for poor children). Second, ensure good quality service delivery through institutional action involving sound governance and the use of markets and multiple agents. This can imply both reforming public delivery, as in education, or privatizing in a fashion that ensures expansion of services to poor people, as often makes sense in urban water and sanitation. Third, ensure the participation of poor communities and households in choosing and implementing services and monitoring them to keep providers accountable. This has been tried in projects in El Salvador, Tunisia, and Uganda. Programs to build the assets of poor people include broad-based expansion of schooling with parental and community involvement, stay-in-school programs (such as those in Bangladesh, Brazil, Mexico, and Poland), nutrition programs, mother and child health programs, vaccinations and other health interventions, and community-based schemes to protect water resources and other elements of the natural environment. There are powerful complementarities between actions in different areas. Because of close linkages between human and physical assets, for example, improving poor people's access to energy or transport can increase their access and returns to education. And improving the environment can have significant effects on poverty. This is well documented in terms of the substantial gains in health from reduced air and water pollution-which have a major influence on some of the most important diseases of poor people, including diarrheal problems of children and respiratory infections.

Q.66 What is the solution given by the author to generate new market opportunities?

A. Creating a sound business environment.

B. Rules and regulations especially in the informal sector should be eased.

C. Private investment will have to be accompanied by public investment

D. By overhauling the banking system

Q.67 What is the tone of the author?

A. Illustrative   **B.** Prosaic

C. Interpretative   **D.** Verbose

Q.68 What can be done to reduce the risk of high volatility in capital flows?

A. Improving banking infrastructure in rural areas.

B. Sagacious use of the opening of the capital account

C. Indiscreet use of the opening of the capital account

D. The closing of the capital account has to be managed prudently

Q.69 What is essential to ensure a proper business ambience for poor households?

A. Regulating institutional reform

B. Regulating foreign investments

C. Streamlining the unskilled labour force

D. Decontrolling institutional reform

Q.70 According to the author, why is it crucial to ensure that there is no bureaucratic harassment for microenterprises?

A. So that microenterprises can expand into the foreign market.

B. So that microenterprises can shrink into the foreign market.

C. So that microenterprises can dominate the market.

D. So that microenterprises can productively function in the market.

Maths and Logical Reasoning

Q.71 What is the HCF of 616 & 32?

A. 8   **B.** 2   **C.** 4   **D.** 7

Q.72 Arc AB is drawn from a circle having a radius of 8 units and centre at O.

Find: $OE =$?

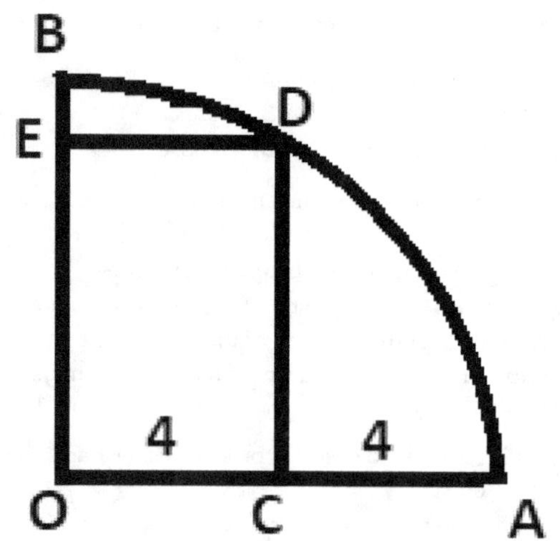

A. $3\sqrt{3}$　　**B.** $2\sqrt{3}$　　**C.** $4\sqrt{3}$　　**D.** $5\sqrt{3}$

Q.73 The average of six consecutive positive even integers is 15. The sum of the greatest and the least is how many times their average?

A. 8　　**B.** 2　　**C.** 4　　**D.** 7

Q.74 How many 2–Digits prime number can be formed using digits $2, 5$, and 7?

A. 0　　**B.** 2　　**C.** 4　　**D.** 7

Q.75 In a one day match of 50 overs, total runs are 282, and run rate for first 10 overs is 3.2 runs & that for last 10 overs is 8.2 runs. Find the run rate for intermediate 30 overs.

A. 8.4　　**B.** 5.6　　**C.** 4.2　　**D.** 2.8

Q.76 If the speed becomes $\frac{1}{4}$ th of the usual speed, then the time is taken to travel the same distance increases by 60 minutes, find the original time? (in minutes)

A. 60　　　　　　**B.** 20
C. 40　　　　　　**D.** None of the above

Q.77 Find the rate of interest, when the principal is Rs. 1200, simple interest is Rs. 432, and time is 6 years.

A. 6%　　**B.** 2%　　**C.** 4%　　**D.** 7%

Q.78 Find the unit digit of 13^{13}?

A. 9　　**B.** 1　　**C.** 3　　**D.** 7

Q.79 $2, 12, 30, 56, ?, 132$

A. 90　　**B.** 100　　**C.** 96　　**D.** 105

Q.80 There are 7 Men and 6 Women. In how many ways can we select 5 members in which at least 3 men should be there:

A. 836　　**B.** 256　　**C.** 495　　**D.** 756

Q.81 Out of the given options, which is the smallest roman numbers?

A. XL　　**B.** L　　**C.** C　　**D.** XLI

Q.82 Average of 5 consecutive integer is 12. Which is the Largest integer?

A. 13　　**B.** 12　　**C.** 14　　**D.** 15

Q.83 $a + b = b - a$, then which of the following is true?

A. $a > b$　　　　　　**B.** $a = b$
C. $a < b$　　　　　　**D.** None of the above

Q.84

For the given numbers:

$6, 8, 0, 3, 1, 6, 9, 3, 12, 3$

$a \rightarrow$ mean, $b \rightarrow$ mode, $c \rightarrow$ median

Which condition is true here?

A. $b < c < a$　　　　**B.** $a < c < b$
C. $b < a < c$　　　　**D.** None of the above

Q.85 If A, B, C and D are equal to $9 : 11, 7 : 9, 5 : 7$ and $11 : 13$ respectively, then which of the following is true?

A. $A > D > B > C$　　**B.** $D > B > A > C$
C. $D > A > B > C$　　**D.** None of the above

Q.86 Probability of selecting a red card or a 6 from pack of 52 cards?

A. $\frac{8}{13}$　　**B.** $\frac{9}{13}$　　**C.** $\frac{1}{4}$　　**D.** $\frac{7}{13}$

Q.87 $\frac{x}{27} = \frac{-1}{9}$, then find the value of x.

A. -3　　　　　　**B.** -9
C. -4　　　　　　**D.** None of the above

Q.88 In a $\triangle ABC$, angle $\angle A = 60°$, angle $\angle C = 90°, AC = 17\ cm$, then $AB = \cdots \ldots cm$

A. 38　　**B.** 22　　**C.** 34　　**D.** 75

Q.89 $Sin\theta = \frac{a}{b}, \tan\theta =?$

A. $\frac{b}{a}$　　　　　　**B.** $\frac{a}{\sqrt{b^2 - a^2}}$
C. $\frac{b}{\sqrt{b^2 - a^2}}$　　　　**D.** None of above

Q.90 What is the angle by minute hand at $12 : 18$?

A. 108degrees　　　　**B.** 96 degrees
C. 64 degrees　　　　**D.** 72 degrees

Q.91 Number of triangles?

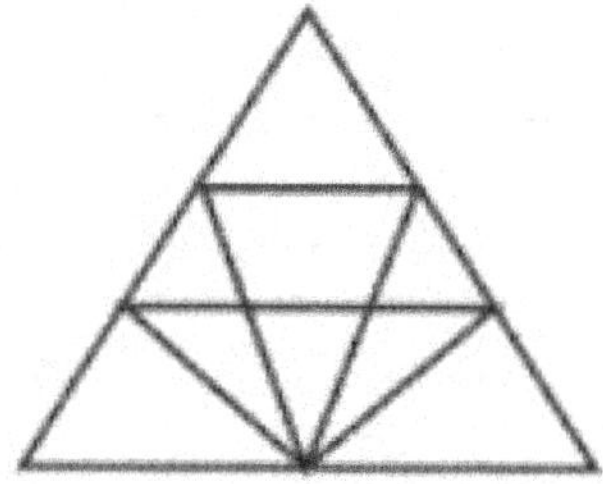

A. 18　　**B.** 12　　**C.** 14　　**D.** 17

Q.92 It is given that on 13th January 2019, there was Sunday, again after how many years, will there be Sunday on 13th January?

A. 11   **B.** 12   **C.** 14   **D.** 17

Q.93 If all the operators change as per the given pattern then which of the following is true?

$$+\rightarrow \div, x \rightarrow +, -\rightarrow x, \div \rightarrow -$$

A. $36 \div 6 + 3 - 5 - 3 = 49$
B. $36 \div 6 - 3 \times 5 - 3 = 49$
C. $36 \div 6 + 3 \times 5 - 3 = 49$
D.   None of the above

Ques (94-95):Direction: These questions are based on the following pie charts which represent the number of boys and girls pursuing courses in Creative Sculpture, Visual Arts, Computer Graphics, Fashion Design, and Hindustani Music in a college.

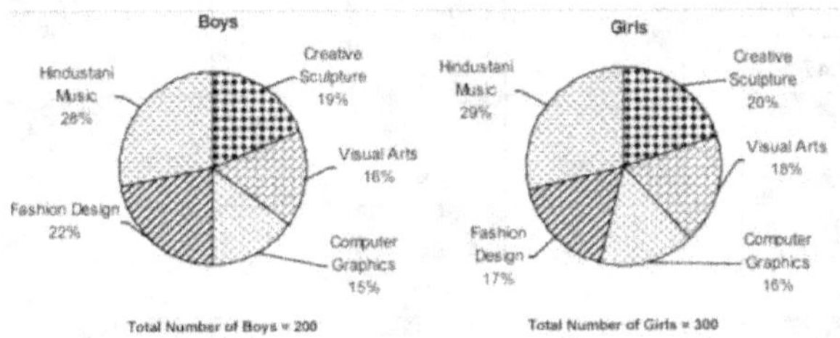

Q.94 How many students are pursuing course Visual Arts?

A. 16   **B.** 32   **C.** 54   **D.** 86

Q.95 By what approximate percentage is the number of students who are pursuing the course Hindustani Music more than the number of students pursuing the course Fashion Design?

A. 49%   **B.** 51%   **C.** 62%   **D.** 71%

Q.96 Three statements are given followed by four conclusions. Consider the statements to be true even if they seem to be at variance from the commonly known facts and find out which of the conclusions logically follow(s) the given statements and choose the proper alternative from the given choices.

Statements:

Some Dollars are Rupees.

All Rupees are Euros.

Some Yens are Rupees.

Conclusions:

I. Some Dollars are Yens.

II. All Yens are Euros.

III. Some Euros are Dollars.

IV. Some Yens are Euros.

A.   Only II and III follow
B.   Either III or IV follows
C.   Only III and IV follow
D.   Only I and III follow

Q.97 Direction: for questions: Select the correct alternative from the given choices.

In a family of five members, P is the brother of Q. R is the sister of P. Q is the sister-in-law of K. T is the daughter of K. How is T related to R, if K has no siblings and P is unmarried?

A. Mother   **B.** Uncle
C. Daughter   **D.** Niece

Q.98 Gaurav works for P hours a day and rests for Q hours a day. This pattern continues for three days and for the next three days he works exactly in the opposite pattern i.e., he works for Q hours and rests for P hours. He rests on the seventh day. Every week he adopts a new pattern and continues working as he does in the first week. The following table shows the daily working hours of Gaurav for the initial three days of each of the four weeks of February of a non-leap year in which 1st was a Monday.

	First week	Second week	Third week	Fourth week
No. of hours worked	3	2	4	6
No. of hours rested	5	7	2	2

If Gaurav is paid Rs. 150 for every hour he works, find is the amount paid to him during the given month. (in Rs.)

A. 16,350   **B.** 15,650   **C.** 14,850   **D.** 13,950

Q.99 If the second half of the following sequence is reversed then which element will be third to the left of the seventh to the right of the fifteenth element form the left?

$$4^* A\ 7@BP\%\#93LQ1?\,N6T©J < R$$

A. 6   **B.** ©   **C.** N **D.** ?

Q.100 The probability of getting at least one head when an unbiased coin is tossed thrice is:

A. $\frac{7}{8}$ **B.** $\frac{1}{8}$ **C.** $\frac{1}{2}$ **D.** $\frac{1}{4}$

// Smart Answer Sheet //

Correct — Indicates percentage of students who answered questions correctly.

Skipped — Indicates percentage of students who skipped questions.

Q.	Ans.	Correct / Skipped	Q.	Ans.	Correct / Skipped	Q.	Ans.	Correct / Skipped	Q.	Ans.	Correct / Skipped	Q.	Ans.	Correct / Skipped
1	A	46.14 % / 28.45 %	17	B	26.42 % / 41.87 %	33	A	46.54 % / 35.98 %	49	B	51.63 % / 43.49 %	65	B	9.76 % / 46.95 %
2	B	42.28 % / 42.48 %	18	A	31.5 % / 41.87 %	34	A	30.49 % / 41.46 %	50	A	49.8 % / 43.29 %	66	C	21.54 % / 47.57 %
3	C	38.01 % / 39.84 %	19	C	42.28 % / 15.65 %	35	A	19.51 % / 41.47 %	51	C	36.79 % / 43.7 %	67	C	12.4 % / 47.97 %
4	D	9.96 % / 42.48 %	20	C	35.98 % / 39.83 %	36	B	34.76 % / 42.48 %	52	C	28.86 % / 43.9 %	68	B	23.17 % / 48.37 %
5	D	25.2 % / 42.69 %	21	A	23.17 % / 39.23 %	37	B	21.95 % / 43.29 %	53	A	45.12 % / 44.11 %	69	D	7.93 % / 47.96 %
6	C	29.88 % / 41.66 %	22	B	13.82 % / 41.06 %	38	C	27.24 % / 41.05 %	54	A	40.85 % / 44.72 %	70	D	29.47 % / 47.77 %
7	A	15.24 % / 43.3 %	23	A	33.74 % / 34.76 %	39	C	38.01 % / 43.49 %	55	B	41.26 % / 45.12 %	71	A	41.67 % / 32.72 %
8	B	32.72 % / 42.08 %	24	C	48.37 % / 42.08 %	40	D	21.75 % / 42.07 %	56	C	50.2 % / 44.92 %	72	C	26.42 % / 38.42 %
9	A	45.33 % / 40.44 %	25	B	44.31 % / 41.67 %	41	D	20.12 % / 36.79 %	57	C	33.33 % / 45.13 %	73	B	34.55 % / 38.82 %
10	B	43.09 % / 41.46 %	26	A	31.5 % / 42.08 %	42	D	36.99 % / 42.89 %	58	A	47.56 % / 45.33 %	74	A	35.77 % / 37.2 %
11	C	23.17 % / 41.46 %	27	B	48.58 % / 37.4 %	43	B	44.51 % / 43.09 %	59	B	46.95 % / 45.53 %	75	B	41.67 % / 38.41 %
12	A	24.19 % / 42.27 %	28	A	51.42 % / 40.65 %	44	A	45.33 % / 43.29 %	60	D	31.91 % / 46.14 %	76	B	35.57 % / 39.02 %
13	A	36.38 % / 38.21 %	29	C	16.26 % / 39.43 %	45	A	35.37 % / 43.9 %	61	D	15.65 % / 47.97 %	77	A	40.04 % / 39.03 %
14	B	50.0 % / 41.46 %	30	B	25.41 % / 42.88 %	46	D	41.46 % / 43.3 %	62	B	36.79 % / 47.97 %	78	C	26.22 % / 40.24 %
15	A	20.73 % / 42.48 %	31	B	38.62 % / 41.66 %	47	C	35.77 % / 43.5 %	63	D	21.75 % / 48.17 %	79	A	34.35 % / 40.45 %
16	C	28.05 % / 42.48 %	32	A	24.8 % / 41.05 %	48	C	37.4 % / 43.49 %	64	B	38.21 % / 47.56 %	80	D	15.45 % / 43.7 %

Q.	Ans.	Correct	Skipped
81	A	20.53 %	41.06 %
82	C	37.2 %	41.05 %
83	D	13.21 %	40.45 %
84	A	23.17 %	42.68 %

Q.	Ans.	Correct	Skipped
85	C	29.67 %	42.28 %
86	D	21.95 %	43.5 %
87	A	44.11 %	42.48 %
88	C	28.66 %	43.49 %

Q.	Ans.	Correct	Skipped
89	B	29.88 %	42.88 %
90	A	23.17 %	42.68 %
91	A	14.43 %	42.07 %
92	A	19.92 %	44.1 %

Q.	Ans.	Correct	Skipped
93	C	21.14 %	43.7 %
94	D	38.82 %	43.7 %
95	B	25.2 %	44.11 %
96	C	28.66 %	44.1 %

Q.	Ans.	Correct	Skipped
97	C	18.09 %	44.31 %
98	D	13.01 %	45.53 %
99	D	22.36 %	44.92 %
100	A	17.28 %	44.71 %

Performance Analysis

Avg. Score (%)	33.0%
Toppers Score (%)	94.0%
Your Score	

General Awareness

Q.1 In which country did chess originate?

A. India   **B.** Iran   **C.** Spain   **D.** Italy

Q.2 Manu Bhaker won gold in the 2018 Youth Olympic Games in _______ sports.

A. 10m rifle   **B.** 50m rifle
C. 25m air pistol   **D.** 10m air pistol

Q.3 Which of the following is an 'inactivated vaccine' or a vaccine developed using a deadvirus?

A. Covishield   **B.** Covaxin
C. Moderna   **D.** Sputnik-V

Q.4 The Sero-survey, that is proposed to be conducted by ICMR for monitoring trends in the prevalence of the novel corona virus, will involve the testing of which sample?

A. Urine   **B.** Nasal swab
C. Throat swab   **D.** Blood serum

Q.5 In which place in Nagaland was a decisive battle of World War II fought?

A. Phek   **B.** Dimapur   **C.** Kohima   **D.** Wokha

Q.6 Find the odd one out:

A. K.K.Shailaja
B. Jacinda Ardern
C. Sanna Mirella Marin
D. Tsai Ing-Wen

Q.7 Which wrestler was awarded the Rajiv Gandhi Khel Ratna Award 2020?

A. Bajrang Punia   **B.** Rahul Aware
C. Yogeshwar Dutt   **D.** Vinesh Phogat

Q.8 Which of the following options is true in relation to an epidemic?

An epidemic ____________.

A. is a sudden increase in the occurrence of a disease with the change of season
B. continues to stay permanently in a region or population
C. always occurs worldwide
D. affects a large number of people within a community, population, or region at a particular time

Q.9 Which of the following musical instruments is Anuradha Pal associated with?

A. Sitar   **B.** Guitar
C. Mandolin   **D.** Tabla

Q.10 Which of the following is NOT a session of the Lok Sabha?

A. Monsoon Session   **B.** Winter Session
C. Budget Session   **D.** Summer Session

Q.11 Black revolution in Indian context is related to _________.

A. petroleum production
B. coal production
C. fish production
D. iron ore production

Q.12 What kind of product was manufactured by the Union Carbide plant in Bhopal, which had one of the worst Industrial disasters in independent India?

A. Plastics   **B.** Paints
C. Leather   **D.** Pesticides

Q.13 India's decision to send Covid-19 vaccine to neighboring countries is being done under the ______.

A. Atmanirbhar Bharat Inititaive
B. Vaccine Maitri Initiative
C. Bharat Vaccine Outreach Programme
D. Vaccine Diplomacy Policy

Q.14 Which was the first book to set the stage for society to change in becoming more environmentally aware?

A. Population Bomb by Paul Ehrlich
B. The Omnivore's Dilemma by Michael Pollan
C. The Lorax by Dr. Seuss
D. Silent Spring by Rachel Carson

Q.15 Greenhouse gases prevent release of heat in the _________.

A. exosphere   **B.** troposphere
C. stratosphere   **D.** thermosphere

Q.16 Which Indian Lunar probe discovered water on the Moon?

A. Chandrayaan-1   **B.** Mangalyaan
C. Cartosat-3   **D.** Chandrayaan-2

Q.17 The year 2021 marks the _________ death anniversary of Mahatma Gandhi.

A. 74th   **B.** 75th   **C.** 73rd   **D.** 72nd

Q.18 The UDAY Scheme implemented by the Government of India since 2015 seeks to_________________________.

A. distribute LED bulbs at a low price to reduce electricity consumption
B. provide life insurance of Rs. 2 lakh for people between 18 to 50 years age group
C. achieve financial turnaround of power distribution companies of the public sector
D. provide LPG connection to BPL families at subsidised rates

Q.19 Which is the state with the highest percentage of the Scheduled Tribes population in India?

A. Jharkhand   **B.** Madhya Pradesh
C. Odisha   **D.** Mizoram

Q.20 The Nobel Peace Prize 2020 was awarded to ____________.

A. World Food Programme

B. Organization for the Prohibition of Chemical Weapons (OPCW)

C. International Campaign to Abolish Nuclear Weapons (ICAN)

D. National Dialogue Quartet

Q.21 Find the ODD one out?

A. M. F. Hussain

B. Pannalal Ghosh

C. Raja Ravi Varma

D. S.H. Raz

Q.22 Who among the following is said to have drafted the U.S. Declaration of Independence with four others?

A. Thomas Jefferson

B. George Washington

C. King George III

D. Abraham Lincoln

Q.23 Which of the following is NOT part of the Sustainable Development Goals?

A. Promotion of decent jobs for all

B. Access to digital technological services for all

C. Access to sustainable energy for all

D. Availability of water and sanitation for all

Q.24 Who was the first Indian woman to be elected as President of the United Nations General Assembly?

A. Indira Gandhi

B. Vijaya Lakshmi Pandit

C. Sarojini Naidu

D. Rajkumari Amrit Kaur

Q.25 Which among the given options is the Indian social reformer also known as the Father of Modern India?

A. Mahatma Gandhi

B. Ishwar Chandra Vidyasagar

C. Raja Ram Mohan Roy

D. Acharya Vinoba Bhav

Q.26 The second largest ocean in the world is ___________.

A. Pacific Ocean

B. Arctic Ocean

C. Atlantic Ocean

D. Indian Ocean

Q.27 Which is the first state/UT to become the first Har Ghar Jal state in India?

A. Goa

B. Kerala

C. Chandigarh

D. Sikkim

Q.28 Who is the current Secretary-General of the United Nations?

A. David Malpass

B. Kristalina Georgieva

C. Antonio Guterres

D. Tedros Adhanom

Q.29 Who was the Commander of the Air India Plane that flew over the North Pole in January 2021 with an all-women cockpit crew?

A. Capt Nivedita Bhasin

B. Capt. Aarohi Pandit

C. Capt. Sarah Hameed Ahmed

D. Capt. Zoya Agarwal

Q.30 Which was the Indian entry for Oscars in 2020?

A. Newton

B. Jallikattu

C. Gully Boy

D. Village Rockstars

Q.31 Drishyam, the Hindi movie released in 2015, was originally made in which Indian language?

A. Malayalam

B. Tamil

C. Telugu

D. Kannada

Q.32 This writer was the first to win the Sahitya Academy Award for English literature. Who was he?

A. R.K.Narayan

B. Raja Rao

C. Ruskin Bond

D. Mulk Raj Anand

Q.33 The book A Promised Land (2020) has been authored by ________.

A. Barack Obama

B. Pranab Mukherjee

C. Malala Yousafzai

D. Nelson Mandela

Q.34 Which among the following Indian freedom movements started with the breaking of the Salt Law?

A. Quit India Movement

B. Champaran Satyagraha

C. Non-cooperation Movement

D. Civil Disobedience Movement

Q.35 What is the name of the Central Government's economic package for the poor to fight the Coronavirus pandemic and lock-down?

A. Prime Minister Kisan Samman Nidhi Yojana

B. Prime Minister Suraksha Bima Yojana

C. Prime Minister Gareeb Kalyan Anna Yojana

D. Prime Minister Annadata Aay Sanrakshan Abhiyan

Q.36 Which of the following hill ranges is dominated by the 'Doddabetta' peak?

A. Nallamala Hills

B. Nilgiri Hills

C. Anaimalai Hills

D. Cardamom Hills

Q.37 Identify the current Lok Sabha Speaker among the given options.

A. Meira Kumar

B. Sumitra Mahajan

C. Venkaiah Naidu

D. Om Birla

Q.38 The main theme of Economic Survey 2020-2021 is ___________.

A. Policy Reforms

B. Saving Lives and Livelihoods

C. Environment and Development

D. Saving COVID-19 Warriors

Q.39 Bhitarkanika National Park is situated in which Indian state?

A. Maharashtra

B. Odisha

C. Himachal Pradesh

D. Madhya Pradesh

Q.40 Name the country that generates all its electricity using renewable energy.

A. Denmark

B. Iceland

C. Costa Rica

D. Bhutan

English Proficiency

Q.41 Direction: For the following questions answer them individually.

"If I were in your shoes, I would put on a happy face," advised Rakesh. No Error.

A. No Error
B. advised Rakesh
C. I were
D. put on

Q.42 Direction: Identify the correct order of the following statements to make a coherent paragraph. The lead sentence has been given.

With its rich pungency and smell, garlic has been both extolled and vilified during its 4000-year history.

A. Later the Greeks and Romans used it for dog bites and bladder infections as well as cures for asthma and leprosy.

B. The ancient Egyptians used it as medicine for more than twenty different ailments including heart disease and tumors.

C. The Israeli slaves when fleeing the Egyptians for the Promised Land complained ofnot having garlic.

D. Although it is sometimes referred to as "the stinking rose" and certainly its smell isoff-putting to many, it still thrives today with even a garlic ice cream available in SanFrancisco.

E. They even fed it to their slaves to give them more strength to build the pyramids.

A. BECAD
B. CEABD
C. DEBAC
D. ABCDE

Q.43 Direction: Fill in the blank to complete the sentence:
Despite being twins, the boys looked so different ____ one another

A. than
B. with
C. to
D. from

Q.44 Which word from the given options is most opposite in meaning to the word in capitals?
IMPEDE

A. fetter
B. speed
C. slide
D. facilitate

Q.45 Direction: Fill in the blanks to complete the sentence:
He was quick ___ arithmetic, but weak ___ languages.

A. in; at
B. at; in
C. at; at
D. in; in

Q.46 Direction: In the following question, one part of the sentence may have an error. Find out which part of the sentence has an error and click the button corresponding to it. If the sentence is free from error, click the "No error" option.
Let us not live here furthermore as it is dangerous to do so, she said. No Error.

A. here furthermore
B. No Error
C. so, she said
D. Let us

Q.47 Direction: In the following question, one part of the sentence may have an error. Find out which part of the sentence has an error and click the button corresponding to it. If the sentence is free from error, click the "No error" option.
Every adult and child knows that success is as much about belief and hard work as about skill. No Error

A. No Error
B. as about skill
C. knows
D. as much

Q.48 Direction: Fill in the blanks to complete the sentence:
The _______ of modern technology do not compensate for the _______ of privacy invasion it harbours.

A. cons; failure
B. wonders; fact
C. tribulations; trials
D. marvels; loss

Q.49 Direction: Fill in the blanks to complete the sentence:
There is _________ on earth I would __________ here.

A. anywhere; be
B. nowhere; rather be than
C. any where; love more than
D. no where; want to be

Q.50 Direction: Identify the correct order of the following statements to make a coherent paragraph. The lead sentence has been given.

The expression "you are what you eat" is becoming clearer with every nutritional study.

A. In brief, most longevity studies indicate that a diet rich in Omega 3s and avoiding sugars and most carbohydrates will add years to our lives, and especially the quality of our lives.

B. However, the problem for most of us in eating a healthy diet is that food is cultural and we tend to eat foods that our culture has instilled in us as good, whether or not they are consistent with these studies.

C. Physically, athletes are learning to avoid carbohydrates if they require bursts of speed in their sports.

D. Even mentally, what we eat can affect performance as many foods such as sugars slow us down and tend to make us lethargic, something we must avoid especially while taking exams.

E. Nutritionists suggest deficiencies in B-12, thiamine, zinc and niacin will result inlower mental performance.

A. BCDEA
B. ABEDC
C. EDCBA
D. CEDBA

Q.51 Direction: Fill in the blank to complete the sentence:
This pandemic has taught us to be more _______ with hygiene.

A. chary
B. tepid
C. suspicious
D. circumspect

Q.52 Direction: Identify which of the given options CANNOT be definitely inferred from the passage given below.

The group was wary of taking the course. The expectations set by the professor were so high, that they seemed near impossible to achieve. There were many readings given and the assignments seems to focus on anything but the readings. It was almost as if the readings were a take off point only. The group was worried that their cumulative grade point would suffer as a result of taking this course.

A. The students may not take the course.
B. The readings were only guideposts for the assignments
C. The professor was very strict.
D. The group does not have faith in its ability to do well in the course.

Q.53 Direction: Fill in the blank with the most appropriate option:

To meet the goals of Atmanirbhar Bharat the universities have started _______studyprogrammes.

A. entrepenurship

B. entreprenuship

C. entrepreneurship

D. entrepnurship

Q.54 Direction: Fill in the blanks to complete the sentence:

The number of people who _____ interested in the play _____ outnumbered by those who already bought the tickets to watch it.

A. is not; are

B. are not; is

C. is; is

D. are; are

Q.55 Direction: Fill in the blanks to complete the sentence:

It is difficult to feel _______ when one is at _______.

A. remorseful; the top of the world

B. enchanted; a birthday celebration

C. favoured by fortune; a loss for words

D. indigent; the mercy of one's creditors

Q.56 Direction: Select the synonym for the word underlined in the statement given below:

He was always looking to save money. After all, one needed to be <u>frugal</u> if one wanted to build a successful business.

A. thrifty

B. wise

C. economic

D. prudent

Q.57 Direction: Which word from the given options is most similar in meaning to the word in capitals when used as a VERB?

MEAN

A. miserly

B. midpoint

C. signify

D. sumptuous

Q.58 Direction: In the following question, one part of the sentence may have an error. Find out which part of the sentence has an error and click the button corresponding to it. If the sentence is free from error, click the "No error" option.

Films are <u>an amazing medium of communicating cultures and history. No Error.</u>

A. cultures and history

B. of communicating

C. an amazing medium

D. No Error

Q.59 Direction: Select the antonym for the word underlined in the statement given below:

They did not know which direction to go in. They were at an <u>impasse</u> about the release date of the film.

A. deadlock

B. breakthrough

C. obstruction

D. debate

Q.60 Based on the information that follows, which of the given options is MOST DEFINITELY TRUE?

There are two containers in a room.

1. One is a box and one is a can.

2. One is small and is green.

3. One of them has toys in it.

4. The can is big.

5. The container that is completely purple has toys in it.

A. The box is big.

B. The can is green.

C. The box does not have toys in it.

D. The can has toys in it.

Ques (61-65):Direction: Read the passage and answer the question:

The target group of major OTT platforms should ideally be "millennials" or the age group of18-35 years. This number, however, is largelydue to the Digital India campaign, increasing the number of smartphone and data users and is also an effect of globalization which has led the population to be more aware. With major data service providers like Jio bringing down data costs, there has been a significantshift in viewership in India with number of Indian users growing at the rate of 4-8%. This essentially means that there is massivepotential for rural India to subscribe to such platforms on a large scale - making rural India also a target group for platforms.In 2017, OTT platforms in India generated INR 2019 crore, this is expected to increase to INR5595 crores by 2022. Digital streamingplatforms overtook film entertainment to rank the third-largest Indian Media & Entertainment sector in 2019, according to the latest EYFICCI IndianMedia & Entertainment Report.When most OTT platforms made an entry in the Indian market, they mainly had catch-up shows. However, with the entry of globalplayers like Netflix and Amazon Prime Video, users are offered a plethora of original content. Hotstar is currently the most popular OTTplatform in India according to data from a mobile advertising and Internet service provider. Although in my opinion, Netflix will be themarket leader in the medium term among millennials as it is agiant global player and it entered India powerful, mainly due to the youth inspired by western culture.

Q.61 Which of the given options best represent the author's purpose in writing the passage?

A. To describe the potential of the OTT platforms.

B. To comment on the importance of the OTT platforms.

C. To highlight the presence of OTT platforms in India.

D. To argue for the advantages of the OTT platforms.

Q.62 Which of the given options is an assumption made by the author?

A. Original content attracts users.

B. Data costs had kept users away till Jio entered the market.

C. The Digital India campaign led to an increase in the sale of digital devices.

D. Mobile interface is essential to attract users.

Q.63 Which of the following can be inferred based on the passage?

A. Rural areas are entirely untapped by OTT platforms.

B. Digital streaming and OTT refer to the same type of platform.

C. OTT platforms will more than double their revenue in just 5 years.

D. Millennials are the only age-group the OTT platforms should focus upon.

Q.64 The author will NOT agree with which of the given options?

A. The ones born between 1985 and 2002 are easily attracted to Netflix.

B. OTT platforms surpassed movies two years ago.

C. Netflix's popularity is solely due to the western influences on Indian youth.

D. Indian players were the first ones on OTT platforms in this country.

Q.65 The passage has most likely appeared in ______________.

A. a brand-building magazine

B. a computer magazine

C. a research journal

D. a newspaper publication

Ques (66-70):Direction: Read the passage and answer the question:

Historians have long argued about what gave rise to the Age of Enlightenment in the eighteenth century. Some have hypothesized that itwas at least in some part due to the riseof coffee houses. That seems a bit farfetched until we look at it more closely.Very quickly after the rise of coffee houses, there emerged a distinction between them and thepubs. Rumors of the health benefits ofcoffee spread and it was soon agreed that coffeehouses spurred more sober, rational thought and sharper political discussion,whereastaverns catered to rowdiness and intoxication. A coffee house was a place to be exposed tonew ideas, current events anddiscussions of how life might be lived. Until this time, a forumto discuss new ideas had not existed. Now, merchants, traders, writers,philosophers, andpoliticians had such a forum. Gradually they found other ways of meeting and coffee housesbegan to wane inpopularity until the Starbucks generation brought them back twenty-fiveyears ago.Some historians claim that coffee replaced "beer soup," which was what most Europeans andAmericans had subsisted on, with a "drug"that now kept them awake and allowed them toconverse well into the night in a far more lucid way. This, they feel, was what gave rise toboththe French and American revolutions. Other historians say that a higher level of leisure hadcreated an environment in which peoplecould afford the time to meet in coffee houses todiscuss the latest farming techniques, business trends and, of course, politics.

King Charles of England actually attempted a ban of coffee houses in 1675, fearing that theymight result in his loss of power or evendecapitation. However, his ministers loved theircoffee so much that they overruled the ban.So, did coffee houses give rise to these meetings or was it the level of leisure that hadsuddenly come about? It does seem logical thatpeople with a clear head would be morecapable of holding onto an idea for a longer period of time, and would have the mental acuitytograsp what each other was saying. So, perhaps it was a happy confluence of increasedleisure and a switch to coffee that enabled somany of those wonderful thinkers to hammerout their ideas for a new nation and those with a scientific bent to come up with so manyofthe major breakthroughs during the eighteenth century in Europe and America.Some of our founding fathers may have sat in these very coffee houses discussing the futureof the colonies or how government shouldbe, noting the pitfalls or failures of the monarchiesof England and France. Perhaps a seemingly harmless thing like the emergence ofcoffeehouses actually influenced our future. Interestingly, almost as quickly as they sprang up,coffee houses began to decline. They hadserved

their purpose and were no longer neededas meeting places for political or literary critics and debate.

Q.66 If coffee was NOT the largest influence on the Age of Enlightenment, what does the author suggest might have been the influence?

A. the revolutionary ideas that were everywhere

B. the King's proclamation

C. the rise in leisure time that Europeans and Americans had suddenly had

D. the closing of many pubs at this time

Q.67 Which of the following most closely suggests the author's attitude about the influence of coffee houses on the Age of Enlightenment?

A. they definitely were the major factors

B. they were definitely an improvement over pubs

C. they were a possible connection, but perhaps not the only one

D. they were more conducive to conversation

Q.68 Which of the following does the author NOT do concerning coffee?

A. indicate that it sharpens the mind

B. mention that it helped people stay up late to discuss things

C. contrast it with "beer soup"

D. demonstrate why it is so healthy

Q.69 Why does the author mention the proclamation of King Charles?

A. to show how kings were bullies

B. to suggest how things got done back then

C. to demonstrate how strongly coffee houses had become part of society

D. to indicate that the King saw coffee houses as a threat to his power

Q.70 Which of the following best expresses the author's purpose in writing this passage?

A. to show how the political thinking behind two revolutions got started

B. to explain how the Age of Enlightenment came about

C. to show why coffee houses are better than pubs

D. to discuss a possible connection between coffee houses and the Age of Enlightenment

Maths and Logical Reasoning

Q.71 If 2 is a root of the equation: $2x^2 + kx + 4 = 0$

A. $k = 6$ **B.** $k = 12$

C. $k = -6$ **D.** $k = -12$

Q.72 The percentage increase in the area of a rectangle when each side is increased by aquarter of its length is ______________.

A. 50.00%   **B.** 66.66%   **C.** 56.25%   **D.** 25.00%

Q.73 The number of ways in which Aman, Anaya, Danish and Nero can stand in a straight line such that, Danish comes between Aman and Anaya and Nero does not come between Aman and Anaya is ______________.

A. 4 **B.** 6 **C.** 8 **D.** 12

Q.74 A Rhombus and a kite both DO NOT have ______________.

A. equal adjacent sides
B. equal opposite sides
C. two acute and two obtuse angles
D. bisecting diagonal

Q.75 Abhay can complete a piece of work in 18 days, Balram in 20 days and Chandan in 30 days. Balram and Chandan started the work but were forced to leave after 2 days. How many days will Abhay take to complete the remaining work alone?

A. 10 days **B.** 12 days **C.** 15 days **D.** 16 days

Q.76 Two guns were fired from the same place at an interval of 6 minutes. A person approaching the place observed that $5\ min\ 52$ seconds have elapsed between the hearings of the sound of two guns. If the velocity of the sound is 330 meter/ second, the man was approaching that place at what speed in kilometer per hour?

A. $24\ km/hr$ **B.** $18\ km/hr$
C. $21\ km/hr$ **D.** $27\ km/h$

Q.77 A positive integer when divided by q leaves remainder 21. When double that number is divided by q, the remainder is 13. Then, q is:

A. 21 **B.** 29 **C.** 39 **D.** 37

Q.78 The least number of complete years in which a sum of money will be more than doubled at 10% compound interest is ______.

A. 10 **B.** 8 **C.** 5 **D.** 6

Q.79 The product of two numbers is 45 and their difference is 4. What is the sum of squares of these two numbers?

A. 106 **B.** 102 **C.** 41 **D.** 104

Q.80 The ratio of simple interest calculated biennially and quarterly at the same rate of interest for the same time period is ____.

A. $1:4$ **B.** $2:1$ **C.** $1:2$ **D.** $4:1$

Q.81 The missing number in the following table is ______.

64	216	512
1000	1728	2744
4096	?	8000

A. 5832 **B.** 7200 **C.** 7648 **D.** 6400

Q.82 The compound interest on Rs. 30000 at 7 percent per annum is Rs. 4347. What is the time period in years for this investment?

A. 2 years **B.** 4 years **C.** 5 years **D.** 3 years

Q.83 Two sets AA and BB are defined as follows:-

$$AA = \{x \mid x \in N, x < 5\}$$
$$BB = \{x \mid x \in N, x^2 < 25\}, n(XX) = \text{number of}$$

elements in XX. Choose the CORRECT option.

A. $n(AA) > n(BB)$ **B.** $n(AA) < n(BB)$
C. $AA = BB$ **D.** $n(AA) \leq n(BB)$

Q.84 The leap day falls on the same day of the week after a gap of at least ___________.

A. 28 years **B.** 7 years **C.** 5 years **D.** 11 years

Q.85 Two fair dices with faces numbered 1 to 6 are thrown and their points are added. The thrower is given Rs. 40 for a score of 12 and he has to pay Rs. 2 if the score is less than 12. What is his expectation about gain or loss per throw?

A. Loss of Rs. $\left(\frac{1}{6}\right)$ **B.** Gain of Rs. $\left(\frac{1}{6}\right)$
C. Gain of Rs. $\left(\frac{5}{6}\right)$ **D.** Loss of Rs. $\left(\frac{5}{6}\right)$

Q.86 For every 60 units that a minute hand moves in an hour, the hour hand moves by______.

A. 15 units **B.** 1 unit **C.** 5 units **D.** 4 units

Q.87 Ranbir's office has two doors facing each other. The front door faces east. He comes out of his office back door and walks 100 metres, turns right and walks 50 metres further. The direction he is now from his office is ___________.

A. North-east **B.** South-west
C. South-east **D.** North-west

Q.88 Among the following options, the CORRECT one is:

$1.$ Rhombus is a cyclic quadrilateral

$2.$ Diagonals of a rhombus are equal

$3.$ A rhombus that can be inscribed in a circle is a square

$4.$ Opposite angles in a rhombus are equal

A. Both 1 and 2 **B.** Both 1 and 4
C. Both 1 and 3 **D.** Both 3 and 4

Q.89 Which of the given statements is an INCORRECT representation of the expression $1\frac{3}{4} \div \frac{1}{2}$ is___________?

A. Number of halves in $1\frac{3}{4}$
B. $1\frac{3}{4}$ times reciprocal of $\frac{1}{2}$
C. Half of $1\frac{3}{4}$
D. The expression is about finding the number whose half is $1\frac{3}{4}$

Q.90 A person goes from X to Y on a cycle at 20 kilometers per hour and returns at 24 kilometers per hour. The method of Central Tendency most appropriate to calculate the average speed would be__________.

A. Geometric Mean
B. Harmonic Mean
C. Arithmetic Mean
D. Weighted Arithmetic Mean

Q.91 The Coefficient of Variation can be measured by
______________.

A.   Standard Deviation and Mean
B.   Quartile Deviation and Mean
C.   Variance and Mean
D.   Range and Mean

Q.92 Complete the following series of numbers:
$6, 26, 126, 626, \ldots\ldots$

A. 3126   B. 3125   C. 3216   D. 3215

Q.93 The seventh term in the series $5, 13, 29, 61,$
is__________.

A. 97   B. 191   C. 253   D. 509

Q.94 An article manufactured by a company consists of two parts: Part I and Part II. In the process of manufacturing of Part I, 9 products out of 100 are likely to be defective. Similarly, 5 products out of 100 are likely to be defective in the manufacture of Part II. What is the probability that the final assembled article will NOT be defective?

A. 0.8465   B. 0.8645   C. 0.8564   D. 0.8546

Q.95 If $\log\left(\dfrac{a}{b}\right) + \log\left(\dfrac{b}{a}\right) = \log(a + b)$

A. $a - b = 1$ B. $a + b = 1$
C. $a = b$ D. $a^2 - b^2 = 1$

Q.96 The surface area of the resultant cuboid that gets formed by placing five ice cubes adjacent to each other, each of whose side is 5 centimeters, is __________.

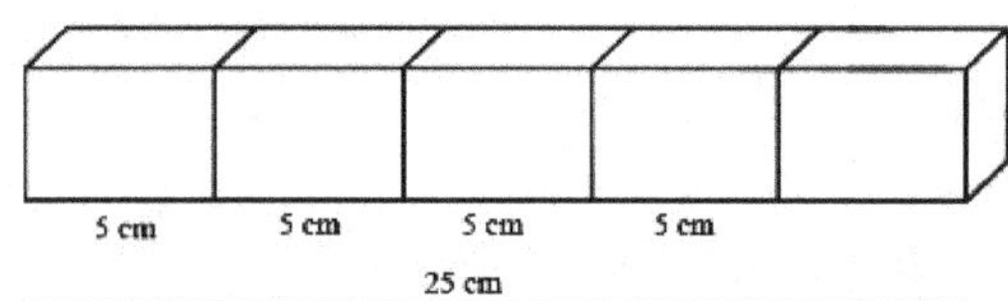

A. $625\ cm^2$ B. $550\ cm^2$ C. $125\ cm^2$ D. $650\ cm^2$

Ques (97-100):Direction: The following table presents Purpose-wise Total Balances (Overdue) of Primary Agricultural Credit Societies (PACS) of some select States of India. Answer the following four questions based on this table.

States	Balances (Overdues) Purpose-wise		
	Agricultural	Non-Agricultural	Others
Gujarat	324455.78	4978.96	13419.82
Karnataka	45064.27	31033.48	7152.67
Kerala	148625.45	1030589.55	505017.31
Madhya Pradesh	155466.25	12301.47	5394.18
Telangana	38759.63	1943.87	2222.15
India	1830035.42	1356970.63	2197801.83

Q.97 Which of the given statements is INCORRECT?

A.   Gujarat has the second highest average overdue.
B.   The average overdue of Karnataka is less than the average overdue of Madhya Pradesh.
C.   The average overdue is the highest in Kerala among the select states.
D.   The average overdue of Karnataka is less than the average overdue of Telangana.

Q.98 The state of ________ has 0.01% of highest Non-Agricultural overdue as a percentage of total overdue.

A. Gujarat   B. Telengana
C. Kerala   D. Karnataka

Q.99 In which state, is the ratio of agricultural to non-agricultural overdue the highest, among the selected states?

A. Kerala   B. Karnataka
C. Gujarat   D. Telangana

Q.100 In the table above, which state shows the highest variability of overdues?

A.   Madhya Pradesh   B.   Kerala
C.   Gujarat   D.   Karnataka

// Smart Answer Sheet //

Correct   Indicates percentage of students who answered questions correctly.

Skipped   Indicates percentage of students who skipped questions.

Q.	Ans.	Correct / Skipped	Q.	Ans.	Correct / Skipped	Q.	Ans.	Correct / Skipped	Q.	Ans.	Correct / Skipped	Q.	Ans.	Correct / Skipped
1	A	52.98 % / 19.64 %	17	C	36.31 % / 34.52 %	33	A	45.83 % / 30.96 %	49	B	35.71 % / 50.6 %	65	D	22.62 % / 49.4 %
2	D	22.02 % / 32.74 %	18	C	22.62 % / 34.52 %	34	D	40.48 % / 34.52 %	50	A	20.83 % / 49.41 %	66	C	30.36 % / 52.38 %
3	B	35.71 % / 32.15 %	19	B	41.07 % / 12.5 %	35	C	47.62 % / 32.74 %	51	D	12.5 % / 49.4 %	67	C	20.24 % / 51.78 %
4	D	29.76 % / 34.53 %	20	A	44.05 % / 32.14 %	36	B	34.52 % / 32.15 %	52	C	25.6 % / 50.0 %	68	D	26.79 % / 50.59 %
5	C	45.24 % / 34.52 %	21	B	32.14 % / 30.96 %	37	D	48.81 % / 34.52 %	53	C	45.83 % / 49.41 %	69	D	25.6 % / 51.19 %
6	A	25.0 % / 32.14 %	22	A	25.6 % / 34.52 %	38	B	43.45 % / 33.34 %	54	B	18.45 % / 50.0 %	70	D	36.31 % / 51.19 %
7	D	30.36 % / 33.93 %	23	B	32.14 % / 30.36 %	39	B	40.48 % / 34.52 %	55	A	28.57 % / 48.81 %	71	C	35.12 % / 37.5 %
8	D	47.02 % / 33.93 %	24	B	45.24 % / 34.52 %	40	B	27.98 % / 34.52 %	56	A	20.83 % / 49.41 %	72	C	26.19 % / 41.67 %
9	D	19.05 % / 34.52 %	25	C	50.6 % / 34.52 %	41	A	24.4 % / 44.65 %	57	C	19.64 % / 50.0 %	73	A	35.71 % / 42.27 %
10	D	43.45 % / 33.34 %	26	C	43.45 % / 34.53 %	42	A	35.71 % / 50.0 %	58	B	20.24 % / 50.59 %	74	B	11.9 % / 42.27 %
11	A	30.36 % / 32.74 %	27	A	38.69 % / 30.95 %	43	D	39.88 % / 49.41 %	59	B	22.62 % / 33.93 %	75	C	23.81 % / 42.26 %
12	D	43.45 % / 33.93 %	28	C	48.21 % / 33.93 %	44	D	25.0 % / 51.19 %	60	D	29.17 % / 49.4 %	76	D	10.12 % / 43.45 %
13	B	46.43 % / 32.14 %	29	D	34.52 % / 32.15 %	45	B	26.79 % / 50.0 %	61	A	29.17 % / 48.21 %	77	B	20.83 % / 44.65 %
14	D	28.57 % / 33.93 %	30	B	35.12 % / 32.74 %	46	A	31.55 % / 48.81 %	62	A	15.48 % / 47.02 %	78	B	21.43 % / 45.24 %
15	C	27.98 % / 32.73 %	31	A	43.45 % / 32.74 %	47	A	11.9 % / 50.6 %	63	B	10.12 % / 48.81 %	79	A	38.1 % / 45.83 %
16	A	36.31 % / 31.55 %	32	A	35.71 % / 32.15 %	48	B	18.45 % / 50.6 %	64	C	14.29 % / 45.83 %	80	C	11.31 % / 45.83 %

Q.	Ans.	Correct		Q.	Ans.	Correct		Q.	Ans.	Correct		Q.	Ans.	Correct		Q.	Ans.	Correct
		Skipped				Skipped				Skipped				Skipped				Skipped
81	A	26.79 %		85	D	11.9 %		89	C	16.67 %		93	D	26.79 %		97	D	14.29 %
		45.83 %				46.43 %				46.43 %				47.02 %				47.02 %
82	A	23.21 %		86	C	27.98 %		90	B	17.26 %		94	B	22.02 %		98	B	12.5 %
		45.84 %				46.42 %				47.03 %				47.62 %				48.81 %
83	C	17.86 %		87	D	25.0 %		91	A	30.36 %		95	B	25.0 %		99	C	18.45 %
		46.43 %				47.02 %				47.02 %				47.62 %				48.81 %
84	A	19.64 %		88	D	17.86 %		92	A	35.71 %		96	B	16.07 %		100	B	10.12 %
		46.43 %				46.43 %				47.03 %				47.03 %				50.59 %

Performance Analysis

Avg. Score (%)	34.0%
Toppers Score (%)	93.0%
Your Score	

// Notes //

// Notes //